To Beach,

Your sensitivity, compassion
and generosity of spirit are
a blessing to everyone you
meet. Thanks for sharing
this humbling & illuminating
work, + thanks for your
friendship—

Sal

The Dawn Is Never Far Away:
Stories of Loss, Resilience, and the Human Journey

J. Scott Janssen, LCSW

Comments and/or correspondence about this book may be sent to Infinity Publishing or:

PO Box 392
Hillsborough, NC 27278

ISBN 0-7414-2258-1

Published by:

INFIN〇ITY
PUBLISHING.COM

1094 New De Haven Street, Suite 100
West Conshohocken, PA 19428-2713
Info@buybooksontheweb.com
www.buybooksontheweb.com
Toll-free (877) BUY BOOK
Local Phone (610) 941-9999
Fax (610) 941-9959

Printed in the United States of America

Printed on Recycled Paper

Published January 2005

This book is dedicated to my parents, John and Judy Janssen, who encouraged me to make the journey on my own terms, and to Sarah, who shares it with me.

Acknowledgments

Several people were kind enough to read the manuscript of this book and offer comments. Tom Beason, M.Div, Director of Spiritual Care, Hernando-Pasco Hospice; a seeker in the tradition of the Irish monks who, centuries ago, placed their flimsy craft into the North Atlantic, trusting the currents to bring them to unknown lands. R. Harrison Grey, D.Min, author, poet, and healer, not to mention one of the most remarkable hospice chaplains I have ever known. Stephen Hawthorne, LCSW, Clinical Associate, Department of Psychiatry, Duke University Medical Center, and my former Clinical Supervisor; other than the hospice families I've been fortunate enough to meet, no one has taught me more about counseling. My aunt, Kathleen Janssen, RN, MS, Director of Quality Management, Riverside Community Care, who has been caring for critically ill patients since before I knew what a hospice was. Linda Jordan, D.Min, Director, Unicorn Bereavement Center, whose skill as a teller of stories is surpassed only by her eagerness to listen to those told by others.

My parents, wife, and siblings (Patricia Hoffman, Dan Janssen, and Sue O'Leary) read the book in its various manifestations. More than any, they insisted that it be jargon-free and easy to read. The book's content and structure owes much to them.

And, of course, gratitude goes to the many families I have had the privilege of knowing and serving. This book is for them too.

Table of Contents

This they tell, and whether it happened so or not
I do not know; but if you think about it,
you can see that it is true.

Black Elk

Introduction

When Teddy Roosevelt entered the door of his New York City home in February of 1884, the twenty-four-year-old politician had no idea that within hours his life would be changed forever. He had rushed back from Albany after receiving an urgent telegram that things were not well. His young wife, Alice, who had just given birth to their first child, was near death in one room and his mother was dying in another. His mother died first. Her once unstoppable vitality disappeared quietly, like a whisper. Alice hung on for another eleven hours before her death left her husband reeling and in shock. Roosevelt's personal journal came to an abrupt end that day, closing with a final entry, "The light has gone out of my life."

Teddy Roosevelt was not one to sit still in his pain. He plunged back into his work, attempting to outrun his grief. When he found it impossible to outrun something embedded in his very fiber, he left politics and retreated into the rugged Bad Lands of North Dakota. For over two years he withdrew into the solitude and the rigors of western life. He wrote a memorial to his wife, worked to exhaustion on his cattle ranch, and reflected that the melancholic sound of doves cooing in the scrubby cottonwoods expressed "more than any other sound in nature the sadness of gentle, hopeless, never-ending grief." Slowly sadness loosened its grip amid the vast, uncluttered landscape of Dakota and his wounds began to heal.

We can all relate to stories like Roosevelt's, where matters of life and death heighten our awareness and remind us of what is truly important. Although it is more common to remember him as a "Rough Rider" or President, it is in his grief that he becomes most human and we are able to find lessons for our own journey. This is a book of such stories, many of them about people struggling with a fatal illness, and of families trying to make the most of the remaining days of a loved one's life. These are drawn from my years as a clinical social worker at a hospice, counseling people facing some of life's most difficult passages.

Few things raise as many important and troubling issues for families as death. It can send tremors to the core of our lives and relationships—shattering longstanding notions of who we are, what's important, what the future holds. At the same time, it reminds us of life's fragility and the need to tend to what matters most. If we listen closely, beneath the storm there is often a steady whisper inviting us to become more loving and compassionate. Nothing reveals this potential better than the real accounts of real people. In his book, *Dying Well: The Prospect for Growth at the End of Life*, hospice physician, Ira Byock, writes that, "Stories are the only satisfying way I know of exploring the paradox that people can become stronger and more whole as physical weakness becomes overwhelming and life itself wanes."

Other stories in this book come from American history. Stories like that of Osceola, the proud Seminole warrior fighting to remain in his home, or of the one-armed adventurer, John Wesley Powell, as he undertakes a hair-raising exploration of the Grand Canyon. At one point during his expedition, Powell found himself dangling above a towering precipice clinging to a small outcropping of rock. He was certain to die unless he trusted that he could let go and lean back into the canyon despite his impulse to hold fast.

I have often told these stories to hospice patients and their families. They offer parallels and insights into the challenges people may encounter as they or a loved one approach death, as well as wisdom for survivors left to continue on their journeys without a spouse or parent.

The connection between people coping with imminent separation and the realm of historical narrative is vital and profound. After all, in its most elemental form history is an exploration of the human story. It is a reflection on how people make sense of things and deal with the uncertainty of the times in which they live. At its most inspiring, it is also the study of how we withstand, even thrive, during times of crisis and sadness, moving beyond our pain to enrich our lives and communities. What could be more relevant to people living the final weeks or months of their lives?

By exploring history we see ourselves more clearly. Before Osceola was transformed into a "historical figure," he was alive with emotions and dreams that anyone can understand. As a boy he endured the confusion and turbulence of war, fleeing with his mother to Spanish Florida in search of refuge. He wrestled with questions about his role in a changing world and worried about his future. As a young man with troubles converging on every horizon, he did his best to adapt and find purpose amid perilous events beyond his control. Although he often suffered, even despaired, he found within himself a fount of strength and resilience that helped him navigate the hardships of his life and, in the end, find some measure of peace.

History is full of stories like Osceola's, illustrating the ways other people, even those who lived long ago, have dealt with the same kinds of challenges we all must face at one time or another. Reflecting on their lives connects us with those who have walked a similar path and borne similar burdens. In remembering history, it is possible to feel the silent accompaniment of kindred spirits as we tread the unevenly cobbled path of our final days, or take care of someone we love.

In a speech to the American Historical Association, historian Barbara Tuchman said: "The story and study of the past, both recent and distant, will not reveal the future, but it flashes beacon lights along the way and it is a useful nostrum against despair." Thus, we may find solace in Osceola's journey. As illness advances, weathering a person's body and consuming his or her thoughts, we may identify with Osceola and be inspired by his spirited humanity.

For centuries stories about people and history have been repositories for deep and enduring truths. In many societies storytellers were, and continue to be, Hermetic figures whose tales bridge the divide between the earthly realm and that of the sacred. Diverse cultures have used narratives in the form of myths, songs, oral histories, dream images, and folktales as the essential building blocks for personal and communal identity. Even the simplest stories often contain profound wisdom skillfully conveyed in familiar images and language. Such stories are also a bridge into the inner world of our psyches. In an article about using children's stories with hospice patients, chaplain Richard Grey reminds us that, even in our modern world, "our stories, tales, poems, and parables possess great value as portals for psychological and spiritual truth."

All of us carry important stories with us wherever we go. We often remember vividly the ones that have touched us deeply and come to embody some important belief or truth. We carry memories of significant personal experiences crafted into stories and added to our unique collection of tales that remind us who we are, and what the world is like. Some of these are unassuming and compact, such as the aphorisms and anecdotes told by a grandparent (as in Chapter Four), others are dramatic and life changing. Some help us in times of trouble, others, if we cling to them when they no longer serve us, can be a hindrance.

For hospice patients and families, there is tremendous value in hearing stories that place their internal narrations into a larger context and offer novel ways of understanding their situation. A good story can help us see and assimilate new truths about our life or circumstances from a comfortable distance, at a safe pace. We are free to identify with central characters and events, yet remain separated by time and context. As Doctor Ofra Avalon puts it, "The working out of a crucial conflict, such as arises from issues around death, will not be possible unless we can provide a safe enough atmosphere...The story provides this safety by containing within its framework the two seemingly contradictory elements of *distancing* and *involvement*..."

My discovery that history holds a rich trove of such stories came while visiting a woman in her early sixties who was dying of bone cancer. Rose was ferociously independent and refused to admit she needed help from her son, Shawn, and daughter, Tamara. She was terrified that accepting assistance would diminish her in their eyes and leave her a "useless burden." For months she fought hard against the steady momentum of her cancer, but eventually she had no choice but to allow Tamara to move into her apartment and, as Rose put it, "start changing my damn diapers."

Much to her surprise, Rose found that accepting help and surrendering arduous tasks did not bring an end to her dignity or degrade the value of her life. Instead, it conserved energy she had been wasting trying to get dressed and figure out which medications it was time to take. Now she used this energy to have conversations with family and friends, and reflect on "what really mattered in life." As she neared death, her emaciated body became burdensome, like a thick waterlogged blanket too heavy for her to lift, but her spirit grew stronger. She gained new insights into her life and a fuller appreciation of, and respect for, her children.

A couple weeks before Rose died, she was trying to describe the paradox of her inner strength increasing as her physical strength waned. She fumbled for words and images but could not find any with enough richness and texture to satisfy her. As she spoke, I remembered a story about the bus boycott in Montgomery, Alabama in 1955, when citizens protesting the racial segregation of public transportation refused to ride the city's buses. It was one of the seminal events of the civil rights movement and the story seemed a nice metaphor of Rose's experience. It was also likely to harmonize with her personal history, since she had often spoken about attending civil rights marches and had even met Martin Luther King Jr. during a visit to Georgia.

The story is about an elderly woman who supported the boycott. She was weary from months of walking and it showed in her bent frame and slow gait. As I told Rose the story I underscored the theme that, although we may be worn down by life's trials and the limitations of our flagging body, our spirit—our deepest and most whole self—can use these trials to grow stronger. Yancey Martin was a young man involved in the boycott and he recalled the story as follows:

> I happened to be in church that day when we had a meeting. That was at Day Street that night. Martin [Luther King Jr.] asked this old lady, he said, "Now listen...you have been with us all along, so now you go on and start back to ridin' the bus, 'cause you are too old to keep walking..."
>
> She said, "Oh no...I'm gonna walk just as long as everybody else walks. I'm gonna walk till its [sic] over."
>
> So he said, "But aren't your feet tired?"
>
> She said, "Yes, my [feet are] tired, but my soul is rested..."

"My feet are tired, but my soul is rested." Rose smiled softly, repeating the phrase as if it were a shawl she was wrapping around her shoulders on a crisp autumn day. For a few minutes we talked about the woman's fatigue and the ardors of walking to work every day. Beneath the old woman's exhaustion was a core of unpretentious strength and, what Rose called, "spirit peace." The story synthesized some of the emerging truths of Rose's experience, for example, that her life had innate value and that inner strength was much more substantive than physical strength. She decided it was, "right on target" for what she was feeling.

The last time I saw Rose she spent most of the visit sleeping. Her respiration was shallow and her blood pressure weak. Tamara knew she was dying. We sat by her mother's bed and talked about Rose's life and the ups and downs of their relationship. As I was preparing to leave, Rose opened her eyes and looked at us.

"Want some water Mama?" Tamara asked. Rose shook her head no.

"Shawn came by while you were sleeping. He'll be back tonight to check in on you." When her mother smiled, Tamara filled her in on some of the neighborhood gossip and read her a card that had come in the mail. All the while Rose looked at her quietly, attentively, but too weak to speak.

When Tamara reached the end of her update, Rose closed her eyes as if preparing to return to the deep transitional sleep that often comes when someone is near death. Before she did, I asked her a final question.

"Is there anything you want Tamara to know before you go back to sleep?"

She opened her eyes and looked at her daughter. In a whisper, she said, "My feet are tired." Then she looked at me and could only muster the word, "But..."

"But what Mama?" Tamara asked. Rose was too tired to answer and she looked at me.

"But my soul is rested," I said. As she drifted back to sleep, she smiled and shook slightly, as though laughing. Then she nodded her head to indicate that, yes, her soul was rested.

The story had remained with her, like a crystalline light, illuminating and affirming her journey.

Rose's story is representative of the chapters that follow and exemplifies the way they are structured. Each one is divided into three sections. The first introduces a person or family and recounts how they tried to cope with the impact of terminal illness. It also identifies one or two of the most difficult challenges they faced and some of the places they found themselves getting stuck. In the interest of privacy, details have been changed and some of the stories are composites. Inevitably, these accounts are compressed to one degree or another. Insights that occurred over the course of weeks or months and resulted from much hard work may seem to emerge suddenly. It is important to remember that sudden insights, though they do occur, are often the culmination of great effort, the dimensions of which are impossible to convey fully in short stories. I have simply tried to capture their essence.

Section Two offers a story from American history that serves as an analogy or metaphor, teasing out the larger elements of the family's experience. These stories offer a broader perspective on the family's situation and point to opportunities they may not have been considering. As with Rose, whose involvement in the civil rights movement and high regard for Martin Luther King Jr. made it likely the story about Montgomery would be one with which she would identify, these stories were chosen not simply because they contain a specific theme or meaning, but because there is something likely to resonate with a particular person or family.

Although these stories usually focus on issues related to separation, they apply to any of life's transitions or big questions. As such, Section Three synthesizes the first two sections and weaves them into a larger fabric upon which we may search for a more thorough understanding of the human journey as a whole.

The chapters are arranged into five parts each of which identifies a fundamental challenge related to death, loss, or transition: Finding Meaning; Facing the Past; Staying Connected; Letting Go; and Moving On. If we are sensitive and know where to look, within each painful challenge resides opportunities for growth, creativity, connection, and peace. The sections are organized to suggest ways of absorbing and processing the impact of these difficult circumstances and making the most of the time at hand.

In the process of distilling the complex and often enigmatic stuff of history into short narratives, it has been necessary to be selective and interpretive. I make no claims that my interpretation of historical events is the only one. As with life, historical investigation and interpretation is a fluid and changeable process, large enough to accommodate many, often discordant, viewpoints. Whatever my limitations as a historian, I have always tried to draw interpretations that are true in a deeper sense, in that they illuminate places within, and beyond, our immediate field of vision that might otherwise have remained in shadow.

Throughout this book themes emerge, such as the inextinguishable power of human resilience, the omnipresence of paradox, and a common longing for love and connection. In the end, however, the main theme is simple and unadorned: Life is a journey. Along the way there will be some hard times that leave us afraid and confused, perhaps filled with sadness or anger. At such times, we endure and grow stronger if we do our best to hold fast to our most compassionate personal and transcendent truths, honoring and supporting those we love. It is my hope that this blending of stories will offer the reader comfort and insight for his or her travels. During difficult times, or simply times when we pause to reflect on how we are living our lives and what it means to be human, may one of these stories alight and give comfort, like an ember of warmth in the hollow of a long and chilly winter.

Section One

Invincible Summer:

Finding Meaning

In the midst of winter, I finally learned that there was in me an invincible summer

Albert Camus

Some challenges, like those that arrive with the diagnosis of a potentially fatal illness, turn our lives upside down. Suddenly the future seems fraught with uncertainty and danger. Roles we are used to playing, routines we are used to following and plans we have made may be thrown into flux or seem unimportant. Still, we may cling to them as a way of seeking distraction or reassurance amidst our fear and sadness. Intense, often conflicting, emotions stir like heavy winds knocking us off balance. Profound questions arise, sometimes at the center of our awareness, sometimes along the periphery. Why is this happening? How can I find strength for the way ahead? What is most important right now? How can I find peace, bring peace to others? What lies beyond the threshold of death?

For some, these thoughts and emotions are unwelcome visitors insinuating themselves into previously orderly lives and wreaking havoc. Many of us try to avoid thinking about such things or try pretending nothing has changed. Others simply wait for them to pass through like waves breaking across the bow of a ship, hoping that once the waters are stilled, the waves won't return. Some of us, however, plunge into the currents searching for answers before it's too late—hoping, perhaps, to make up for lost time, or to use what time remains as wisely as we can.

Whatever our response, unsettling thoughts and emotional pain are likely to ebb flow, often along side of joy, hope, laughter, and love. Understandably, we may label those things that distress us as "negative" and try to find ways to minimize them. But like love and hope, they are also a part of our path. Often, the harder we try to escape our sadness the more powerful, adaptable, and patient it becomes. Such feelings are not our enemies; they are a part of our humanness. It often takes more energy to avoid or repress painful thoughts and emotions than it does to make peace with them. The walls we build trying to protect ourselves may leave us feeling isolated and misunderstood.

To their surprise, many people find that their deepest pain can be an avenue into their deepest insights and possibilities. Opportunities for growth and meaning always abound within the icy seas of distress. Whether this means finding greater empathy and appreciation for a loved one, as with Robert in Chapter One, or an enhanced sensitivity to the value in simple moments of closeness and connection, as with Lizzie and Ray in Chapter Two, the lessons we learn about ourselves and others at such times can be significant and invaluable. Sometimes, as in Chapter Three, those lessons endure long beyond the death of a loved one, bringing comfort and transformation to those, like Bev and Ike, who are left to continue the journey.

The stories in Section One are about such lessons. They underscore the fact that times of crisis and difficult change can lead us toward wisdom, illumination, and a more unconditional expression of love. If we open ourselves up to such things, our pain and stress will find their proper perspective within the larger dimensions of our journey.

Chapter One
Cabeza de Vaca:
Growth Within Suffering

After Robert's back surgery, his doctor told him to stay off his feet while he recuperated. He may as well have instructed him to float through the air or dance on the head of a pin. It was hard enough for Robert to sit still under the best of circumstances and these were among the worst. Months earlier, he had injured his lower back jumping over a steel rail while pursuing a shoplifter at a local shopping mall. Money was tight and, in addition to his job as a police officer, he had been working part-time as a security guard. "I always tell the new cops," he said, "that flying is for the birds and the rest of us should keep our feet on the ground, then I go and mess my back up tripping over a rail."

The timing couldn't have been worse. His wife, Sandy, had Carpal Tunnel Syndrome in her wrists, a painful condition caused by repeating the same physical movements over and over. It had become so stressful she had recently been forced to quit her job as a medical transcriptionist. Robert would be out of commission for several months and was getting the run around about his workman's compensation claim. They were both in pain, the bills were piling up, and neither was able to work. As if this weren't enough, Robert's mother, Tessa, had been diagnosed with lung cancer and had moved in with them after the rest home in which she had been living informed them that the facility could not meet her increased needs. By the time Tessa began hospice care, Robert was starting to envy some of the people he had put in jail, joking that at least they had some predictability in their lives.

Robert was a tall, robust, muscular man whose quick wit and kindness were often camouflaged by his seriousness and mercurial sarcasm. Even his back pain and regular doses of morphine hadn't muted his bustling energy. At times, as he lay on the couch unable to move, he seemed like a pressurized barrel about to fly apart.

As for Tessa, Robert was quick to inform me that cancer was the least of her worries. In fact, she was unperturbed by the diagnosis, insisting that her physician had been tricked by "the mist" into misreading her diagnostic tests. As far as she was concerned, she was perfectly healthy. When I asked Robert what she meant by "the mist," he rolled his eyes and threw his hands up. "Mom has schizophrenia," he said, as though trying to find meaning in her words was senseless. "She's always been in the mist."

Schizophrenia is a baffling and complex mental illness about which Robert had become an informal expert. He figured he'd spent enough time in psychiatric hospitals talking to doctors and psychologists to make him either crazy or brilliant. He wasn't sure which. Although schizophrenia affects people differently, the disease has some common features. In Tessa's case, these included delusions, compulsive behaviors, hallucinations, and paranoia—a combination that often twisted her reality into a surreal, sometimes frightening experience. Although medications had helped her maintain a delicate balance, she occasionally felt threatened by the concerns of her inner world. Threats of which she thought the rest of us were unaware because the mist was marching us slowly, unsuspectingly into psychological bondage.

For as long as Robert could remember, his life had been cut by the sharp edge of crisis. As a child he was afraid to make friends, lest they find out something was wrong with his mother. His father had tried to insulate him from the effects of Tessa's psychosis, but it was like "trying to hide an elephant under a napkin." He expected Robert to be secretive about family matters, to soothe Tessa whenever she became anxious, and accept without question her odd demands and compulsive personal rituals. "She had a ritual for everything," he remembered. "One before she got out of bed, another before she went to sleep, and probably twenty more throughout the day." She was terrified that if she ever forgot one of them something bad would happen. Without siblings to divide the weight of his parent's complex demands, Robert's early life had been stressful and confusing.

Tessa had expected him to be obedient and to validate beliefs and behaviors even a child could see were bizarre. If he didn't comply with her requests, her reaction could be unpredictable and dramatic. "She might have thought I was under the influence of the devil," he recalled, "or that my body had been taken over by evil spirits." He worried that if he simply went along with her he would become lost in an alternate world of horizonless delusion, but if he didn't acquiesce, things might escalate quickly into anger and chaos. His solution to this dilemma was to placate Tessa by appearing to go along with her, while giving little or no credibility to her words or behavior.

This strategy became even more important after his father died from a sudden heart attack when Robert was only seventeen. It was a crushing loss. His father had been like a sturdy lighthouse guarding treacherous reefs and shoals. "Whenever things were getting out of control," he recalled, "I'd look up and see Dad, steady and solid." It was unimaginable that he was gone, especially at the very time when Robert, who had been working at a woodchip factory, was hoping to leave home and start a new life. As if overnight, he became solely responsible for looking after his mother.

Tessa's grief was all-consuming. As Robert put it, "it was like someone tossed a match into a river full of gasoline." Her already disorganized thoughts became a cacophony of jumbled suspicions and paranoid allegations. Where was her husband? Who kidnapped him? Why wouldn't anybody tell her the truth? She simply could not comprehend that he was dead. When she retreated into the root cellar and refused to come out, Robert was at his wits end. "She was convinced," he said, "that Dad was hiding down there in a secret chamber and she could communicate with him when no one was around."

His father had repeatedly driven home the need to protect Tessa from the scrutiny of others and take care of her alone (in fact, she hadn't yet been diagnosed with schizophrenia). For a young man confronted with such complicated pressures and responsibilities, it was overwhelming. His life was a maelstrom of combustible emotion that built, at times, to near panic. He agonized about whether to seek help, knowing that doing so violated a fundamental family rule. Finally, after she had been in the cellar for a week, Robert decided to call the sheriff. Years later, he still felt the intersecting tides of shame and relief that had rushed in along with the county patrol car.

He was afraid of what his mother's response might be and what might happen once others knew she was "different." At the same time, he was relieved to share the burden of her care and shed the loneliness of their family secret. Looking back, he saw this as a turning point. "I just shut myself down," he said, "until I was numb. I decided Mom was crazy, and I needed to treat her that way from there on out."

It was a decision that ossified into a cold personal truth as Tessa was hospitalized time and again over the ensuing years. Every time things went awry he grew more detached until finally her crises seemed like part of a bland routine. Amid the well-ordered halls of the state psychiatric hospital, he stopped thinking of Tessa as his mother who happened to be struggling with schizophrenia, and began thinking of her as a schizophrenic who happened to be his mother. Her illness defined everything.

By the time she was "permanently placed" in a nearby rest home, Robert was intent on separating his world from hers, determined to make a "normal" life for himself and his family. The separation was not difficult. He was used to dividing the world into broad categories of people. There were good guys and bad guys, strong people and weak people, people who gave a damn and those who didn't. Adding another division was easy—now there were those who were crazy and those who were sane.

Viewing Tessa's life as a bundle of symptoms clustered around a mental illness took the pressure off of him to fix things or stem the swells of her anxiety and delusions. If her behavior was strange at times, it was the illness, something he could not control and for which he was not responsible. He no longer second-guessed himself or wondered if he had done something to trigger his mother's behavior. He no longer had to walk the fine line of listening to what he called "crazy talk," without disputing it on the one hand, or getting drawn into a flickering world of unreality on the other. Instead, he could detach himself and respond with the coolness of a surgeon about to operate on a stranger.

While this perspective protected him from the emotional gyrations that had haunted his youth, he lost something of irreplaceable value. Somehow he'd forgotten that beneath the clatter of Tessa's alternate world, she nourished an enduring spark of love and humanity—the essence of who she really was. In her heart she was a kind, generous, and nurturing soul filled with compassion for those who suffered. When Robert was younger, he had been adept at seeing this even when she assailed him with torrents of verbal chaos. Now it had been many years since he had known this dimension of his mother's life. It had disappeared into the perplexing shadow-world of her schizophrenia and, for Robert, looking for it was pointless. Taking his mother seriously in any way, he believed, would only "encourage her and get you into trouble." As with many things in his life, this was not negotiable.

At first glance, the effects of Tessa's cancer were difficult to see. She was a large woman, in no danger of wasting away from disease-related weight loss. She dressed herself and moved around the home without assistance. The only outward signs that something was amiss were her occasional use of an oxygen concentrator and strict avoidance of going up or down stairs. She was congenial and liked to laugh. Her round face was effervescent and expressive. She fidgeted constantly as she talked. Initially, she was cautious about answering questions, asking several times if the hospital had sent me to bring her back. Despite her suspicions, she was soon at ease and came to relish the opportunity to talk about her life.

She seemed unfazed by the events around her. Since intensified levels of stress had preceded many of her psychiatric crises, Robert and Sandy had insulated her in a blanket of routine and predictability. She didn't know money was tight or the extent of Robert's physical pain. She flatly rejected any notion that she had cancer much less that it was terminal. Her days were alive, however, with drama of another sort.

Once she was comfortable with our visits, she drew a vivid and textured picture of her extraordinary inner world. She said she received messages regularly from the voice of a spirit she called King Alfred. Faces appeared on the walls of her room and her two songbirds, Micky and Spud, were, in reality, diminutive and feathery friends through which she communicated with "higher beings."

Tessa believed that the people of the world belonged to a single family and that we were in the process of ridding ourselves of the mist—an imperceptible haze of negative energy separating each person from his or her most advanced state of spiritual development. She referred to this state as *empathassion*. A contraction of "empathy" and "compassion." These were qualities that, if fully developed, would burn the mist away like dew evaporating under a summer sun.

Every thought and action affected the mist in some way depending on a person's intentions, making it stronger or weaker. A great cosmic war was being fought between spirits who wished to strengthen the mist (stone ones), and those who wanted to see it disappear. Tessa believed that she was an important intermediary between King Alfred, who was leading the fight against the mist, and the larger human family, naively oblivious to the momentous events unfolding beneath our noses.

Although her world was full of what most would regard as strange sensations and enigmatic ways of thinking, in its center was an oasis of latent sanity. She had a warm and genuine desire to help others and to develop a keener, more compassionate sensitivity to suffering of all kinds. "Every time I make someone laugh," she said, "the mist gets a little bit weaker."

I encouraged Robert to join Tessa and I during our visits, but he preferred to speak privately since, as he put it, "She knows I don't listen to her when she talks crazy." Their interactions revolved around practicalities, like what she wanted for lunch or whether she needed a pain pill. "All I care about now," he said, "is making sure Mom is comfortable for however much time she has left." It was one area, at least, over which he had some control.

Perhaps his focus on Tessa's physical comfort was related to his own intense pain. Robert was fond of reminding me that his fellow officers had called him "the conquistador," a nickname given by a friend who worked in the motor pool. The conquistadors were tough, battle-hardened men. In the sixteenth century they conquered much of Mexico and South America for the Spanish Empire. He was proud of the nickname; it captured how he saw himself and how he wanted to be seen by others. Lately, however, the back pain was getting to him and he was not feeling much like a conqueror. Despite his stoicism, it was wearing him down like a stone eroded by sandy desert winds. He was frightened and unable to bridle the intensity of his frustration and anger. Immobilized much of the day, the conquistador was sliding into depression.

Along with receiving a crash course on the consequences of physical pain, Robert's convalescence was also giving him an uncomfortable familiarity with intense mental anguish. Sitting on the couch and bristling with anger at his inability to move around freely, at times he clenched his fists as he railed about being "cheated out of my life." Just weeks before, he had been one of the strongest officers on the police force, now his body seemed frail and unresponsive. Anguish, depression, anxiety, a body whose delicate homeostasis had been bluntly interrupted—these were things that had always characterized Tessa's life, but never his own. Now the tables had turned.

He lost interest in things. His once considerable energy slackened beneath the gravity of burdensome thoughts. It became harder for him to see beyond the unhappiness of his immediate experience. He had never felt such disheartening sadness. Suddenly, the simple categories into which he'd always divided the world began to lose their meaning. He no longer felt strong, and he questioned whether he was sane. Depression became the solvent into which his timeworn categories dissolved, leaving him confused and disoriented. Ultimately, it would challenge him to think about himself and others in new, more humane ways.

After he had spent several of my visits pretending he was fine, Robert slowly delved into the psychological firestorm testing the limits of his endurance. He was ashamed that, as he saw it, he couldn't provide for his family. Unmoored from the status and esteem he had derived from his job, and unable to do more than simple tasks, he felt "useless." He was convinced he was a burden to his wife. He worried about the future and ruminated constantly about his circumstances.

With Sandy's encouragement, he spoke to his doctor and agreed to try an anti-depressant. It was a big step, not just because of his stalwart intention to do things without asking for help, but because his mother's experiences with unwanted side effects and improper dosages had given him an intense distrust of medications. He found, however, that although it was no panacea for his emotional pain, the medicine gave him a reserve of energy with which to deal with things more constructively.

A few weeks later, Robert asked if he could join Tessa and I during our visit. "I guess I just want to see how Mom is doing with all that's going on," he said, fidgeting nervously as I helped him up from the couch. I asked about his change of heart and he managed a smile. He told me he had been thinking about many things lately, especially the fact that his mother would not be around much longer. Chronic back pain had taken much away from him, but it had given him ample time to think about things that were important. This was giving him a new clarity and compassion for Tessa's battle with mental illness.

After some initial awkwardness, the two of them settled into a bantering, humorously oppositional style of sharing memories and reflecting on their lives together. Neither one was willing to surrender his or her version of events, but each indulged the other in misrecollections. From then on, our visits were spent jointly. When she could, Sandy sat with us and offered her perspective as they sifted through the complex strata of their shared experiences. These visits became an important time when they could talk openly, acknowledging the challenges and affirming the strength of their enduring bond.

Robert's staunch refusal to let Tessa's delusions go unchallenged proved pliable. He learned to suspend his protests and enter his mother's world—exploring its unique dimensions without correcting her. In doing so, he rediscovered the wellspring of kindness and love beneath the distracting facade of paranoia and delusion. One day, while Robert and I were standing on the front porch near the end of our visit, he mused that, when he was a kid, no matter how chaotic things got his mother had always found ways to let him know that she loved him.

"I'd forgotten about that," he said, "until the other day."

"What reminded you?" I asked.

He wasn't sure, but such spontaneous memories were happening more frequently.

As Tessa's condition deteriorated, she had less stamina for conversation and often became short of breath. Robert, on the other hand, began to feel less pain and was able to move around more freely. Although he continued to contend with psychological pain, it was less enveloping. He cut down on his back medications, hoping to reduce the sleepiness that accompanied them and restore even more of his energy.

All the while, he was wrestling with an embryonic and emerging fact: Something inside him was different, but he wasn't sure what. He intuitively knew this, though frankly, he wasn't sure he liked it. His rigid views about his mother, himself, and the world, no longer worked. Everything, it seemed, was more multifaceted, refusing to fit into the neatly crafted mental boxes that had always been so convenient and reassuring. It was as though he had been washed up on some strange land far from any familiar paths or landmarks, uncertain of his bearings or how to find his way home.

He grasped for a place to anchor himself and gain understanding. Eventually he decided to approach the situation as though he were investigating a crime scene. It was his job to figure out what, why, and how things had happened. "I guess it started," he said, furrowing his brow and rubbing his balding forehead, "when I hurt my back." This had given him the opportunity to deepen his empathy for, and insight into, his mother's situation in a way that all of his prior ordeals had not.

He saw many parallels between his struggles and Tessa's. Things like a pervasive sense of vulnerability, losing control, and seeing one's life unexpectedly career off course. As had his mother, he felt the eruption of volatile emotions and labored with the irrational thoughts that often accompanied them. And like Tessa, he had been mystified about how to reduce their powerful convections. He had also learned what it meant to rely on medications to steady these fearsome churnings and to struggle with the tedium of sitting on the sidelines as others engaged in activities no longer available to him, simple things like having lunch with a friend or driving to the store. Perhaps most importantly, he now understood what it was like to have a quiet, inexplicable feeling of otherness—of being in some way different, abnormal.

As Robert reflected, he could see that the labels he had affixed to his mother's life were misleading. He was awed by the realization that, while Tessa had struggled nearly all of her life with such challenges, they had nearly driven him "off the deep end" in only a few months.

Sometimes it is in our deepest and most desperate suffering that we find our most enduring insights. This was certainly true for Robert. His suffering was giving him a compassionate and animated sensitivity to the challenges of Tessa's life. It was also helping him see her creativity and strength. I suggested that what he had gained was, in its essence, empathassion.

He smiled and said, "You bet."

Even positive transformation and growth, however, often occurs in the shadow of fear, ambivalence, and resistance. Robert was grateful to have a deeper understanding of his mother, but it came with a cost that went beyond his physical and emotional pain. His previous way of grouping people, events, and ideas, had been consoling in its simplicity. Imbuing things with ambiguity and the capacity for change was unsettling, leaving him, he said, "feeling like I don't know who I am anymore." He was being beckoned to live his life in a different and, as yet, undefined way, to let go of old ideas without the benefit of time-tested new ones. For all his resilience and adaptability, it was something he had never done before.

Robert's early life had been awash in chaos and uncertainty. To survive he had carved out a few unbending rules around which he could find stability within the seemingly endless volatility. One of these rules was that people didn't change. Now, he knew this wasn't true because *he* was changing. He was shedding old beliefs much like a snake sheds worn-out skin. Unfortunately, his old stories merely reinforced these beliefs. He had no language for what was happening, no stories or images to serve as mileposts as he made his way forward into unexplored, potentially frightening lands

I decided to offer him a story that mirrored his emerging insights and might serve him in this journey. Remembering the pride he took in his nickname, the conquistador, I asked if he had ever heard of Cabeza de Vaca. He laughed and asked if this was one of Tessa's secret messengers. I told him that he was a conquistador of the most tenacious sort. In 1528 Cabeza de Vaca was one of the few survivors of an ill-fated quest for gold and glory in the wilds of Florida. He endured eight years of unimaginable suffering and, by the time he emerged, he had discarded many ideas about who he was, who the native inhabitants of America were, and how he would live his life. In the crucible of his backbreaking hardship, he found deeper, more fundamental truths than he'd ever imagined.

Robert was intrigued and had me pronounce the name again.

"Cabeza de Vaca," he said, "Now that I can pronounce his name, tell me his story."

II

In April 1528, a one-eyed, red bearded Spaniard named Panfillo de Navarez led three ships carrying some four hundred men into a harbor along the Gulf Coast of Florida near present-day Tampa. His second in command was Alvar Nunez Cabeza de Vaca, a leathery soldier also serving as the expedition's treasurer. It was Cabeza de Vaca's job to keep track of the riches they expected to find when they cut their way through towering forests and cane-filled swamps in search of Cibola, an imaginary kingdom of staggering wealth. Their expectations were grandiose and their disdain for the Indians of the New World was absolute. They saw themselves as strong and noble, the Indians as weak and conniving. For these Spaniards the world held no subtlety and their beliefs were as inflexible as Castilian steel. In their minds, there were superior people like themselves who were destined for glory, honor, and wealth, and then there were those, a majority of the earth's population, whose destiny was to live in the shadow of obscurity. When Cabeza de Vaca gazed out on the coast of Florida, he could not have conceived how his suffering during the next several years would shatter these simplistic notions and transform him.

Navarez foolishly divided his force and marched three hundred soldiers inland. The rest went north with vague instructions to sail the ships to a place where the two groups would rendezvous; it was a place that existed only in their hopeful imaginations.

As the land force pushed its way through dense forest, their treatment of the Indians was harsh and frequently brutal. Cabeza de Vaca and his companions considered all Indians savages, deserving no kindness. The welfare of the natives was of no concern to the Spaniards and they were no more sensitive to an Indian's pain than they would have been to that of a pack mule.

When the conquistadors discovered "small amounts of gold" among the Timucuan tribe, they demanded more. Eager to rid themselves of these violent invaders, the Timucuans told the strangers that they would have to travel far away to find more. "They indicated to us," Cabeza de Vaca wrote, "that very far away was a province called Apalachee where there was much gold, and…a large quantity of everything we wanted."

As the clattering band of heavily armed soldiers headed north in search of the Apalachees (who lived near present-day Tallahassee), native tribes avoided them like they would a swarm of bees. The terrain was difficult to cross. Fallen trees, marshes, and thickets seemed to block every step. The heat and humidity, combined with lugging heavy weapons and supplies, taxed their strength. Soon the meager rations of biscuits and bacon were depleted and some of the men were reduced to eating palmettos. By the time they finally reached the Apalachees, there were many who, Cabeza de Vaca recalled, "besides great fatigue and hunger, had sores on their backs from carrying their weapons in addition to the other things they had to carry."

The Apalachees, it turned out, had no gold, but they were very skilled at launching arrows with such accuracy that, to Cabeza de Vaca, it seemed they "never miss[ed] anything." Beating a hasty retreat amid a flurry of skirmishes, the demoralized soldiers found their way back to the Gulf Coast and dropped from exhaustion. They were starving. Many were sick and "in such a condition that there were few who could be of any use." Some, like Cabeza de Vaca, had been injured and they prayed their wounds would not become infected. Fifty were dead. The expedition that had once boldly entered the forest with dreams of conquest and riches had been quickly transformed into a desperate band struggling to survive.

With their ships nowhere in sight, those who could work set about building barges from fallen pine trees. Although they had no tools, no knowledge of shipbuilding, and little chance of surviving anything but the most placid seas, they saw no choice but to try to sail for one of the Spanish settlements in Mexico. Six weeks later, through necessity and raw determination, they dragged five crude rafts into the Gulf of Mexico. The vessels each held about fifty men and, according to Cabeza de Vaca, were "caulked with palmetto fiber, and we tarred them with a kind of tarry pitch made...from pine trees; and from the same palmetto fiber and the tails and manes of the horses we made cords and rigging, and sails out of our shirts, and from the juniper trees that grew there we made the oars that we believed we needed."

Several weeks later, two of these waterlogged vessels carrying a handful of woeful Spaniards washed ashore on a small island they dubbed the Isle of Ill-Fortune (present-day Galveston, Texas). They were cold, parched from thirst, and their bodies were skeletal with the effects of chronic hunger. Most of them, including Cabeza de Vaca, collapsed on the beach so tired that, "scarcely half a dozen...could get up from the ground." When they were found by a group of Karankawa Indians, the forlorn party must have looked like some melancholic drift of jetsam splashed up by frigid waters indifferent to their suffering.

Had circumstances been reversed, the Spaniards likely would have been unmoved by the Karankawa's plight,

27

but the Indians were sympathetic and eager to help. They brought food and, seeing that the naked, emaciated conquistadors were freezing in the chill November wind, built fires to warm them as they made their way to a nearby village. Despite these acts of compassion, most of the eighty or so men who washed ashore died. When a "stomach ailment afflicted the Indians" and killed half of them, things changed quickly. The Indians blamed their Spanish visitors for the sickness and, rather than continuing to treat them as weary guests, enslaved them.

For Cabeza de Vaca and his dwindling companions, it was an inconceivable link in a growing chain of doleful events. They saw themselves as conquerors, favored by God and harbingers of the most powerful nation on earth. Many were aspiring to ascend the social hierarchy through glorious conquest. Most envisioned *owning* slaves. Once they had debated whether Indians were even human, now they were in bondage to them. Any assumptions they had about themselves or their future not already savaged by months of punishing hardship must have been whisked away in the rush of these new torments, like salty spray dispersed in a winter gale.

Cabeza de Vaca was separated from his friends and forced into labor that, ordinarily, any Spaniard who fancied himself a gentleman would have petulantly refused. His life became a monotone of privation and anguish. He was reduced to the sad anonymity of a slave, ordered about by people who were barely eking out survival by subsisting on thin seasonal fare such as berries, cactus, fish and nuts. At times, he was immersed in water for so long while digging for edible roots that the mere touch of a twig or blade of grass was enough to lacerate his skin. He endured humiliation, ill treatment, and unrelenting hunger. Assailed by a skin-sizzling sun, plagued by bloodthirsty mosquitoes and nearly freezing in the cold mists of winter, his former life must have seemed like a surreal hallucination. Finally, unable to bear it any longer, he decided to escape to the mainland of Texas.

He waited until his captors were occupied with moving their village and quietly slipped away. After stumbling onto the mainland he learned that, "owing to the constant state of war" among the various tribes of eastern Texas, "there was not much traveling or trading." As an outsider with no tribal affiliation, he posed little threat and could "go into the interior of the country as [he] liked..." He became a trader, carrying goods such as shells, snails, and beads from the coast and exchanging them further inland for pelts, dyes, flint, and ornaments. "Everywhere I went," he said, "they gave me good treatment and food on account of my merchandise."

Although his circumstances had improved, they were far from desirable. Hunger was constant, as was the danger of harsh storms, cold nights, predatory animals and withering heat. He also had to contend with the psychological suffering of being separated from his home and family, adrift in a strange land, uncertain of survival, and strangely alone.

Somehow, he reunited with the only other survivors of Navarez's fatal debacle—Alonzo del Castillo, Andres Dorantes, and a Moroccan named Estaban. The four decided to try to make their way overland to Mexico. They cast a bizarre, otherworldly shadow as they traveled together speaking in a strange tongue, communicating with the Indians through hand signs and fragments of native dialect. Coming from a land behind the eastern horizon and belonging to no tribe, their scraggly beards and unfamiliar skin pigmentation branded them with an inescapable otherness.

Word spread that these outlandish strangers had supernatural powers and could cure sickness and injury. When Indians arrived seeking help, the surprised Spaniards offered prayers, genuflected a few times, and blew on each petitioner in his or her turn. Amazingly, Cabeza de Vaca reports that time and again Indians from diverse tribes found relief from their afflictions after these simple ministrations.

As they traveled from one village to another, great crowds of people began following them in a long human caravan. Celebrations were held everywhere they went. Grateful Indians showered them with whatever gifts they could offer which the Spaniards distributed among their followers. The rugged conquistadors who had come to take things by force were now sharing what they had with friends they had previously despised and considered inferior.

Cabeza de Vaca had come as a warrior intent on pillaging this New World and subjugating its people. Now, after descending into the humiliations of slavery and losing everything that had been the bedrock of his identity, the Indians hailed him as a healer and bringer of peace. The befuddled Spaniards had ceased being conquerors and had been transformed by their suffering into what the Indians called, "children of the sun," holy men capable of penetrating the veil of the heavens.

In the course of his travels, Cabeza de Vaca gained affection for the Indians. He shared in their struggles, learned their languages and customs, donned their simple clothing, and even acquired their mannerisms and tattoos. Though their lives were hard, he admired their capacity for generosity and love, friendship and grief. Just as he and his three companions "shed our skin like snakes twice a year" because of the heat, Cabeza de Vaca was shedding rigid ideas based on ignorance and misunderstanding. He was seeing in his Indian host their full and irreducible humanity. He was now convinced that if the natives were "to be brought to be Christians" and assimilated into the Spanish empire, it would have to be done not by force and violence, but "by good treatment…and no other will suffice."

He respected the Indians and relied on them for protection and encouragement. When several of them died from an illness, he and his Spanish companions, "felt such sorrow about this that it could not have been greater, for in addition to seeing those that were dying we feared that all of them would die, or that…they would leave us all alone..."

Despite their improved status, the ardors of traveling continued to wear Cabeza de Vaca and his companions down. Even after they'd traded the lean and dusty desert for mountain forests, they were hounded by the relentless elements. Cabeza de Vaca, recalled that they:

> developed great sores on our chests and backs, which hurt us badly because of the large loads we carried, which were very heavy and caused the cords to cut into our arms. And the land is so rugged and heavily forested that we often sought firewood in the woods, and when we had finished getting it blood would run in many places from thorns and thickets we encountered, which broke the skin wherever they touched us.

Without calendars, clocks, or the many festival days of his Christian faith to measure the passage of time, his life unfolded with the phases of the moon and the movement of the seasons. Amid the vast Texas space, Cabeza de Vaca must have wondered if he would ever again set foot in Spain. His contemporary, Gonzolo Fernandez de Oviedo, was later astounded when he learned that Cabeza de Vaca and his companions "did not even have any way of knowing in what longitude or latitude they roamed when they were lost." Whenever they came upon a new tribe, they carefully gathered information about what lay ahead and whether there were others who looked Spanish. When they could, they moved west and south toward Mexico. Ultimately, they traversed some six thousand rugged miles.

When they crossed the Rio Grande into present-day Mexico they saw unmistakable signs of Spanish soldiers out searching for slaves to dig in silver and gold mines to the south. Villages and fields lay destroyed. Indians were harder to find since, "all the people were hidden in the woods, fleeing so that the Christians would not kill or make slaves of them..." Despite Cabeza de Vaca's newfound abhorrence for slavery, he was eager to find his countrymen. Traveling with a few Indian friends, he moved ahead of the main party.

In March 1536, he spotted a small group of Spanish

soldiers. They mistook him for a native and would have enslaved him, but when he spoke their native tongue they were stunned to realize he was Spanish. They were "thunderstruck," Cabeza de Vaca recalled, "They went on staring at me for a long space of time, so astonished that they could neither speak to me nor manage to ask me anything."

By then Cabeza de Vaca was changed in ways even he could not fathom. Eight years of indescribable hardship had fashioned him into a different person. He was no longer completely Spanish nor was he Indian: He was of both worlds. If he harbored any hopes that his kinsman would hear his message that friendship and respect were the way to live in peace with the Indians, these were quickly dispelled. Unfortunately, the thick mist of brutality and greed that had once blinded him continued to grip the soldiers. Instead of seeing the Indians as potential allies, they saw only slaves. He tried to protect his friends from the insidious violence of such men, but in the end, he could not.

When the slavers told the Indian's that they had come from the same distant land as the four healers, the Indians knew better. They said the Spaniards were lying. They pointed out, Cabeza de Vaca remembered, that:

> ...we came from where the sun rises and they
> from where it sets; and that we cured the sick
> and they killed the healthy; and that we came
> naked and barefoot and they well dressed and
> on horses and with lances; and that we did not
> covet anything, rather we returned everything
> that they gave us and were left with nothing,
> and the only aim of the others was to steal
> everything they found, and they never gave
> anything to anyone...

The Indians knew instantly what it would take Cabeza de Vaca years to understand, he was forevermore to be a child of the sun living in a land encumbered by pockets of thick mist and rigid darkness.

III

As the mill of human suffering turns, it has the potential to grind our capacity for deep compassion into dust, or bring it more fully into view and fill us with its healing power. It is often at times when our pain—whether physical, emotional, or psychological—is most acute, that we discover who we are and who we may become. In Robert's case, it opened him up, as if cutting furrows into the ground of his existence, and planted seeds bearing the promise of enriched insight and sensitivity.

Although this was a profound gift, it did not extinguish his pain. As Tessa approached death, Robert's sadness increased. He recognized, however, that his sorrow was the price he was paying for learning some important things about life and awakening to new meaning.

He appreciated the parallels between Cabeza de Vaca's story and his own: the way myopic beliefs can break down beneath the weight of new experience, and how suffering can season us with the potential for growth and understanding. He also appreciated that this was a tough, tenacious man, like himself, who learned that true strength has more to do with one's heart and spirit than the ability to use force or act decisively.

Another part of the story that rang true to Robert was that beneath the burdens of journeying through great hardship, there abound countless opportunities for acts of love, kindness, and connection. Even amid the constant cadence of privation and conflict, Cabeza de Vaca's concerns for the Indians, and theirs for him, were expressed simply and profoundly.

"If I hadn't been knocked off balance," Robert acknowledged, "I'd never have understood or appreciated Mom the way I do now." In the final analysis, he reckoned, if "going through all this stress with my back and being outta' work and fighting with depression is what helped me to see things more clearly, then sign me up. As far as I'm concerned, it's a pretty good deal."

As his recovery progressed, Robert assisted Tessa whenever he could. Things he'd once done perfunctorily, like getting her an extra blanket or a spoonful of ice cream, became important expressions of love. "I can't change that she's dying," he said, "but I can sit with her and read her a story or make sure her lips aren't too dry. I want to do little things like that."

Sometimes little things are bigger than they appear, especially when they convey empathy and compassion. The mist had lifted, taking with it all inclinations toward detachment and separation.

Robert's newfound patience was tested when Tessa's paranoia intensified. It was impossible to avoid the fact that she was deteriorating. Rather than attribute this to her cancer, Tessa was sure it was the result of some malignant force bent on killing her. When breathing became difficult for her, she grew anxious. She insisted her windows be sealed with masking tape and refused to take the morphine prescribed for her respiratory troubles. She was convinced the doctor wanted to poison her. Whenever Robert tried to coax her into taking her medicines she became agitated and clamped her jaws tightly in defiance.

Months before, he would have gotten angry and made her take her medication "whether she liked it or not." The result would have been another battle of wills and lingering resentment. This time, he didn't argue or ride roughshod over her objections. He decided to do something different, something, he admitted, that "scared the hell outta' me." Instead of trying to orient Tessa to his world, he entered hers.

For the first time in years, he paid close attention to Tessa's words and the images she used and took them seriously. If she said a medication was poison, instead of insisting that she accept his reassurances, he asked what he could do to help. When she gave him unintelligible instructions about finding "the king," he assured her that he understood, left the room, waited a bit, put some food coloring in the morphine and returned saying the king had advised that she take this drink. It felt awkward at first; after all, it flew in the face of much of what he had come to believe. But compassion, and his desire to sooth his mother's distress, emerged as higher priorities for him than retaining the cooler contours of what he'd often been told were "appropriate non-reinforcing responses" to Tessa's paranoid delusions.

In some ways this was a relief. Rather than resisting her, he simply accompanied her. To his surprise, he found he could do so without losing his perspective. By standing beside her as a loving son, instead of in front of her as the "sane one," he was even able to get her to take an increased dose of her medication.

As he took care of Tessa, his grief was complicated by the symptoms of her schizophrenia. His mother appeared to have no knowledge that she was going to die. It was not a matter of avoiding something she preferred not to think about—no mere repression or denial—she truly did not equate her physical decline with illness and didn't understand she was dying. Thus, Robert was faced with the challenge of knowing his mother would soon be gone and wanting to find a way to say goodbye, while at the same time being limited by Tessa's lack of comprehension and anxiety about discussing death.

He gave her ample opportunities to ask questions about what was happening or discuss any concerns she had, hoping to get some glimpse of how she was doing inside, but to little avail. She would not, or perhaps could not, talk about dying. Robert was left trying to find creative ways of communicating, such as talking about other people who were ill, hoping they could discuss things indirectly.

Each day became as important as life's final sunrise. He practiced patience like a monk practicing prayers. A month earlier he had longed to return to work, but now he wanted to spend as much time with Tessa as possible. "I don't even know if I want to keep on being a cop anymore," he said with visible anxiety, "but I'll deal with that identity crisis after Mom is gone."

In the days ahead, doubts about being a police officer

fused with other questions (about his role as a son, and a husband) as he developed a new way of understanding himself in light of his recent insights. In the following months, Robert's ambivalent return to the police force would stand like a distant reflection of the hardship Cabeza de Vaca faced trying to fit back into sixteenth century Spanish society. As with most who find ways to transcend self-limiting ideas and restrictive worldviews, there was a period of mild disorientation as a familiar world lost its worn assumptions and casual predictability and the two conquistadors began to live with new eyes, able to see further and more clearly.

Cabeza de Vaca's written account doesn't give a good picture of what it was like for him once he returned to Spain. After a joyful and a triumphant homecoming, however, it was clearly a mixed experience. His life-changing ordeal in the New World had made it impossible to return to the life of a Spanish noble without doubts and misgivings.

"For the rest of his life," according to writer David Duncan, "Cabeza de Vaca would try to convince his fellow Spaniards that the best way to conquer Native Americans was to be firm, but also to show kindness and respect—a notion other Spaniards dismissed as the Quixotic impulse of a man who had gone native far too long."

For months Cabeza de Vaca spent time writing an account of his odyssey and trying to finagle an appointment from the Crown. In 1540 he was made governor of a large area encompassing present-day Argentina, Uruguay, Paraguay, and part of Peru. When he arrived, he found the region in disarray and the thin population of Spaniards embroiled in political intrigues and senseless clashes with native tribes.

With little mastery of the disingenuous and subtle rituals that attended the life of an administrator, Cabeza de Vaca was an ineffective governor. He raised the ire of his fellow Spaniards when he insisted on humane treatment of the region's Indians and passed an edict forbidding slavery.

This made it clear to his associates that he was not a typical functionary of the King, but a man who saw, and demanded that others strain to see, alternate ways of living their lives.

Not surprisingly, he won little favor among many of the Spaniards and a faction seeking his demise soon formed. By 1543, as he lay weakened by illness, a group of these bickering subordinates hatched a plot against him, clapped him in irons and sent him back to the King.

He spent much of the rest of his life trying to clear his name and regain his former prestige, never entirely at ease with the treacherous workings of court politics and the life he was trying to recapture. After his wanderings in North America, he no longer fit neatly into this world. His suffering had unearthed deeper insights and sensitivity than were known to the unreflective men around him who were focused on personal gain and power. It had made him a soldier for peace in a land of warriors bent on violent conquest. This is one reason Cabeza de Vaca remains "one of the more paradoxical figures of the *conquista*—mystical yet pragmatic, moralistic yet highly ambitious, a proud *hidalgo* and longtime professional soldier who endured slavery and torture at the hands of the Indians during his years lost in *La Florida*, only to become one of their greatest defenders."

Although his experience deepened his wisdom and compassion, in many ways it made his life more challenging. Such is often the case when someone grows beyond the barren field of rigid convictions he or she shares with others and alights on a new path. Hardship followed Cabeza de Vaca to the end of his days, but so did the resilience and quiet courage born in the fires of the arid, bone-bleaching deserts of Texas and the snake-infested coastlands of Florida. Probably he would have agreed with Robert's assertion that it was worth the price.

Tessa slipped into a coma a few days before she died. Almost simultaneously Robert's back pain intensified. Rather than increase his medications and retire to his bedroom, he decided to use enough medicine to "take the edge off" his discomfort without causing too much sleepiness. He settled down on the bed in Tessa's room, next to her hospital bed, and watched over her until she died.

I didn't see Robert until a month after the funeral. Most of our visit was spent talking about Tessa and reflecting on her last few weeks. Robert said she had "woken up out of her coma" in the pre-dawn hours of the day she died. For a few minutes, he mused, she "looked at me and talked with me just as clear as a bell," before sinking back into silence. "She told me she loved me," he said, "and she said she knew it'd been hard on me all these years and that she was sorry. Then she said she had to go and that she knew I'd be okay."

In that moment, she was perfectly lucid. He likened it to his mother "coming out of a fog for just a minute and telling me straight from the heart that she loved me and she wasn't afraid anymore."

"It's kinda funny," he said, as we rocked on battered wicker chairs sitting on the front porch, "All my life what I saw most when I looked at Mom was her mental illness and now that she's gone it doesn't really seem important. I'm just glad I was able see that before she died, instead of after."

I asked him what he had said to her when she had awakened momentarily. He smiled and looked directly into my eyes, contemplating how to answer.

"I guess I told her the same thing she told me."

What went unsaid was that such a moment probably wouldn't have happened if he had not dispelled the fog of his judgments. He was there beside her when she emerged from the shell of her coma (and the cloud of her psychosis), ready to hear her words in their crisp, full clarity. And ready to respond from his heart.

Chapter Two
California Gold Rush:
Golden Moments in a Frigid River

Lizzie liked the facts straight and undiluted. The facts were, at thirty-three, with two young children and a husband, she had a cancerous brain tumor that was growing quickly and would probably kill her within six months. It was likely she would become disoriented and need help with the most basic tasks. She knew her path would be difficult. In her mind, as she tried to chart out her future she imagined one catastrophe after another. Her deepest fear was that one day she wouldn't recognize her husband, Ray, or her kids, Tad age seven, and Dana, age four. She was haunted by the thought that when the children were grown they would have no memory of who she was or how much she loved them. She worried their only memories would be of her struggling in the darkness of confusion, saying things she didn't mean and vibrating with the jerky spasms she was sure would occur as she lost control of her muscles.

Another fact was that Lizzie had not been sitting still during the preceding months. After chemotherapy failed to stop her disease she began giving away possessions that had sentimental value. Lightening her load so she could travel unencumbered on the road ahead, she had carefully matched each object with the person she believed would most appreciate it. An autographed photograph of Elvis Presley had gone to her sister-in-law and her collection of seashells to a nephew. The necklace with a "magic amulet" she had gotten while hiking in Ireland went to a friend who had always admired its luminosity and delicate metalwork. Some people thought she was being morbid, but it was comforting for her to find homes for things Ray and kids might not want; she stopped worrying about everything winding up in the trash.

As special keepsakes for Ray and her children, she had come up with a creative idea. She bought a tape recorder and a box of cassette tapes. Several times a day she sat with the tape recorder and talked about her life. She spoke in detail about the days her children were born, how she and Ray met, the things that made her laugh and things that made her sad. Woven throughout were her hopes for Tad and Dana as they grew up, and encouragement for when times got tough. And, of course, there were many expressions of her unconditional love.

She had even coaxed Ray into talking as well. He answered questions as she interviewed him or he played guitar as she sang the folk ballads they loved. Now and then, she simply recorded Dana and Tad playing in the family room—wrestling with their father, arguing about video games, or pretending to be astronauts.

Every night, without fail, she made a copy of the day's recordings and placed one tape in a box for Tad, the other in a box for Dana. She called these her "treasure chests." When the boxes were nearly full she made separate tapes for each child, putting each in its proper box. Then, she put a handmade card on top, wrapped the packages tightly and put her tape recorder away. She instructed Ray to "bury them on a desert island" until Dana was eighteen, at which time he was supposed to dig them up and deliver them. Secretly, she had made a treasure chest for Ray and given it to his mother for safekeeping.

By the time Lizzie finished the project she was having difficulty remembering words and was beginning to lose her short-term memory. She braced herself for more changes. The next several months were difficult as Lizzie and Ray tried hard to keep things "normal" for the kids— waking them for school, helping with homework, and going to soccer practice. Despite their efforts to insulate the children, they could not hide the many doctor appointments, mommy's hair falling out, or sudden glimpses into the pain behind the fragile veneer of normality, like seeing their mother silently crying as she tucked them into bed. Tad and

Dana knew things were not normal, but they joined their parents in pretending otherwise.

Prior to her diagnosis, Lizzie had developed a great deal of strength lifting weights and running. She had even competed in two triathlons. Months after her cancer treatments she was still physically strong and able to do most things for herself. She needed prompts from Ray, however, to remember things like how to get her jacket on and where to put the dirty dishes. Remembering things in general was more difficult. Conversations were harder for her to follow and, at times, seemed to move so fast she could not keep up with them. Her mind was still basically sound, but around its edges she was sliding into confusion.

Her doctor recommended an anti-depressant but she refused, telling him she was on enough pills already. She would move forward on her own terms, making her own choices. If this became impossible, she trusted her family to act on her behalf and do what they thought was best.

Her strength was still evident the morning we met. Her handshake was firm and she easily restrained their medium-sized collie, Maxwell, when I rang the doorbell. Lizzie was cheerful and at ease discussing her illness, but seemed uncomfortable whenever the conversation focused on her for more than a few minutes. When this happened she steered the discussion toward Ray or the children as quickly as she could. Ray seemed tired. He had rearranged his work schedule so he could be home during the day and was not getting much sleep. "Even when I'm in bed," he admitted, "I don't sleep much." His days were filled with caring for Tad and Dana, managing household affairs, and keeping an eye over Lizzie's shoulder.

Just a year earlier, Ray and Lizzie had assumed they were at the beginning of their lives together. It was a painful process, absorbing the realization, still almost unbelievable, that they were actually near the end. When talking about their relationship they had learned to compress the beginning, middle, and end of the story into a mere ten years; or as Ray put it, ten years and three months. The story began

41

with a chance meeting at a nearby botanical garden, the middle was somewhere around the time Dana was born. Now they were talking openly about living in the closing chapter, one that Lizzie predicted would be over before her thirty-fourth birthday.

Lizzie's parents lived nearby and were struggling with similar issues. "Parents aren't supposed to bury their children," her mother said, choking back a swell of emotion, "They're supposed to carry on *our* memory, not the other way around." It was unfathomable that she and her husband would outlive their daughter and be left to speak of her in the somber, lonely intonations of past tense. "I fought in the Korean War," her father said, "and saw buddies of mine floating dead in the Yalu River. When the fighting was over, the river looked like it was made out of blood. It's the only thing I can think of to compare this to, but this is worse." Like Ray, they felt sad, and they felt cheated.

Lizzie was declining more quickly than her cheerful personality and firm handshake suggested. She was losing her coordination and having occasional hallucinations. I quickly learned that I would have to introduce myself to her on each visit, since she had no memory of the previous one. Each time I went she was weaker, less focused. Although Ray decided to take a leave of absence, he found that taking care of Lizzie and the kids was almost more than he could manage.

Lizzie's physical needs had increased, but the real challenge was her behavior. Two months after our first visit she was confused most of the time, suffering from distressing hallucinations and periods of paranoia. Once she locked herself in the bathroom and Ray had to pry the doorknob off with a screwdriver and hammer to get in. Some nights she would wake up screaming, afraid that people were in the room trying to hurt her. Dana and Tad withdrew from her and became anxious whenever she was near. Her worst nightmare, it seemed, was coming true.

"I'm worried about the kids." Ray admitted one day as we watched them sitting in the living room drawing pictures with crayons and colored pencils.

42

As if responding to his cue, Tad jumped up and ran over to show us a picture of a racecar. "What should I draw next?" he asked.

"Why don't you and Dana each draw a picture of your family?" I suggested.

They set themselves to the task and Tad was done quickly. Like his racecar, he was fast and liked to finish first. He showed us a crayon portrait in which he and Dana were very small, standing together in a corner of the page. In the middle was a large green lizard with a face drawn on its belly. Ray was dwarfed next to the creature and was holding its hand. I asked him where his mother was.

"That's her in the monster's tummy," he said.

"How'd she get in there?"

"He swallowed her."

"Why'd he do that?"

"Because he's bad and he likes to make people cry."

"Why does he like to make people cry?"

"Because he's real mean and no one likes him."

"What's the monster's name."

"Cancer-Man."

"What's going to happen to your Mom?" I asked.

Tad shifted his gaze to his feet and grew quiet. He looked at his father as if trying to gauge the impact his words might have, seeking permission to answer. Ray nodded gently and told him it was okay. Finally Tad said, "He's going to kill her."

It's common for parents to try to protect their children from pain and hardship by avoiding direct conversation or discouraging questions about illness and death. Many find it hard to explain what is happening and resort to bland, potentially confusing euphemisms like "Mommy is sleeping" or "She is going on a long trip." Sometimes, in attempts to reassure children, parents even portray death as a happy experience by over-emphasizing that someone has "gone to heaven" or "become an angel." Such explanations may be offered out of love and compassion, but in the absence of broader discussions they can confuse children and leave them to sort things out on their own, drawing conclusions based on fear, limited life experiences, and immature levels of cognitive and emotional development.

When Ray and I discussed the situation openly with Tad and Dana, he discovered they were much more aware of what was going on than he had realized. In the absence of honest information, they had come to some troubling conclusions. Tad, for example, was afraid he had caused Lizzie's disease by being "bad." Dana was worried that Ray was going to "catch" cancer and that she and her brother would be left alone. Once the subject was out in the open, Ray's sensitivity and ability to speak in ways his children could understand opened the channels of communication. Thereafter, he made a point of giving Tad and Dana opportunities to ask questions, keeping them apprised of what was happening with their mother; and what was likely to happen next.

When it appeared that Lizzie was living her last weeks, her parents hired a professional caregiver named Toni to help out during the day. This was a big relief to Ray; it allowed us to talk while Toni sat with Lizzie. We were sitting at the kitchen table one morning; his face was suffused with sadness and exhaustion. With his head down in his left palm he said, "It feels like ninety-five percent of my life with Lizzie right now is pure hell." Watching her struggle while feeling powerless to change the fact that she was "slowly fading away" had worn him down. If he could have traded places with her he would have done it without hesitation, if there were a treatment with even a remote chance of curing her he would have sought it however expensive or far away. But he had fantasized about such things enough to know they were not possible.

Hearing Lizzie shouting from their bedroom, he got up from the table and went to check on her. When he came back he was smiling. He laughed, shook his head, as if surprised, and said, "You know what? Ninety-five percent may be hell, but that other five percent is pure joy. And it's all worth it for a single one of those moments."

"It looks like you just had one of them," I said with a smile.

"Yeah, I did."

"Is it something you're comfortable sharing?"

"It's kinda hard to put in words," he said. "Sometimes it's just a feeling, like a minute ago when she started singing a lullaby the way she used to, right out of the blue. It reminded me..." His voice trailed off as though disappearing down a gently cresting bluff.

"It reminded you...?"

"Reminded me of a look she had in her eyes when we brought Tad home after he was born."

As the challenges of terminal illness accumulate and nerves wear thin, it is easy to lose sight of such moments as Ray was describing. They can be fleeting—unless we watch closely for their arrival we may miss them. As our conversation turned to these moments Ray began mentally sifting them from the recent days. They were moments of closeness and small expressions of affection that, in spite of all the suffering, arrived every day without fail. They were, he thought, "like finding a treasure buried under a mountain of crap."

While we were talking about ways he could hone his sensitivity to these moments, Ray suddenly had an idea. He remembered the tape recorder Lizzie had put away months earlier and got up to see if he could find it. After some searching, he dug it out from under a pillow on a shelf in their hall closet. He brought it back to the kitchen table, tested it, and found that it worked perfectly. "Those tapes aren't quite finished," he said, smiling broadly like a boy about to go on a treasure hunt. "I'm going to catch some of those moments if I have to tape ten hours of hell to do it."

I asked what he had in mind and he explained that he was going to let the tape player record their interactions whenever he was with her. "Then when I catch one of those moments," he said, "I'll transfer it to another tape."

"What will you do with it?" I asked.

45

"I don't know. Maybe I'll hide it away and just know that it's there." Soon Ray would be digging through the sand and rock of the days ahead, in search of buried gold.

After he explained his plan, I asked if he and Lizzie had ever sung a ballad called, "The Days of Forty-Nine." He thought it sounded familiar but couldn't recall it. I explained that it was about the California Gold Rush in the late 1840s. People came from all over the globe looking for shiny nuggets, but by the time most miners finally made it to California the surface gold was gone and digging it out of rivers and rock was much harder than they had anticipated. Probably ninety-five percent of what they went through, I speculated, had more to do with hard work and frustration than gold. Still, most persevered, although many ultimately left with empty pockets. Some of the lucky ones got rich, others left with a small cache of treasure extracted from months of hardship and sacrifice. I offered to tell him about the "Forty-Niners" and he quickly agreed. "One of the things Lizzie always loved about ballads," he said, "was all the stories."

II

By 1848 John Sutter had built a thriving empire in the present-day state of California. His large estate boasted a ranch, fort, blacksmith shop, and store. He had herds of cattle and sheep, fields full of crops and an orchard full of fruit. Although his success had been dependent on his professed allegiance to Mexico, when California had recently been ceded to the United States Sutter had shifted with the prevailing winds. He was not picky about alliances as long as they were good for business.

Americans had already been trickling in along the Oregon-California trail and Sutter figured when more arrived they would need beef and leather from his ranch, supplies from his store and timber from the sawmill he planned to build. He had already sent one of his foremen, James Marshal, to a bend of the American River to construct the mill. What lumber Sutter didn't use he planned to float down the river and sell in Yerba Buena (San Francisco), a small town of about eight hundred, known for its trade in cowhide, tallow, and its role as a supply port for Yankee whalers.

Little did Sutter know he and Marshal were on the cusp of a discovery that would captivate the world. Soon men would throng to the rough trails leading into California, joining thousands doing backbreaking work in icy rivers searching for tiny nuggets of gold.

On January 24, 1848, while Marshal was inspecting a mill race that his men were digging, his eye, he later recalled, "was caught by something shining in the bottom of the ditch...I reached my hand down and picked it up; it made my heart thump, for I was certain it was gold." He quickly returned to consult with Sutter. The two performed some rudimentary tests and agreed it was gold. Given the tenuousness of Sutter's claim to the land, both agreed to keep things quiet, but, not surprisingly, news got out and spread throughout the region.

Almost over night most of the inhabitants of San Francisco packed up and headed to the American River, eager to strike it rich. As news traveled, others followed suit. Walter Colton, who was living in Monterey, recalled that "the blacksmith dropped his hammer, the carpenter his plane, the mason his trowel, the farmer his sickle, the baker his loaf, and the tapster his bottle. All were off to the mines."

News took longer to reach the eastern states, at first trickling in as rumors and suspiciously unbelievable anecdotes. President Polk confirmed these accounts in his message to Congress that December. "The accounts of the abundance of gold in that territory [of California]," the President announced, "are of such an extraordinary character as would scarcely command belief were they not corroborated by the authentic reports of officers in the public service."

His words were a catalyst inspiring tens of thousands

of Americans to head west. Men like William Swain of Niagara County, New York, who otherwise would never have thought of traveling thousands of miles from their friends and families came down with "gold-fever" and set out with dreams of becoming millionaires. They would join thousands already working the rivers and thousands more coming from places like Mexico, South America, Hawaii, and Australia. So many people would come to California the next year that they would be known collectively as "Forty-Niners."

What the President's words had not foretold, however, were the hardships involved in getting to California. He had also failed to hint that finding gold would be far more difficult than simply reaching into a river and pocketing a few nuggets. Swain and his companions would learn that the hard way.

For those in the eastern United States, there were three ways to get to "the diggings." The easiest was by ship around Cape Horn and on to San Francisco, but this could take six months and passage was expensive. A second option was to travel by ship to Panama, cross the Isthmus, and hop a ship to California. This was quicker but one had to contend with the cholera and yellow fever epidemics raging through Panama. Many thousands chose the third option of going overland.

The overland route was grueling and demanded that one go across vast plains, rough mountains, and scorching deserts. The first challenge, though, was simply getting to one of the "jumping off" towns on the Missouri River—such as Independence or Saint Josephs—that marked the beginning of the western trails. These towns were on the fringe of the frontier and reaching them was not easy. By April 1849, about thirty thousand gold-seekers had jammed themselves into these towns with more arriving every day. They scrambled to find supplies, buy wagons and form themselves into traveling groups known as companies. They broke teams of oxen or mules, dashed off letters to family and poured over maps and travel guides trying to decide their precise route. Some would head down the Santa Fe Trail before going west along various intersecting trails, others would take the trail recently blazed by the Mormons on their exodus to Salt Lake City. Most, however, decided to follow the Oregon-California Trail.

Despite their eagerness to get moving, it was mid-April before the wagon trains could safely head out. The trick was to leave late enough in the season that there would be enough grass to provide forage for teams and livestock, but early enough to ensure the wagons wouldn't be trapped in the Sierra Nevadas during winter. Just two years earlier this is what had happened to the Donner party and the results were well known. Trapped by mountains and heavy snow, more than half of the eighty-seven men, women, and children, died of starvation, and some of the survivors had resorted to cannibalism. This stood as a gripping cautionary tale for all but the most foolhardy of the would-be prospectors.

In addition to gold-seekers crowding the Missouri that spring, there was a cholera epidemic raging along the river. Many Forty-Niners never made it beyond Independence or Saint Joes. They died from the disease and were buried, often by strangers, long before they could place a foot in the golden waters of a California stream. William Swain, writing in his journal, noted that "Cholera is the prevailing topic, and you hear but little else spoken of." Despite hopes that they could leave this scourge behind once they were underway, the pestilence would dog them all the way to the Rockies, killing thousands.

When the first companies rolled onto the prairie the wagons were packed to the breaking point. Many became mired and sank into a quagmire of earth drenched from rain and melting snow. Wagons broke axles and cracked wheels as teams of oxen strained under the heavy burdens. Men and animals constantly slipped and accidents, sometimes serious ones, occurred. To move ahead many had to lighten their loads. Things were hastily thrown onto the prairie and left behind.

By the time wagon trains began reaching Fort Kearney, in present-day Nebraska, some men had already had their fill of trail life and turned around, preferring the safety of home to the more perilous prospect of hunting for riches. The agonies of sloughing through mud and rain, going without sleep, managing unruly oxen, and the ever-present specter of accidents and disease had made it clear that finding gold would involve more danger, fortitude, and sacrifice than most had dreamed.

Fort Kearney, located on the bank of the Platte River, stood as a reminder to companies that they were entering "Indian territory." Although hostilities with tribes were rare, most of the travelers viewed Indians with apprehensions rooted in misguided stereotypes. Forty-Niners were more likely to die from their own accidental gunfire or that of friends than from conflict with Indians, but many lived in fear of attack as they journeyed west.

From Kearney, they began a three hundred forty mile stretch along the Platte to Fort Laramie. Along the way, rain and mud were replaced by withering heat and thick clouds of dust that choked lungs, irritated eyes, and coated clothing. Death from cholera continued. It killed quickly. Graves dug and abandoned in haste were a common sight along the trail. Prospector David Dewolf, recalled that it "would make your heart ache to see how some of the companies buried their dead. I have visited graves where the person was not buried more than twenty inches deep and found them dug up by wolves and their flesh eaten off and their bones scattered to bleach upon the plains."

There were plentiful sources of frustration—the rigors and monotony of trail life, the slow pace of advance, disagreements within companies, and separation from loved ones. G.W. Thissel, on the trail that year wrote that "If there is anything that tries a man's patience and brings out his combativeness…it is a trip across the plains…If there is any indication to shirk or do any little mean trick or slightest tendency to hoggishness, it will soon develop."

Animals died from exhaustion. As the first wagons

reached Fort Laramie, many oxen and mules lay dead along the plains and the wagons once again had to be lightened. Things that had seemed essential in Independence were now encumbrances to be sold, given away, or left along the trail.

Making matters worse, the Platte coughed up great swarms of mosquitoes which one letter-writer described as "abundant and unmerciful." Storms, sometimes with pelting hail, slowed the wagons and caused some men to wonder why they had ever left home. River crossings could be deadly and needed to be approached with special care. At one crossing it was reported that nearly thirty people drowned that year. Even shallow rivers could be dangerous, especially for those inexperienced at driving teams and livestock. Wagons could be ferried, but oxen, mules, horses, and cattle, were usually driven into the water.

By the time the Argonauts began rolling up the steady grade of South Pass in the Rockies, the way behind was strewn with discarded supplies. Broken wheels, cracked axles, abandoned wagons and furniture, dead animals and haphazard graves (some without so much as a simple marker) marked their passage and bore witness to their struggle. Many more had turned around; some had already arrived home with stories of travail and hardship. From his New York home George Swain wrote his brother, William, that "The stories of returning emigrants make the plains sound like a kind of Golgotha, inhabited by savages and armed with storms, pestilence and famine to obstruct your passage to the golden land." Perhaps more would have turned back as they entered the Rockies had they known that the hardest days were still ahead. The price for the chance of finding a few nuggets was growing higher every day.

Between South Pass and the treasures of California, rivers flowed across the Forty-Niner's paths as though intentionally laid out to frustrate them. In some places steep grades or stretches of desert fought them for every step. And then there were the Sierras, which William Swain called the "team-killing, back-breaking, legs-soaring mountains." These were stark, punishing mountain ranges with treacherous rocks, deep ravines, and lethal blizzards.

Shortly after crossing South Pass the trail began to split and companies had to make choices based on little or no reliable information. Should they take Sublette's Cut-off or the Mormon Trail? What about Hudspeth's Cut-off? Lassen's Cut-off? Carson's Cut-off? Some even took Hastings Cut-off despite the fate of the Donner party. Whatever path they chose, the men all shared common hardships. Supplies were often dangerously low and some companies faced starvation. After many weeks on a diet with little variety, many began to show symptoms of scurvy. Making matters worse, a new, potentially fatal, disease known as "mountain fever" was added to the list of woes besting the weary Forty-Niners.

In addition to physical challenges and dangers, there were psychological and emotional ones. Privacy was nonexistent, tempers were tested and conflict and disagreement was common. The men were separated from loved ones, packed together day after day with others eager to be at the end of their journey. At night they slept on the ground or wooden wagon planks. Many must have wondered, at least occasionally, if they would ever see their wives or children again. Would a handful of yellowed letters sent hurriedly from the trail have to stand as the only reminder for children of a parent who had died in a distant land? If so, would these speak truthfully of that parent's life, and of the love and hope they had harbored for their children?

Animals began to die in massive numbers, killed by the desolate heat and alkali sand of the Blackrock desert, the menacing Sierras, and sheer exhaustion. J.G. Bruff, writing from Rabbit Hole Spring, said that, "There was scarcely space for the wagons to reach the water holes because of the ox carcasses..." More wagons were abandoned, battered beyond repair or too difficult to pull forward. Some men left their companies and headed out on foot taking nothing but backpacks. Some companies disbanded, leaving every man for himself. With winter descending and many in danger of freezing to death, the army's fledgling Pacific Division sent out rescue parties to bring in stragglers. If they had not done so, many more would have died on the trails to California.

Many Forty-Niners downplayed the hardships in their letters, wanting to protect wives and children from worry. Others, like Andrew Orvis, had no qualms about vividly describing the rigors of their ordeal. After finally making it to California, Orvis wrote his wife that, "you will shed tears when you come to know how much I have suffered and the hardships I have encountered. If it had not been for you and the children to think of, I should certainly have given up and died."

Despite all the hardships and frustrations involved in the overland journey, and the many who had died or turned back along the way, the majority of those who set out onto the prairie in April and May made it to California still optimistic they would strike it rich. Some ninety thousand souls made their way to the goldfields that year, joining thousands who had arrived the year before. By then, the surface gold that had once been so plentiful was gone. There was still gold left, but it was much more difficult to get and there were many more people out digging for it. Now, rather than simply dipping a pan into the water and sifting through sand and pebbles, men had to dig through tons of earth and divert streams and rivers. Dreams of instant riches were quickly dispelled, like fragile gossamer threads borne away by a strong gust of cold air.

With so many treasure hunters crowding the region, simply finding a place to prospect could be a challenge. Nearly every foot of riverbed from the Feather River to the Mariposa had a crew of miners parked on it. Before they could even stake a claim, however, most new prospectors needed to buy supplies. Purchasing these proved to be no easy task. Prices were exorbitant and most exchanges were done in gold dust, flakes, or nuggets. Countless journals and letters complain of the high prices for everything from picks and shovels to the delivery of a letter. To some, it seemed the merchants were the only ones striking it rich.

Once supplied, most miners worked in groups. The labor was intensive and strenuous. Dams needed to be built, rivers channeled, earth shoveled. The work required lifting, sifting, hauling, smashing, and pulling, often while standing in ice-cold water or balancing on piles of slippery rock. One miner figured that finding gold combined "the various arts of canal-digging, ditching, laying stone walls, ploughing, and hoeing."

Living conditions were difficult. Men were crammed into tents or hastily built shelters. Accidents were common, so were illnesses like dysentery, scurvy, and pneumonia. Alonzo Delano wrote in his journal that many simply "rushed to the mines and went to work...without tents, many without blankets to shield them from the cold night air, living on pork and hard bread...Hundreds have been stricken down by disease; many died, while others have been unfitted for work for the rest of the season..."

After months of working hard, paying outrageous prices and possibly succumbing to the temptations of towns like San Francisco or Sacramento, most prospectors had very little gold to show for their efforts. Many had none. Although some had indeed struck it rich, most were lucky to return home with a few flakes or nuggets stashed away. The days and nights spent on the trail and in the diggings often boiled down to a few precious flecks drawn from the otherwise stingy earth. For every nugget found there was a week spent straining across rivers or through prairie mud. For each golden rock, a day and night had been lost bent over with dysentery or the aches of relentless labor.

For many, these few flecks made it all worthwhile. Others walked away with a treasure of even greater worth measured in transcendent flecks of insight, perspective, or understanding. In a letter to his brother, William Swain wrote that he would not choose to "traverse the same route under the same circumstances, even were a princely fortune the sure reward. But were I to be unfortunate in all my business here and arrive at home at last without *one cent*, I should be ever glad that I have taken the trip to California. It has learnt me to have confidence in myself, has disciplined my impetuous disposition and has learnt me to think and act for myself and to look upon men and things in a true light."

Some, of course, went home bitter and disappointed, but many, like Swain, returned with a small pouch of another kind of gold. The kind no cardsharp, whiskey dealer or grasping merchant could touch. Gold that had been chipped away from the rock and sifted from the sand of difficult experience, and from days spent prospecting in a river larger than the American or the Sacramento: the river of one's life.

III

When we are engaged in difficult tasks or laboring in the frigid streams and stony rivers of sadness, grief, and uncertainty, it can be hard to remember that along side the rough gravel and swirling detritus of the riverbed there are nuggets of gold. These take many different forms. Perhaps it is something important that we learn about ourselves, or others, that we could not have learned under easier circumstances. Maybe it is an enhanced awareness of our resilience and capacity for sacrifice or a gentler acceptance of our limitations. Some gold may appear as mere moments during which we find reassurance, peace, or happiness amid the churning waters. All of these stand and, if we nurture them, grow in our lives as part of our own personal cache of treasure. When our labors are over, or even as they continue, if we have been attentive to this gold we may look back and be glad to have prospected so well despite the hardships endured.

I only saw Ray one more time before Lizzie died. On that visit he said he was "finding some gold dust down in the diggings." He had even bought another tape recorder; a voice activated one, so he could let it run in the background whenever Lizzie was awake. At night he sifted out the moments he wanted to save and recorded them from one machine to the other. He estimated that for every hour of recording, he probably got three or four minutes of gold. In the process, he learned to pay close attention to these moments and appreciate them more deeply. Even when sadness and frustration arrived, as they often did, he did not lose his bearings and was able to stay focused.

I asked him if there were any themes emerging in what he was extracting from his hours of taping. Without hesitation he said there were two things: songs and laughter. More than at any other times, it was when she laughed and sang that Ray could "see her spirit." "You never know when she is going to do either, or even why she does it," he said, "but when she does, I can see her come out, for just a minute from behind her illness." Armed with his tape player and deepened awareness, Ray rarely missed even a fleck of Lizzie's spirit as it sparkled beneath her confusion.

The same was true of the time he spent with Dana and Tad. Once he stopped trying to insulate them from what was happening and allowed them to ask questions and express feelings openly, he was able to support them better. Tad became less withdrawn and stopped hiding in his room. Dana stopped clinging to Ray and following him wherever he went. Ray also created ways for them to stay connected with their mother. When the kids realized Lizzie wasn't mad at them, that her seemingly strange words and behaviors were due to the illness, they were more at ease going into her room. Although Lizzie was sleeping most of the day, Ray and the kids set aside a special time every afternoon when they all sat in her room and told her about their day, read her stories, or sang one or two of the songs she liked. "What started as special time for the kids," Ray said, "turned into a special time for me too." Focusing on the golden moments buried in life's silt and grit had changed everything. Truly, he was prospecting well.

By autumn of 1850, William Swain had also prospected well, but he had little gold to show for it. Like many Forty-Niners, he was disillusioned and tired of the rough life and bald avarice of the mining camp. Most of all, he missed his family. As thousands more made their way to California over the same trails he had taken the year before, Swain wanted to go home and be done with his quest for riches. When he received a letter from his brother assuring him there was no shame in returning without gold, it was all he needed to start packing his bags. "You have friends who will meet you just as cordially unsuccessful as successful— and more so," his brother had written, "for we are sure you have suffered, suffered, suffered..."

Shortly thereafter, Swain joined the swelling ranks of those leaving California. He booked passage on an ocean steamer and headed for Panama. This time he would skip the overland journey and return home as quickly as possible.

In the decades before his death in 1904, William Swain rarely traveled much beyond the boundaries of his thriving farm, but he constantly returned to his experiences in California. His grandchildren grew up hearing stories and reading the many letters he had sent from the trail and mining camps. His participation in the gold rush was one of the most important and formative experiences of his life. As years passed, he regularly affirmed his claim from the gold fields that, regardless of the hardships of the trip and his failure to get rich, the journey had been well worth it. The experience had deepened his self-confidence and made him more discerning about his companions. The inexpressible joy he had felt when reunited with his family reminded him of the wealth he had always possessed, but had at times failed to appreciate.

On July Fourth in 1849 Swain had written a letter to his wife, Sabrina, while camped a few miles from Fort Laramie. "If it were consistent," he had confessed, "I should long for the time to come when I shall turn my footsteps homeward, but such thoughts will not answer now, for I have a long journey yet to complete and then the object of the journey to accomplish." In the years after his return, it became a family tradition to read this letter every July Fourth and hear stories of his adventures. In the end, they surely would have all agreed that William Swain had accomplished much more than he had ever envisioned, and his reward was more durable and precious than mere gold.

Lizzie died peacefully in her home. About two months after her funeral, Ray was surprised when his mother stopped by with a box full of tapes for him. Initially, Lizzie had asked that it be delivered on the first anniversary of her death, but on reflection she had decided that a "mother's intuition" would be a better guide and she had asked Ray's mother to listen to hers. On hearing Lizzie speak directly to him, her voice strong, her mind clear, Ray was ambivalent about his mother's timing and wondered if "it was just making me feel worse." But he soon found comfort in her words of encouragement, especially as they related to his new role as a single father of grieving children. After a week or so, Ray realized he had been given a deep vein of golden ore.

Lizzie's worries about Dana and Tad turned out to be unfounded. Despite their young ages, they both have many warm memories of her, the richness of which suggests they will be enduring ones. It will be several years before Dana's eighteenth birthday. For now, two chests of treasure are buried away in a safe place. If unearthing them prior to the appointed day seems right, Ray has decided to do so, citing a "father's intuition" as a fair gauge to use when charged with protecting such a valuable store of gold.

Chapter Three
Joshua Slocum in the Strait of Magellan: Creating Positive Change in the Face of Resistance

"How come we can't get around this?" Bev was frustrated and it showed.

All Ike could do was throw his hands up and shake his head. They had grown apart during the many years of their marriage and they wanted to find a way to regain their closeness, but felt stuck. Finally, Ike suggested that, "Maybe if you just learned to relax some, we wouldn't always get like this." Looking back, he acknowledged, he should have known it wasn't a good way to put things.

Bev felt blamed and responded with angry criticism.

We had explored this pattern several times, the way a single word or sentence, a facial expression or tone of voice could quickly lead to an argument that neither wanted to have. By then, they understood some of the ways they pushed each other's buttons. We had discussed strategies for changing these patterns, but it kept happening anyway. It was as though they were constantly moving in opposite directions, like small boats caught in conflicting winds. Changing things was hard; their patience was wearing thin.

They had been married almost forty-four years, raised seven children and had several grandchildren. For most of their lives they had taken care of Bev's brother, Dean, who was born with Cerebral Palsy. Dean, in his early fifties, had been receiving hospice care for about nine months. He had already lived well beyond the most optimistic guesses of his doctor and had shown few signs that his condition was deteriorating. According to the hospice nurse, there were small "indications" that he was declining, but no one else could see them. This, and the very fact he had lived into his fifties, was a testimony to the care and love he received from Bev.

Much of her life revolved, as it always had, around her brother's needs and comfort. She frequently sacrificed her own well-being while attending to his—working to the point of exhaustion, neglecting her elevated blood pressure, chronic arthritis, and need for sleep. Although Dean was not able to speak, Bev seemed to know intuitively what he needed and how to reassure him.

Initially, my visits were cordial but short. Bev was reluctant to discuss her internal experience, preferring more general topics of conversation. Ike was usually working down at his automobile repair shop and, if not, he usually found a reason to go there shortly after I arrived. They described themselves as simple country folks and tended to keep their thoughts and feelings to themselves. Bev rarely spoke about herself, much less about the details of her and Dean's frightening childhood. It was over and done with and there was no point in bringing it up, besides, it was nobody's business but hers and her brother's.

Over time, however, she came to appreciate the opportunity to discuss what it was like caring for Dean and her anxiety about his impending death. In doing so, she made several references to their early years. It was impossible, she said, "to understand why I protect him so much, and baby him the way I do, unless you know what we went through."

Keeping her memories buried for so long had not mitigated their fury. When Bev began exploring these childhood years she was surprised at the intensity of the emotions they evoked. "It feels," she said, "like it just happened yesterday."

Vivid memories of her father came flooding back. He had been a violent man, full of rage and hatred. He had made her life nearly unbearable. He was physically abusive, regularly assaulting Bev and her mother, Geraldine. On three occasions he had choked Bev so violently that she had lost consciousness. She was never sure if he had intended to kill her or just scare her. Once, at the age of eleven, she stole a box of rat poison from a hardware store, intending to put it in her father's food. For weeks she agonized over whether to kill him before finally deciding to pour it down the outhouse.

"Sometimes I think I shoulda done it," she said coldly.

"Why didn't you?"

She thought about it and said, "Maybe I was scared. Or maybe I didn't want to be like him."

"How did you want to be?"

"I wanted to be like the opposite of everything he was."

He drank heavily, his most savage abuse coming when he was drunk. She remembered listening for clues to what might be in store for them whenever he came through the door at night. "I could always tell," she said, "when he'd been drinking by the way the dogs acted. If they were quiet when he got out of the truck I knew we were in trouble, if they barked, we were probably going to be safe that night."

Geraldine tried her best to protect Bev, but it was impossible. She tried to distract her husband's rage and direct it toward herself, but he knew he could hurt her more by attacking Bev. The more she tried to protect her daughter, the more angry and vindictive he became. Bev and her mother shared lives under siege. A siege that was invisible to neighbors who thought, or who chose to think, they "were just one big happy family." Every day they had walked on tenterhooks hoping to avoid an explosion, knowing that no amount of accommodation or compliance could guarantee their safety.

Dean was not a target of his attacks, but of his neglect. Her father treated him, Bev said, "like he was a useless piece of furniture to be put away and forgotten about." Bev helped with his care, often looking after Dean when her mother was recovering from at attack. When her father was killed in a bar fight, Bev was relieved and didn't shed a tear.

Whenever she talked about her father, her voice vibrated with anger as sharp as a thunderclap on a winter night. It was not hard to understand why her rage was so strong, even after forty-five years. Still, I asked her why she thought it had remained so fresh.

"Where do you want me to start?" she quipped.

"What comes to your mind first?"

She looked annoyed. "What comes to mind first is how that bastard stole twenty-five years of my mother's life and stomped on them. He made her life a hell and she was stuck there."

"How did his violence affect you?"

She started to speak, then stopped, as though catching the thought before it was spoken. She finally said, "Sometimes I think it made it impossible for me to trust people, or to feel like I can rely on them."

"Even Ike?"

"Yeah," she admitted.

"What stops you from trusting him?"

She changed the subject.

Bev had met Ike when he was on leave from the army, shortly before her father was killed. Growing up in a small town, they had seen each other from time to time but had never spoken. Bev was "amazed" at his good manners and "the way he smiled all the time." Although she had vowed she would never get married under any circumstances, she felt safe with him. A year later, after he returned from the army and landed a job as a mechanic, they were engaged. "I was scared," she said, "because Mama had gotten stuck after marrying a man who seemed like a decent fellow. But I just had a strong feeling about Ike, that it was okay."

Bev's instincts were well founded. Slowly, her fears of getting *stuck* as her mother had been began to fade as she realized the depth of Ike's kindness. In those early years they did many things together. On Saturdays they often borrowed a trailer from a neighbor, loaded up their rowboat and headed for a nearby lake. They would spend the entire day paddling, trading off from time to time on the oars, although Ike was quick to note that he had always offered to do all the rowing, but "She'd have none of it." Soon, they were bringing their first child along, and Bev finally agreed to let Ike do the rowing. "It wasn't because I couldn't do my share," she pointed out, "but only because I already had my hands full."

They had only been married three years when things changed dramatically. Geraldine had a stroke that left her unable to walk without assistance and she and Dean moved in with them. By then, they had two children and were scrambling to take care of the family and pay the bills. Somehow they found enough space in their tiny home so that Ike didn't have to sleep in the truck.

Almost overnight, Bev and Ike were given new responsibilities and pulled in different directions. This made it difficult to find time for each other. When Geraldine died several years later, there were four children and Dean's needs had increased along with the expense of his medical care.

There were always things that had to be done. In addition to supporting Dean and the kids, they ran a small farm raising pumpkins and Christmas trees to supplement their income. To make ends meet, Ike worked overtime. Later, when he took over as manager of the automobile shop, his workload became even more demanding. Bev stayed busy at home from early morning until very late at night. "There were days," she recalled, "when between the kids and Dean and the farm, I didn't have time to stop and eat." By the time Ike returned from work and the evening chores were done, there was no time for anything other than catching a few hours sleep before they got up and did it all over again.

Pulled into separate spheres, Bev and Ike began living what they referred to as "separate lives." With little time to reflect on what was happening and many demands to distract them, the distance between them grew. As the years passed and Ike's shop expanded, the situation only got worse. It was as though they were living on different coasts of the same broad ocean. By the time the last of their children left home, Bev and Ike were like strangers, their separation wielding the weight of a long-standing habit.

Rather than face the problem, they ignored it. "I guess we were too scared or too pessimistic," Bev said, "to admit what was going on." Bev made Dean the center of her attention, telling herself she was the only one who knew how to take care of him. Ike poured his energies into his work, telling himself he needed to be there to keep an eye on things or the business would fall apart. Along with separation came feelings of resentment and of being unappreciated. Arguments were common and there was tension whenever they were in the same room.

During the time hospice was involved two things converged that made this situation even more difficult, and made addressing it unavoidable—Dean caught pneumonia and appeared to be dying, and Ike was nearing retirement. The two things that were providing a buffer between them—the demands of Dean's care and Ike's responsibilities at work—would be soon gone. They would no longer be able to hide behind them. Also, in light of these twin specters of death and retirement, they were filled with an acute awareness that they were getting older. Silently, each had been taking stock of their lives and reflecting on their mortality.

It is common to have such thoughts while caring for someone with a terminal illness. Questions about one's own death are normal. Caregivers may even experience the lingering tides of grief long since laid aside, as memories of others who have died return to their minds. In Ike's case this was particularly vivid. When he had been a teenager one of his younger sisters had died at home after a short struggle with influenza. As Dean attempted to fight a respiratory infection, his lungs filling with fluid, his brows dripping with fever, Ike began "reliving" the days long before when his sister had endured similar symptoms before she had died. "I watched Mama take care of her," he said, "just like I'm watching Bev take care of her brother. And I watched her die, just like Dean is dying now."

Bev was also mulling over equally serious thoughts. Taking care of Dean had transformed her life as indelibly as would his death. She knew that dramatic changes lay ahead and she worried she might be left to grieve Dean's death with little support from Ike. It was even possible she would find herself in a relationship, though not violently abusive, as seemingly constricting and inescapable as her mother's had been.

Motivated by these private reflections, Ike began staying for my visits and he and Bev started talking openly about their relationship. They had spent a lot of time and energy finding ways to avoid talking, so the first few conversations were hard. Finding common ground was difficult and tempers often flared. Once, Bev jokingly suggested I bring a lion tamer with me on subsequent visits to keep things from getting out of hand.

Gradually though, a picture emerged of what had happened and what they wanted to do about it. They still loved each other, but, in many ways, they no longer knew each other. Without Dean, the children, or the repair shop to hold their attention, they would have to find a way to get reacquainted. Swallowing hard, trusting in their mutual commitment, and, as importantly, their shared sense of humor, they plunged into the job of reconnecting. They learned to communicate more openly and attempted to become more forgiving of each other's foibles (real and perceived). By doing so, they realized how much they missed talking without an undercurrent of anger, blame, and competing agendas muddling things up.

They quickly created small, but significant, changes in the way they interacted, finding great satisfaction in this. They began to laugh together and interrupted each other less often. As often happens, however, the smooth sailing and excitement of the early part of a new journey soon gave way to difficult seas and strong headwinds. The old patterns they were trying to escape proved resilient and adaptable. After their initial flourish of success, they again found themselves getting angry and avoiding each other. Discouraged, they questioned whether their efforts were worth pursuing, each blaming the other for not really wanting to change or for not caring enough to follow through.

Dean's respiratory infection was less virulent than expected, slowly clearing up, much to Bev's relief. The owner of Ike's shop asked him to work an additional three months to train the new manager. These things, combined with their disappointment and waning motivation to talk, reduced their sense of urgency about the impending changes.

Ike missed a couple visits and appeared to have no intention of continuing our conversations. Bev wondered if the joint visits had been a mistake. Still, she could not accept that after Dean died she and her husband might be like strangers living in the same house. She had spent much of her early life feeling unloved and unsafe. The thought of living the last part of her life the same way was painful and unsettling.

Fortunately, Ike's absence turned out to be temporary. When he returned, they reflected on the initial enthusiasm they had had for trying to navigate through difficult relational straits toward deeper closeness. They discussed their discouragement about being blown off course in spite of their heartfelt efforts. It was on this visit that Ike, frustrated and feeling a little hopeless, had suggested that Bev "relax," and once more they had found themselves feeling angry and misunderstood.

When things calmed, I asked if they had ever encountered a storm when, years earlier, they were out on the lake in their rowboat. They both remembered one storm that had come up out of nowhere. They were so far out in the water that day that the shoreline wasn't visible. They laughed recounting their efforts to reach the beach; afraid they would capsize at any moment. Neither was sure they could swim hard enough, or even in the right direction, to make the shore, but slowly, methodically, they found their way.

I suggested this was a good analogy for their situation and asked if I could tell them the story of Joshua Slocum sailing in the Strait of Magellan. The Strait, marking one of the few passages between the Atlantic and Pacific, has long challenged mariners with its fierce squalls and treacherous currents. In 1896 Joshua Slocum, while completing history's first solo circumnavigation of the globe, found himself struggling through the Strait's narrow channels, buffeted by waves, lashed by rains, and threatened by hostile coastal inhabitants. Despite these and other challenges, he kept plodding forward. Even as he was swept back time and again, he remained focused on his ultimate goal of reaching the Pacific, confident that if he was patient he would eventually get there.

Laughing at my suggestion, Bev said, "Anything's better than listening to more of Ike's nonsense." Taking the humor, not the bait, Ike laughed and said, "You go on and tell us about this here Slocum fellow. At least one of us will listen with good manners." After the laughs subsided, I offered them a story.

II

In the winter of 1892 Joshua Slocum was down on his luck. Nearly fifty, out of work and virtually penniless, he was unsure of his next move. Since the age of sixteen he had worked on the water and he longed to return as captain of another ship, but after making inquiries on the Boston waterfront, he had found that "there were not enough ships to go round." He could have found work on a steamer, but in a day when most freighters were replacing wind power with steam, Slocum moved by the sail and he refused to change. With few options left, he was beginning to feel stuck.

While he was walking on the wharves trying to turn something up, he ran into an old friend, Eben Pierce, retired from the whaling trade. Pierce saw Slocum's plight and offered him a ship. The *Spray*, he admitted, was in need of repairs, but if Slocum was willing to put in the work, it might once again be seaworthy. In fact, it would take a great deal of work since the vessel was rotting in a Fairhaven pasture and had not been afloat in seven years. Most passersby assumed the *Spray* would be hauled off as salvage, its days as an Atlantic oyster sloop long gone. But Slocum, an accomplished shipbuilder, was confident he could repair the ship's rotting hull and dilapidated floorboards, and that he and the *Spray* would once again ply the seas.

Slocum landed at Fairhaven the next day eager to size up the job and begin working on the restoration. For the next thirteen months he worked on the *Spray*. He felled an oak with which to rebuild the keel, hauled in pine for planks, curved saplings for ribbing and brought in spruce for a mast. He planed, sanded, scraped, bolted, caulked, sewed and tied until finally both he and the *Spray* were ready for launch.

Roughly thirty-six feet long and fourteen-feet wide with two cabins, the vessel quickly became his home. Now the question was, what to do next? He tried his hand at fishing but concluded, with dry humor, that he "had not the cunning properly to bait a hook." Occasionally he chartered the *Spray* for short passenger cruises but found little satisfaction in this line of work.

By the spring of 1895 Slocum had decided on a daring plan, he would sail alone around the world. So far as anyone knew, nobody had ever attempted a solo voyage before. Most who watched him weigh anchor that April and sail out of Boston Harbor doubted it could be done. More than a few were convinced he would be lost beneath the waves and never seen again.

Slocum had no such misgivings. Talking with a reporter, he explained that he would simply "sleep in the day time and keep the boat going at night...When it blows too hard I shall get out my sea anchor, batten everything down tight, and go below for a sleep and let the gale blow itself out." As for his route, the first stop after loading provisions in Gloucester was his childhood home in Nova Scotia, Brier Island. He hadn't been back since running away from home thirty-five years earlier and signing on with the first schooner willing to hire a green hand. Perhaps Slocum realized the dangers of his impending journey more than he let on and wanted to see his home one more time, or maybe he wanted to start this new chapter of his life from the place of his birth. Maybe he was just nostalgic. Whatever his reasons, something drew him home.

From Nova Scotia he intended to sail across the Atlantic to the Mediterranean Sea. He figured he would sail through the Suez Canal and make his way to the Indian Ocean. Helped along by the dependable winds of the Gulf Stream, he made good time in the Atlantic. After several days he had worked out a system for tying the *Spray's* rudder in a fixed position so it would sail on its own while he rested or did chores. When he arrived on the edge of the Mediterranean after a month of sailing, he was in good spirits. By then he had adjusted to the stark solitude that, early on, had left him "drifting into loneliness, an insect on a straw in the midst of the elements."

At Gibraltar, British authorities persuaded Slocum to change his route. They informed him that the Mediterranean and Red seas were home to pirates; a small vessel traveling alone would be an irresistible target. He decided to heed their advice and cross the Atlantic again, this time on a southwesterly course with the goal of making his way to the Pacific by going around the tip of South America. Ironically, as soon as he left Gibraltar a swift moving ship full of North African pirates chased him, but he managed to outdistance them after their ship was swamped by a well-timed wave.

For anyone else, crossing the Atlantic alone would have been suicidal, but after decades at sea Slocum was a nautical jack-of-all-trades. Part oceanographer, part meteorologist, part astronomer, he could read the wind, clouds, and stars. He could decode subtle messages in the surface of the water, the sounds made by sea birds or the feel of a breeze. Part mechanic, part homemaker, he could set sails, splice rope, repair hulls, sew, cook, and wash clothes all in the course of a day. He was a one-man crew and his second voyage across the Atlantic went as well as if he had been accompanied by a full set of deck hands.

He made landfall at Pernambuco, on the coast of Brazil, in early October, staying long enough to make some repairs on the *Spray* and purchase supplies. Soon he would be approaching Cape Horn—the tip of South America—where some of the world's most treacherous, unforgiving waters waited. At the Cape, the Atlantic meets the Pacific creating mountainous waves, whirlpools, and thundering gales of sail-tearing, rig-ripping winds, often accompanied by hail, snow, or sleet. Some of the worst sailing conditions on the planet guarded the transition from one ocean to another. Rather than rounding the Horn, Slocum decided to go through the Strait of Magellan—a winding channel, over three hundred miles long, between the southern tip of Chile and the island of Tierra del Fuego. Although this route offered protection from the open ocean, it would be no easy journey. Slocum knew the Strait had been making ghosts of seafarers for centuries. The next months would be some of the most challenging and dangerous of his life. Making headway would require patience, persistence, and a willingness to keep trying in spite of many setbacks and the powerful winds that would blow him off course.

In January 1896, he was sailing cautiously along the Patagonian coast nearing the Strait. As if warning him of what lay ahead, Poseidon sent a "tremendous wave" crashing down on the *Spray*, which Slocum described as "the culmination…of many waves." Acting quickly, he lowered the sail, lest the ship capsize, and hurried up the rigging to the peak halyard, hanging on with all his strength as "a mountain of water" crashed over the boat and left him dangling high in the mast, sopping wet. He must have been quite a sight, holding on high above deck, drenched and dripping like a soaked oilcloth rag. The wave, however, was just the beginning of his ordeal.

As the *Spray* approached the Strait's entrance, the water was rough, the waves choppy. According to Slocum, the wind was "blowing a gale [that] sent feather-white spume along the coast." Once in the narrow channel, he recalled that, "long trailing kelp from sunken rocks waved forebodingly under [the *Spray's*] keel, and the wreck of a great steamship smashed on the beach abreast gave a gloomy aspect to the scene."

Almost as soon as he had entered the narrows, a tremendous squall swept down with a force that threatened to push the *Spray* back into the Atlantic. For thirty hours Slocum strained to hold the rudder and adjust the sails in the face of this furious storm. When the winds finally subsided, despite all of his exertions the sloop was in nearly the same place as when the storm had started. Sometimes, simply holding one's ground can exact a heavy toll. By the time Slocum landed in Punta Arenas, a coaling station on the tip of Chile, he must have been exhausted.

The Chilean Port captain advised him not to proceed without hiring a crew to assist in repelling attacks from the gangs of native men that often preyed on smaller vessels. Slocum, however, could not find anyone willing to join him so he prepared to continue his voyage alone. Fortunately for him, a farseeing fellow captain gave him a bag of carpet-tacks, a gift Slocum would find "worth more than all the fighting men and dogs of Tierra del Fuego."

As he departed from Punta Arenas he kept his rifle and pistol loaded. He had fair winds that day and sailing was good. Night, however, brought his first experience with the frightening squalls called williwaws. He described their awesome power as "compressed gales of wind that Boreas handed down over the hills in chunks," noting that, a "full-blown williwaw will throw a ship, even without sail on, over on her beam ends..." These harrowing winds resisted his every effort forward, pushing against him all the way to Fortescue Bay. Worn-out and glad to be alive, he dropped anchor for a much needed rest.

The next day Joshua Slocum headed into gales so powerful they seemed animated with a will bent entirely on stopping him. He tried to move forward but couldn't. After only three miles, for which he exchanged a great deal of sweat, he slipped into a cove to sit out the storm, afraid that if he did not, the *Spray* would go down. For the next two days he waited for the tempest to subside as he tossed and rolled, satisfied simply to remain afloat. When the gusts finally slackened he raised sail and resumed course.

Not far from the cove, he met a threat as dire as any that nature had presented. Bearing down on the *Spray* were several canoes paddled by men from Tierra del Fuego. It was plain their intentions were hostile. The leader of the group matched the description of a man nicknamed "Black Pedro," whom Chilean authorities suspected was responsible for several murders. Slocum fired his rifle a couple times and they retreated back to the bay, unwilling to risk a full attack. Rather, they would bide their time and wait for an opportunity to take the *Spray* by surprise.

For the next two weeks the vessel inched forward against wind, rain, sleet, large waves and strong currents. Slocum was often forced to retreat or seek whatever shelter was available in order to ride out the storms. Although his sights were on the Pacific, many days found him no closer to his goal at nightfall than he had been when the sun had come up.

By early March, the end of the Strait was finally in view although another squall was brewing. The *Spray*, Slocum later remembered, "plunged into the Pacific Ocean at once, taking her first bath of it in the gathering storm." For a moment it looked like the feisty captain would sail clear. Visions of sailing up the Chilean coast must have flashed in his mind and lifted his spirits. But the storm that greeted him in the Pacific was too fierce to take head on. Rain fell as if thrown down in sheets, waves the size of tall buildings rolled with horrifying pitch tossing the *Spray* as through it were a speck of wood. Whips of lightening lashed the water's surface. The wind was so destructive Slocum had to lower all sails and let the gales and water take him wherever they pleased.

It must have been a hard pill to swallow, knowing that just as he had finally made it through the Strait he was being pushed back into the Cape he had tried so hard to avoid. He had no choice, "No ship in the world," he wrote, "could have stood up against so violent a gale." Moving toward the Pacific was no longer his chief concern as he struggled to keep from being wrecked by foaming waves.

For four days he was pushed back. During that time he slept little and worried a lot. His face bled where it had been pelted by sleet and hail, his hands were raw from pulling on wet ropes. The *Spray's* rigging and sails were in tatters and Slocum feared he would be pushed into the grip of Cape Horn. To make matters worse, in the midst of the storm's kaleidoscopic fury, he had lost his bearings. When the seas finally settled, it was nighttime and Slocum had no idea where he was. The next morning, he realized he was drifting into one of the most difficult waterscapes any sailor could imagine. It was a place known as the Milky Way, a name that came from the countless rocks jutting just beneath the water's surface. These stony sentinels stretched like stars in a night sky and stirred up breakers, threatened hulls, and churned up currents. Many ships had already gone down in this place. Charles Darwin had come this way on the *Beagle* and written that, "Any landsman seeing the Milky Way would have nightmares for a week." Slocum, familiar with Darwin's account, noted that mariners had nightmares as well.

He knew that if he could navigate this maze of rocks and waves he would be able to re-enter the Strait of Magellan through the Cockburn Channel, which was still preferable to trying to round South America in the open ocean. Cautiously, he found his way through the treacherous labyrinth back into the Strait. By the time he made Punta Arenas he had mended his sails and weathered another attack by Fuegians. This time they had attempted to board his vessel when he was asleep, only to find that the carpet-tacks scattered strategically on deck played havoc with bare feet.

In the days ahead, Slocum would continue to sail into the powerful williwaw gales. Snow, sleet, and breaking waves seemed like daily fare, and the natives were an ever-present threat. It would be the middle of April before he found his way into the Pacific without being tossed back toward the Cape. In the end, his trip through the Strait took almost as much time as his two Atlantic crossings combined.

Moving forward was slow and arduous, on some days impossible. Many times he had been blown back by winds and waves, left to retrace his earlier progress over again.

But the transition from one ocean to another is no easy journey. It can be frightening sailing away from the shores of a familiar coast in search of new waters and new possibilities. It takes time, patience, and a willingness to continue sailing even while being pushed back by unfriendly winds. As Slocum headed north into the Pacific, a final wave, larger, he recalled, "than others that had threatened all day," broke over the *Spray* and seemed to "wash away old regrets."

III

On any journey there are bound to be capes and barriers that obstruct or hinder us. As we attempt to find our way around them or chart our way through their intricate channels, we may have to work hard, enduring many setbacks before we finally succeed. It can be discouraging to find ourselves losing ground, at times winding up back where we started. With each setback, however, we have the opportunity to grow wiser and more familiar with the way ahead.

Sometimes these obstructions are tangible, such as the white-capped waves Joshua Slocum found in the Milky Way or the pressures Ike and Bev faced as they worked to pay their bills and care for their family. Others exist more in our minds, often reinforced by habits and emotional patterns. For Bev and Ike these included the hopelessness they occasionally experienced and the painful patterns into which their interactions had calcified.

When major life changes appear on the horizon, as with Dean's terminal condition and Ike's retirement, they often mark a transition from one chapter of our lives to another. At such times, many people find themselves reflecting on life's larger questions. How have I lived my life? How have I treated others? How will I handle the changes ahead? How much longer will I live? How much longer does my spouse have? Is this how I want my life to be? In the swirl of these questions, Bev and Ike realized that they had been allowing a williwaw of misunderstandings and hurt feelings to foster a pattern of separation. The time had come to chart a new course.

Once he was in the Pacific, Slocum charted his course for the island of Juan Fernandez off the coast of Chile. After the pounding the *Spray* had taken, the island was a good place to make repairs and catch up on some rest. From there he sailed west, breaking his solitude only occasionally to lower anchor at various islands on his way to Australia. A highpoint of these short respites came on Samoa where he had the chance to meet the widow of Robert Louis Stephenson. In 1890, she and her husband had settled on the island—when her husband died she had decided to stay.

At New Guinea Slocum arrived in the aftermath of a misbegotten gold rush that had led to far more misery than riches. After witnessing the grisly plight of destitute miners straggling in from the Mai-Kusa River, he arranged to give a lecture on his travels in order to raise money for their aid. "He would have been a hardened wretch," Slocum recalled, "who could look on and not try to do something for them."

From Australia he sailed west. By March 1898, he was in Cape Town, South Africa. Tension there was palpable. He left this troubled settlement only months before the entire region exploded into the depredations of the Boer War.

The vast Atlantic once again stood between Slocum and home as he plunged in for one last crossing. As he had throughout his journey, he continued to encounter storms. In June, not far from New York, he was overtaken by one so fierce that the *Spray's* rigging began to shred and one of its masts snapped off. For several days he worked indefatigably to stay afloat as his ship rocked, its sails ripping from their jibs like paper. By the time the storm blew through, Slocum was "tired, tired, tired of baffling squalls and fretful cobble-seas."

Bev and Ike were tired as well. They had spent years drifting apart. The currents that separated them were difficult to sail beyond. Meaningful change, the kind that creates a lasting transformation in the deep layers of who we are and in our relationships, rarely comes in an instant. It usually follows in the wake of slow and steady movement over time, often amidst heavy winds and numerous setbacks. Knowing this helped them keep their situation in perspective. While we were discussing the story of Joshua Slocum, Bev wondered if she and Ike had been "pushed back into the Strait." Ike laughed and said, "Now wait a minute, we still have to get through that old Milky Way first."

After his respiratory infection, Dean's condition had visibly worsened and he began declining at a steady pace. Ike decided not to postpone his retirement and, without the demands of work, he began helping Bev with Dean's care, or as he put it, "Bev finally *let* me help." It was another step in getting reacquainted. As the days passed, small steps accumulated as they made headway toward mending their marriage. Tempers still flared, misunderstandings still occurred, but the havoc these created was less destructive and storms abated more quickly.

When Dean died, Bev's pain was dense, like cold sea mist. It was, she thought, "about the hardest thing I've ever had to go through." Ike tried to be supportive, but often questioned the value of his efforts. For years he had fixed things down at the shop. He was good at it, but there was nothing he could do to fix Bev's sorrow. No belt he could replace or part he could install would counter the deep hollows of her grief. They would both have to be patient.

Without Dean as the center of her life, the world seemed strange and unfamiliar to Bev. It helped, though, that she and Ike were no longer leading separate lives. Once again, she was beginning to see Ike's gentle spirit as he stood by her in her grief. Slowly, the lens of distrust through which

Bev had long filtered the events of her world began to lose its distorting tint. "I still don't trust people, especially men," she said, "but I'm finally learning to trust Ike. When I look back, I should have done it a long time ago."

In the crush of her brother's death, Bev rediscovered the instinct that had told her long ago that Ike was the perfect companion for her life's voyage. Like a weary mariner returning to a familiar dock, she knew she was home safe.

On June 3 1898, Joshua Slocum was safe as well. He sailed the *Spray* into the Acushnet River and onto Fairhaven where he tethered the plucky ship at the same dock he had left nearly three years earlier. "I secured her," he recalled, "to the cedar spile driven in the bank to hold her when she was launched. I could bring her no nearer home."

Bev's fear that she would be stuck after Dean died abated slowly. The way ahead, though difficult at times, was navigable and rewarding. Such fears and concerns stood like reminders of what may have been if she and Ike had not joined hands and tacked into, rather than away from, the winds confronting them.

It took a long time before Bev began to regain her balance. After several months, tentatively at first, as though doing something awkward, she and Ike started going out to dinner or a movie. For years they had not been able to do this, since one of them always had to be home with Dean. The last time I spoke with them on the telephone they had even been out to the lake and rented a rowboat. This time they stayed close to shore and Ike joked that, "Now that I really need the help, I can't get her to paddle." They were planning to visit the ocean in a couple weeks. Bev asked if I remembered the story I told them "about that guy who had so much trouble getting around South America?"

I told her I did and she laughed. She asked how long Slocum's trip had taken.

"About three years," I said.

I could hear her turn her head and say to Ike, "I think we're going to make it a little ahead of schedule for a change."

77

Section Two
Looking Deeply Into the Shadows: Facing the Past

*The secret of life is in the shadows
not in the open sun; to see anything
at all, you must look deeply into
the shadow of a living thing.*

Ute saying

When death or another of life's transitions—predictable or otherwise—arrives on the horizon, it's not just our future and our present that are shaken; it is also our past. Along with questions of what tomorrow will bring, we may find that memories that have slumbered dormant for years are stirred and brought to the surface of our awareness. Some of these thoughts will recall happy experiences and things we are thankful for or proud of, such as how we have raised our children, stood by friends, or the simple moments of pleasure we have enjoyed.

Some memories, however, may sweep in like an unwanted gale bringing bursts of guilt, regret, unresolved grief, an awareness of frayed connections, or unrealized hopes. It is natural that our past should assert itself during these times. One of the challenges of coming to terms with our mortality is the urge to reflect on, or in some cases the urge to avoid reflecting on, the nature and meaning of our lives. When we are at a crossroads, running out of time, we may suddenly see our journey as a whole—as though the many events and experiences we have compartmentalized, and others we have "forgotten about," are bound together and placed before us.

Often, it is the things that we have tried to forget or hide from, or the things that have fallen apart or managed to elude our grasp, that trouble us most. To be human is to be imperfect. Few can look back on their lives without finding pockets of deep pain, things left undone, or hopes that were unfulfilled for one reason or another. Often, as with Nell in Chapter Five, we try to bury such things in the vault of our unconscious mind, only to find that they emerge stronger, more vividly, during times of stress. Maybe, as with Luke in Chapter Four, we have always been aware of such things in the back of our minds and suddenly they become amplified, threatening to distort our vision beyond all perspective. For others, like Paul in Chapter Six, the fears and doubts we have tried to elude by constructing walls and forging personal defenses may become an overwhelming cascade, dashing our fortifications and leaving us in a state of anxiety and confusion.

Whatever the challenges of such reflections and experiences, there is also a gift: the potential to finally grieve, find forgiveness, or see more deeply into the value of our lives. We may even learn that it is our pain, fear and unaccomplished dreams—in short, all our rough edges that we have tried to avoid or overcome—that most bear witness to our humanness, resilience, and courage.

To face the present and the future, it is often necessary to face the past. The stories in Section Two illustrate this theme and, I hope, provide illumination whereby others can do so as well.

Chapter Four
Salem Witch Trials: Affirming Life at the End of One's Journey

Luke's grandmother was a strong woman. Before she died, as though by sheer willpower, she had imparted her strength to him and demanded he use it wisely. She had raised him while his mother and father were working as sharecroppers, digging under a pitiless sun in the sandy clay of eastern Georgia. He had been thinking about his grandmother a lot since being diagnosed with pancreatic cancer. It had helped him survive an operation, as well as seemingly endless rounds of chemotherapy. Now that the disease was spreading and there was nothing to cure it, thinking about her eased his mind as he absorbed the fact that he was dying.

His grandmother's name was Shaante, but he had always called her Mima. "She was five when slavery days ended," he said, "and she remembered how her mother took her around, after the (Civil) War," looking for members of their family that had run off or been sold away. During his first fifteen years, she had told him many stories and offered ongoing "instructions for life"—pithy anecdotes, Bible verses, and earthy aphorisms like: "You can catch flies with honey, but use a strong poison when it comes to the rats," or "Bow your head to the Almighty, but make everyone else look up." None of these instructions though, were delivered with such seriousness as the two upon which Luke had tried to live his life:

Don't go chasing pots of gold, 'cause under all the glitter ain't nothing but dust.

Dig ditches 'til sundown if it helps you get

by, but never sell your soul. Always stand for something higher, if you don't, you're nothing but a slave.

For a young boy with black skin growing up in Georgia during the 1940s and 50s, her message was empowering and defiant. "Momma used to yell at Mima about putting things in my head," he recalled. His mother was afraid Luke would get killed if he stood out from the crowd or failed to cultivate the proper appearance of deference, even obsequiousness, usually demanded by whites in the segregated South. The arguments between his mother and grandmother embodied tensions he would live with all his life. Shaante instilled an uncompromising sense of self-esteem and a conviction that he deserved respect and opportunities to excel. His mother, however, was keenly aware that they lived in a world often bent on making him behave as though he were inferior, and where those who stepped out of line might wind up on the bottom of a river under a pile of tractor chains.

He learned to wear a mask in the presence of white people, especially the ones who owned the stores, held title to the land, or ran the local sheriff's department. He concealed his confidence, lest he be labeled a troublemaker. Even after mastering this facade, he lived with the constant threat that he might become a target if "something bad happened, and people started a mob." His wife Norma grew up in the same community; she likened such things to witch hunts in which local whites "went looking for someone to blame for something and you just knew it was going to be a black man."

Despite the complexity, most people understood the rules of the game and lived relatively peaceful lives. Luke's life had been quite adventurous, though fraught with many ups and downs. As often happens when a person reaches the twilight of his or her life, he was looking back and taking stock.

"Mima always told me I was going to do great

things," he said, "Big things to change this world." But when he measured his life against the unbending yardstick of his grandmother's words and hopes, he felt he had "messed things up and let people down." In his mind, he hadn't done the grand things Shaante had predicted (perhaps demanded). In fact, living by her precepts had been difficult and had often brought consequences that were disastrous to his family.

He had constantly stood up for what he had thought was right and had gotten knocked down time and again. It had made for a hard life. Opposition and false accusations were more often his reward than gratitude whenever he challenged perceived injustices. The good things, he thought, went to those who simply accepted things, even morally offensive things, without protest. Life, it seemed, came down to a fundamental, and frustrating, choice. You either preserved your integrity by speaking out and demanding change, accepting that you may be greeted with hostility, or you ignored injustice and shared in whatever benefits came to those who conformed, while losing your integrity. The choice had never seemed fair. For much of his life he had expected some pivotal moment of validation to soothe the sting of his many sacrifices, but it had never come. Now, as he was dying, he was questioning the path he'd taken and wondering if he had made a mistake.

Luke's memories were condensed into stories that, like his grandmother's, were rich in personal meaning and, for him, replete with universal truth. Invariably these stories underscored the hardships he and his family had faced in pursuing lives guided by conscience. One story was that of his "other than honorable discharge" from the military. As a young man he had surprised his family and Norma by deciding to join the army. There were few opportunities in his hometown and, after watching his parents break their backs tilling someone else's land for years, he had no intention of becoming a farmer.

"I was ready to get as far away as I could," Luke recalled. "Mr. Truman had integrated the army years before and I thought maybe it was a place I could be judged for who I was and not be expected to use a separate restroom."

"I thought he was crazy," Norma remembered. "I told him, you never took orders from anyone but Mima and now you're going to join the army?" After pretending to be angry with him, she packed their bags and warmed to the idea of seeing some of the world beyond the loamy Georgia low country.

They wound up stationed in Japan, on the island of Okinawa. Unlike many of his fellow soldiers, Luke developed affection for the Japanese people who worked on the base and whom he met around town. After a few years, he was able to carry on a basic conversation in their language. Norma also developed an affinity with her host country, regularly blending the disparate cuisines of mainland Japan with the Sea Islands of her childhood. A conspicuous minority of unruly soldiers, however, frequently harassed the locals and occasionally committed crimes against them. When civilians complained, it was common to dismiss their concerns, blame them, or give the offending soldier an ineffective slap on the wrist. Most soldiers accepted this as the way things were, but not Luke, he spoke out.

For months he complained to his commanding officer, requesting an investigation into the complaints. When his protests fell on deaf ears, he went higher in the chain of command and wrote a letter to a lieutenant colonel. "When they finally got back to me," he said, "it was like getting pushed into a hornets' nest."

His commanding officer's rage teetered on the edge of psychopathology and Luke was upbraided for breaking the chain of command. Shortly thereafter, he was accused of using government property without proper authorization and threatened with a court marshal. He had used a jeep and the requisition order had suspiciously wound up missing. His commander claimed Luke had stolen the vehicle and hauled him before the metaphorical gallows reserved for those brave souls who stand up against injustice, even when doing so imperils their well-being. "They were after me," he said, "from the time I started protesting until the door hit me on the way out."

Luke was dismissed from the military and he, Norma, and their twin daughters, Ruby and Rita, returned to Georgia with no money and no jobs. "If I'd kept my mouth shut," Luke said, "I'd be living on a military pension right now." Instead, he had fought the good fight and been railroaded by unsympathetic guardians of the status quo.

Other events followed that further disillusioned him. He found work at a funeral home and did odd jobs as a welder (a trade he'd learned in the military). Norma cleaned houses while her sister watched the children. Somehow, they managed to make ends meet. Around 1964, Luke "got the call" and began preaching occasionally at their church. "I thought I was going to be a minister for sure," he remembered. He studied the Bible with a burning desire to unlock the secrets of every parable, verse, and psalm. "He was good," Norma recalled, laughing as she pretended to stand at the pulpit, imitating his authoritative bearing and raising her arm as if pulling back a thin curtain separating this world from the Divine. "Whenever he raised that arm," she said with a laugh, "I knew the heavenly spirit was rising and the Holy Ghost was coming down."

At last he had found his niche. It was a role well suited to his passion for social justice, his moral courage, and his innate qualities as a leader. With the civil rights movement building momentum and churches often the nuclei of protest and strategy, he believed this was where his grandmother's prophecy that he would do great things would finally be fulfilled.

He found, however, that the parishioners at his church were less eager to push for reform as openly as he was. "I really got people riled when I started planning to take a group of young folks with me to attend the white church across town," he said. "I figured all these folks were rushing to desegregate soda counters, buses, and movie theaters, why not the house of the Lord?" Looking back, he had more compassion for the temperate stance of his pastor and the church deacons, but at the time he was impatient with what he saw as foot-dragging hypocrisy. Amid perplexing and impassioned church politics, he was quietly asked to tow the line or find another place to worship. With Norma's support, he chose the latter. Once again, his stand on principle had led to ostracism and misunderstanding. It did not, however, dilute his resolve when it came to raising his voice against injustice.

In 1968 Ruby and Rita were in ninth grade and, for all practical purposes, the schools were still segregated despite a Supreme Court ruling, over ten years prior, ordering them to integrate as quickly as possible. "Near as I could make out," Luke said, without a hint of humor, "that meant sometime around when hell froze over." He went down to the local school board and asked to see the Superintendent. When the secretary said he was unavailable, Luke sat in the office all day before the man snuck out the back door. When Luke showed up the next day with the same request, the secretary called the police and he was taken to the sheriff's office for several hours and "questioned." Word travels fast in a small town and within a few days all the women whose houses Norma cleaned had informed her they no longer needed her services. One even suggested she put a muzzle on Luke, before he got into trouble. "I told her," Norma recalled, "if I had a muzzle I knew just where I'd put it, and it wasn't on my husband."

Luke was not easily discouraged. He wrote letters to President Lyndon Johnson and Supreme Court Justice Thurgood Marshal complaining about his county's resistance to desegregation. Norma searched for other work, but was unable to find anything. When the welding jobs suddenly dried up, they worried. "It wasn't that there weren't jobs out there," he said, "it was that nobody wanted to hire us. Black folks were afraid we'd get them into trouble and white folks didn't like the way I'd speak out."

Things got so difficult they finally decided to move to Newark, New Jersey, where Norma had some cousins. "We were a little fearful," Norma said, "because we'd seen

Newark on television when they had a big riot up there and people got killed. But we wanted a fresh start, and we knew we could stay with my people 'til we got settled."

They stayed in Newark for ten years but never felt at ease there. It was a big, noisy place. Something always seemed to be boiling just below the surface, ready to explode. Luke got a job collecting coins from washers and dryers in a chain of Laundromats owned by a group of local businessmen. Norma decided not to work so she could keep a closer eye on the kids. Without her income, it was difficult to pay the bills. During winter, their apartment was so cold Luke collected empty bleach bottles and brought them home so Norma could fill them with hot water, wrap towels around them, and tuck them into bed with Rita, Ruby, and their son Lemeul.

Luke's job required him to carry large amounts of cash, so he was vigilant and careful. He kept meticulous records of the daily collections and kept his eyes open. As such, he knew that one of the men who owned the Laundromats was associating with people reputed to be criminals. Luke began to suspect his boss was using the laundry business as a smoke screen to hide profits made by a network of petty thieves and heroin dealers. "I guess they took the phrase money laundering seriously," he observed acidly. Once again he was faced with the choice between remaining silent and tacitly accepting something he believed was wrong or speaking out despite the conflict that was sure to ensue.

"I actually thought about keeping my mouth shut that time," Luke confessed. "I was tired of always having the rug pulled out from under me, plus I was worried about my family." After agonizing about the situation and talking it over with his wife, he decided to confront the man. "I pulled out the heavy artillery on that one," he joked, "and asked Mima's spirit to walk beside me that day and keep me from getting shot."

Fortunately, his boss discussed the matter calmly and insisted Luke's concerns were ungrounded. After a tense conversation, Luke was mollified enough to admit he was mistaken and apologize. Nonetheless, he kept his eyes open and began asking questions around the neighborhood. When he confronted his boss again, he was certain the Laundromat was being used for criminal purposes and no denials would sway him. Seeing Luke's determination, the man offered to cut him in on the money if he kept quiet. When he refused, the man threatened Luke's family. "I don't know if I quit or got fired," he said, "because they happened at the same time." Either way, he was out of a job, concerned about the safety of his family, and unsure what to do next, his life, yet again, turned upside down as the result of his moral courage.

Luke called a man who co-owned the business to report what was going on. During their conversation, he mentioned his desire to return to Georgia. The man offered to help him finance a Laundromat in the Atlanta area if he agreed to share the profits for five years and pay back the initial investment over time. He and Norma waited until they had looked at the deal's fine print, then jumped at the opportunity.

Their years in Atlanta were uneventful compared to other chapters of their lives. There were no gut-wrenching choices to be made, no dramatic moral battles to be fought, no upheavals with which to contend, just the ongoing attempt to live comfortably and provide for their family. Eventually, they gained a level of prosperity that allowed them to do something they had never done before, save money.

Luke never forgot his grandmother's emphasis on improving the lives of others and her expectation that he do things on a scale larger than his own backyard. He convinced Norma to set aside some of their savings each month so one day they could create a trust fund to help poor children go to college. For almost eleven years they deposited as much as they could into an account earmarked for this project. Unfortunately, when Luke was diagnosed with cancer, the bills (even with their health insurance) were so overwhelming they were forced to use the trust money to offset their lost income and pay for treatments and medications. For Luke, it was a blow as staggering as any he had ever received.

When they reached the end of his medical options, he and Norma moved in with Ruby and her family, in North Carolina. "I came here to be around my family until I die," he explained. Lemeul was nearby, attending graduate school and working as an English teacher. Rita lived in Georgia and was able to visit regularly. When I met Luke he'd been weathered by illness, but still exuded calm strength. He enjoyed playing the role of wise old granddad and used his waning energy to tell stories and share his own version of instructions for living.

He was resigned to death, but he worried about Norma, money, and being dependent on others. His biggest concern, however, could be traced back to the words of his beloved grandmother. More than anyone else, she had strengthened his resolve to live in accordance with a higher law governed by moral principles and the courage to speak against injustice, regardless of the consequences. He had done his best to uphold these standards and had paid a high price. It had caused anxiety and distress for people he loved and often left him floundering. It had ended his career in the military, closed the door on his aspirations to become a minister, alienated friends and created enemies.

Looking back, he wondered if it had been worth it. Wouldn't it have been better, not to mention easier, if he had simply acquiesced and reaped the social and material rewards claimed by those willing to conform? As far as he could see, he had not made the world better; he only caused his family pain. Had the seemingly ephemeral reward of preserving his integrity been worth it? Maybe it would have been better to have simply avoided life's battle altogether.

"What good did it do?" he scowled, as though daring me to try to convince him that his sacrifices had made a difference. It was a poignant dilemma.

For many of us, when we look back, there are things we would do differently or choices we would reconsider. For

Luke, it was his entire life that was being questioned. Whether he affirmed or renounced it was more than an abstract exercise in homespun philosophizing, it would determine the way he lived his final weeks, and the way he died.

Norma and his children had tried to reassure him that he had lived well and, as far as they were concerned, his life had been a model of unassuming virtue. Its meaning resided in the example he provided for others and the many lives he had touched, not in his social status, wealth, or any other misguided measure one attempted to apply. They believed it, but he didn't.

In his mind, he imagined what his life might have been like if he had simply gone along. He saw himself as a brigadier general, respected by straight-backed soldiers and a grateful nation. He imagined himself pacing near his pulpit before a thriving congregation, a leader in his community and among his peers. Such fantasies are a pass-time most of us have engaged in, but for Luke it crossed the line from harmless daydreaming into the realm of painful rumination.

"If only I'd been able to change things. Then I'd know I did the right thing." Time and again the thought returned, as though some spectral visitor impervious to closed doors and drawn shades. When he was younger, he had believed that good works and humane intentions would, in the long run, be validated and appreciated by others. Now he doubted it, and in so doing he questioned the essence and meaning of his life.

It's hard to look back on your life and wish you had lived in a different way. We had several conversations exploring these inner churnings. During one of these, I asked what he'd say to his grandmother if he could speak with her again. After thinking about it, he returned to her two ironclad rules. Along with his spiritual beliefs and the welfare of his family, they had formed the sturdy pillars upon which all of his choices had been made and they had provided solace during difficult times.

The first rule—don't go chasing pots of gold—was

an admonition against striving for material rewards or succumbing to their temptation, because, in the end, they were mere illusion. Viewed through this lens, his life was a resounding success. Several times he had sacrificed his own comfort and security in pursuit of some higher principle, always trying to focus on the deeper truths buried beneath the ground of our existence, like dormant seeds waiting to flower.

The second rule—work hard but never sell your soul—reminded him that there was no shame in doing honest work as long as you didn't betray your integrity or values. Here again, his life was a success. Time and again he and Norma had scrambled to survive and at times went hungry, but their children were always loved and protected.

"If Mima was here now," he said, "I'd ask how I did, and how come all those great things I was supposed to do never happened?"

I asked what he thought she would say. He thought about it and smiled. With eyes slightly glassy from unborn tears, he said, "She'd tell me we're not promised great things just for doing right, and if we're expecting some kinda reward we better look inside ourselves, or to God, to find it."

I suggested that doing our best to uphold a law higher than our own self-interest is synonymous with doing great things.

"I'll have to think about that one," he said in a fatigued tone that suggested it was time to move on to less intense contemplations.

He had used a lot of energy thinking things through and answering questions, so it wasn't a surprise when he suggested that I do some of the talking for a while. There was a dog-eared copy of the play, *The Crucible*, on a nearby table. I asked if he was reading it. He explained that Lemeul had left it there for one of Ruby's daughters who needed it for a high school class. I picked it up and thumbed through it. I told him it was about the Salem witch trials of 1692. Arthur Miller had written it as a cautionary tale after the hysterical excesses of Senator Joseph McCarthy's witch hunt against alleged communists in the 1950s.

I suggested that this episode in Salem, Massachusetts three hundred years earlier had a striking relevance to his life and his struggle. Many innocent people had been killed in Salem because they chose to stand up for their principles and act in accordance with their conscience, rather than give in to pressures to conform and accept injustice. Though they were intimidated and pressured to back down, many chose to die rather than compromise their integrity. What sacrifice could be greater?

I handed him the book and asked if he wanted me to tell him the story of what had happened.

"After a build up like that," he smiled, "you're not leaving 'til you do."

II

When the first ships loaded with English Puritans landed along the stony coast near present-day Boston in 1630, they quickly set to work building what they believed would be a "city on a hill," standing in the open for all to see. It would be a beacon in the wilderness for those who sought to live a Godly life. In a world full of conflict, temptation, and vice, they intended to hold themselves to a higher standard and live in accordance with strict moral principles, free from the bondage of greed and duplicity.

They inhabited a world where God's presence was personal and immediate, infusing everything from the first shoots of corn rising from spring ground to the pang of conscience following a selfish thought. The devil was a real and palpable presence as well, an evil force constantly probing the hearts of God's Elected, searching for weaknesses in the wall of their faith and the firmness of their resolve.

The existence of witches was virtually unquestioned. Anyone with the temerity to doubt their reality might find himself or herself hauled before a magistrate to explain such dangerous thinking. The veil separating this world from the supernatural one was thin and porous. It was the job of every good Puritan to be vigilant and root out those, such as witches, who conspired with evil.

By 1692, although some of the religious zeal of the first settlers had waned, this was still the world of Salem, a thriving seaport north of Boston, and the adjacent community known as Salem Village. While the town was a busy commercial center, the village was oriented toward agricultural pursuits and had recently petitioned to become a separate municipality. Town officials had denied the request, but the village was allowed to establish its own church and, at the time, it was shepherded by Reverend Samuel Parris.

In the dark, frigid days of January 1692, Parris's nine-year-old daughter, Betty, and his niece, Abigail Williams, began experiencing strange and frightening symptoms that the minister was at a loss to explain. The girls' bodies, as described by Boston merchant Robert Calef, contorted into "sundry odd postures and antic gestures," and they began "uttering foolish, ridiculous speeches, which neither they themselves nor any others could make sense of."

Parris called on physician, William Griggs, who couldn't find any organic cause for the girls' behavior. When other young women began experiencing similar fits and spasms, the doctor surmised that they were being tormented by *maleficium*—evil magic, possibly conjured by witches. To Samuel Parris, it seemed the devil was launching an attack on God's earthly kingdom.

He enlisted the help of neighboring ministers, such as John Hale of Beverly and Deodat Lawson of Boston. Together they prayed and fasted, hoping the afflictions would subside. Although they tried to keep the situation from becoming widely known, rumors spread and soon suspicion and speculation obscured fact and reality.

In a misguided attempt to unmask the witch, or witches, among them, Mary Sibley advised one of Reverend Parris's slaves, an Indian woman named Tituba, to bake a "witchcake" from rye flour and some of the tormented girls' urine. To Parris, such an act smacked of satanic divination. When he learned of it, he was irate. He exclaimed to Goodwife Sibley that, because of her meddling, "the Devil hath been raised amongst us, and his rage is vehement and terrible..." Rather than snuff the incipient flames of anxiety, Mary Sibley and Tituba had unwittingly fueled them and cast suspicion upon themselves.

Parris again called on his fellow ministers, as well as influential members of the village, for advice. They suggested he, "sit still and wait upon the Providence of God...and to be much in prayer for the discovery of what was yet secret." By then a month had passed and several other young women had started experiencing the same mysterious convulsions. Pressure was put on the girls to identify their tormentors. Two of them accused Sarah Good, Sarah Osborne, and Tituba of being witches. They claimed to have been assailed by the disembodied specters of Good and Osborne and "most grievously" tortured by them.

On February 29, the three bewildered women were charged with witchcraft and jailed in Salem Town. The next day they were hauled into a meetinghouse full of spectators and interrogated by magistrates John Hathorne and Jonathan Corwin. From the start, the officials considered them guilty and harangued them in accusatory tones with leading questions. Sarah Good was the first to be questioned. A snippet from her ordeal, as recorded by Ezeckiel Cheever, conveys what lay in store for those who followed (Q = question; A = answer):

Q. Sarah Good what evil Spirit have you familiarity with?

A. None.

Q. Have you made no contract with the devil?

A. No.

Q. Why do you hurt these children?

A. I do not hurt them. I scorn it.

Q. Who do you employ then to do it?

A. I employ nobody.

Q. What creature do you employ then?

A. No creature but I am falsely accused.

In a departure from standard judicial procedure, the magistrates directly addressed the small group of accusing girls during the hearing and instructed them, "to look upon [Sarah Good] and see if this were the person that had hurt them..." They said it was, and suddenly, as if in confirmation, the girls "were all tormented" with fits and seizures. The crowd was stirred into such fear that before the questioning was complete, even Sarah Good's husband had joined the accusers in offering testimony against his besieged wife whose pleas of innocence were all but drowned out.

The interrogation is an example of what would occur time and again during the next several months as more people were accused and more hearings held. The presiding magistrates and judges assumed the accused person was guilty and tried to force him or her to confess. The core group of young girls leveling many of the accusations was present and questions were addressed directly to them. Often, they appeared to be overcome by dramatic displays of bewitchment that were immediately attributed to the accused, or to Satan acting on that person's behalf.

Spectators participated spontaneously, defendants were tortured and harassed, exculpatory evidence was dismissed. Fear was so pervasive that testimony that would never have been allowed in a legitimate legal proceeding became the basis upon which suspects were condemned. Most significant was so-called, "spectral evidence," in which accusers claimed that a person's apparition had appeared before them and had attempted to convince them to become a witch. Puritan courts usually barred such "evidence" because these claims were impossible to prove and an accuser might have ulterior motives. With emotions high and fear running rampant, Salem became a deadly exception to this time-tested legal practice.

At the end of the first hearing, all three of the accused women were found guilty and shipped to jail in Boston to await criminal trials. The crisis might have ended there but Tituba, under intense pressure, confessed that she and her co-defendants were guilty of plotting with the devil. She said there were seven other people throughout Salem and Boston that were also witches, although she didn't know their identities. Later, Robert Calef reported, Tituba recanted her testimony, explaining that, "her master did beat her, and otherwise abuse her, to make her confess and accuse...her sister-witches; and that whatsoever she said by way of confessing, or accusing others, was the effect of such usage." Regardless of the dubious nature of her claims, Tituba's allegations intensified people's fear and sparked further accusations.

Although the band of apparently possessed girls remained at the forefront of the accusers, many others joined them. By the time the next hearing was held, Deodat Lawson wrote, people were so frightened that all who attended were "struck with consternation, and they were afraid, that those that sate next to them, were under the influence of Witchcraft." In this ocean of panic, simply being accused of practicing the demonic arts was tantamount in many people's minds to guilt.

Some, however, were more cautious. Most of these held their tongues or expressed their concern in a manner calculated not to arouse distrust. Some gently reminded their fellow townspeople that the devil had many ways of deluding them, and it behooved the faithful to be scrupulous in matters of assigning guilt and innocence. A few spoke out more forcefully, none as adamantly as John Proctor, a sixty-one year old tavern keeper. He was critical of the judicial proceedings and openly stated his disbelief that so many of his neighbors could be witches. When his wife, Elizabeth, was accused, he vehemently defended her innocence.

Not surprisingly, John Proctor was soon accused of witchcraft as well. One of the "afflicted" girls, Mary Warren, worked at his tavern. She testified that once when she was in the throes of one of her fits Proctor had snarled that "if ye are Afflicted I wish ye were more Afflicted…because you goe to bring out Innocent persons." Samuel Sibley told the court that Procter had told him that he thought the afflicted girls should be taken to the "Whipping post" since, "if they were let alone so we should all be Devils and witches quickly."

Proctor's courage to speak out was rare. The social pressure against doing so was great and most people, including the magistrates, genuinely believed that the accused were guilty. In their minds, Proctor's willingness to openly question the court and attack the credibility of those who bore witness against Satan's conspirators, much less defend the accused, were acts worthy of condemnation. By speaking out against injustice, he had placed himself at risk of being hauled before the magistrates, and ultimately, before the gallows.

Fear permeated Salem like the heavy mist of a dank, slow-moving fog. When some of the girls accused George Burroughs, a former minister of Salem Village, of being the ringleader of the ever-widening coven of supposed witches, most were ready to believe it. The fact that Burroughs had moved to the wilds of Maine was immaterial. Within a few days a warrant for his arrest had been filed and a constable was on his way north to drag the reverend back to Salem.

By the end of spring, many more hearings had been held and the magistrates had judged everyone guilty, including George Burroughs and John Proctor. But these were not the criminal trials necessary to dispense ultimate judgments. No such trials could be held until the new colonial governor, William Phips, arrived from England. The prior governor had been ousted in 1689 and thus, throughout the first months of the witch crisis, the legal system of Massachusetts was in a state of confusing interregnum.

Week after week innocent people were accused, warrants issued, arrests made, hearings held, and alleged witches thrown in jail, yet not a single trial was held. When Governor Phips finally sailed into Boston Harbor on May 14, the climate in the region bordered on hysteria. Thirty-eight people were packed into the jails at Salem and Boston awaiting trial. Five others had succumbed to the dogged pressures of the magistrates and simply confessed they were witches. Hundreds of aroused Salemites had stepped forward and joined in the hailstorm of accusations against their neighbors.

Phips quickly established a "Court of Oyer and Terminer," composed of nine judges, to take control of the situation and administer the trials. On June 2, they convicted Bridget Bishop of witchcraft. A few days later, in a scene that would be repeated in the months to come, she was placed in a wooden cart and rolled up the rocky bluff to "Witch's Hill" and hung.

She went to her death knowing she was innocent, refusing to confess to a crime she had not committed, despite the concerted efforts of an intimidating array of learned judges bent on making her do so. She could have saved her life by confessing to the crime and giving the court a few more names. Instead, she chose to abide by a higher law, higher even than self-preservation.

In the wake of her death, murmurs could be heard that the proceedings, and the accusers, were going too far. Several ministers sent a letter to the court urging "a very critical and exquisite caution" in their judgments. Although the clergymen applauded the judges' zeal to root out and prosecute Satan's minion, they advised against placing too much weight on dubious forms of evidence such as spectral visitation. This, they warned, might result in a "long train of miserable consequences..."

One of the judges, Nathaniel Staltonsal, resigned in protest over the tactics of the first trial. Reverend William Milborne circulated two petitions defending several of the accused as "persons of good fame and unspotted reputation." In light of what the court had allowed to "pass for evidence," one of the petitions stated, the signatories had "great grounds to fear that the Innocent will be condemned." When Governor Phips got wind of what Milborne was up to, he quashed the petitions before they could be submitted.

Another petition was circulated defending the innocence of Rebecca Nurse. Others began questioning the credibility and motives of the young accusers. In the face of social pressure and the threat of dire personal consequences, people of moral courage were standing up. Such objections, however, were anemic compared to the power of fear and the livid righteousness that infused a majority of those living in Salem and its environs. Most were intent on making sure that other "witches" either confessed and recanted, or dangled from the end of a rope.

The court next convened on June 28. This time it completed five separate trials. As before, none of the defendants would admit guilt despite intense pressures to force confessions. Once again the court considered animated testimony accompanied by the dramatics of the tormented girls. All five of the defendants were found guilty. All five were sentenced to death. Even on the scaffold they refused to give in to last minute demands to confess. Sarah Good retorted to a minister that, "I am no more a witch than you are a wizard, and if you take away my life, God will give you blood to drink."

Six people were dead and none of them had admitted to being witches, yet those who had confessed seemed in no danger of facing Witch's Hill. By then it was evident that the surest way to save one's life was simply to confess to the crime. Historians Davidson and Lytle describe the dilemma: "Those who were wrongly accused quickly realized that if they did not confess, they were likely to be hung. If they did confess, they could escape death, but would have to demonstrate their sincerity by providing details of their misdeeds and names of other participants. The temptation must have been great to confess and, in so doing, to implicate other innocent people."

In addition, a confession would spare one from the tortures legally employed under English law. John Proctor, for example, complained that when his son William was arrested for wizardry, "he would not confess that he was

100

Guilty, when he was Innocent," and colonial officials "tied him Neck and Heels till the Blood gushed out at his Nose..."

Before the witch hunt ended, at least fifty people had confessed to crimes they most certainly did not commit. Robert Calef chided that, "though the confessing witches were many, yet none of them that confessed their own guilt, and abode by their confession, was put to death." Others had shown profound moral courage and chosen to die rather than violate their morals, implicate others, or condone the workings of a court wracked by paranoia. More than any others in Salem, these people exemplified the values and hopes of their Puritan ancestors who had intended to live their lives in accordance with the highest spiritual principles.

When the executions failed to calm the community's fear, John Proctor was certain he and the others scheduled to be tried next (including his wife), would simply be scapegoats given over to the shrill cry for death to all who refused to admit guilt.

On July 23, while locked in Salem prison, he petitioned several Boston clergymen to intervene. The "Accusers and our Judges, and Jury..." he wrote, had "condemned us already before our trials." Unless the trials were moved to Boston where they could be conducted fairly and dispassionately, he warned, the "shedding of our Innocent Bloods" would be the result. Petitions that gathered fifty-two signatures were circulated on behalf of the Proctors attesting to their innocence and moral rectitude. Others even defended them in court against their accusers.

In the end, nothing could stop the feverish momentum of anxious persecution. The Proctors, along with George Burroughs and three others were sentenced to hang. No one, it seemed, save those who compliantly acknowledged guilt, stood a chance before the increasingly fatal calls to appear before the Court of Oyer and Terminer.

Elizabeth Proctor's execution was postponed in consideration of the fact that she was pregnant; it was ordered that she be hung after the child was born. On August 19, John Proctor, George Burroughs, John Willard, George

Jacobs, and Martha Carrier were allowed to address the crowd gathered to witness their executions. When Burroughs eloquently asserted his innocence and flawlessly recited the Lord's Prayer (something a witch was supposedly not able to do), Calef reports that many were so affected that "it seemed to some that the spectators would hinder the execution." Were it not for a somber warning from Reverend Cotton Mather to allow the hanging to proceed, and claims by the accusing girls that they had seen an apparition who "dictated" the words of the prayer to Burroughs, the sporadic but growing voice of moral outrage may have stopped the executions on the spot. As it were, the hangings proceeded without further incident, leaving five more people dead.

Despite the executions, the prisons continued to fill and anxiety floated freely like leaves dispersed in an angry wind. To some, including a growing number of ministers, the number of accused defied believability and the strange behavior of the afflicted girls began looking more and more like malicious antics at best, and Satan's work at worst. Cotton Mather began to suspect that the devil's goal was not to convert witches, but to divide the people of Salem and set them, "hotly and madly, mauling one another in the *dark*."

Amid growing dissent, the judges continued to put relentless pressure on the accused. One of these, Mary Tyler, so overwrought by the abuses and threats, later said she had "wished herself in any dungeon, rather than be so treated." She finally confessed that she was a witch only because she was, "so terrified in her mind," as she put it, that she would have "owned, at length, almost anything [her accusers and judges] propounded..." Unfortunately, confessions such as these, even though they were given under extreme duress, only served to increase the fervor of the accusers.

By the time the court reconvened in September 1692, some two hundred persons stood accused, including many of the colony's most reputable and pious members. During this session, five persons were found guilty, but pardoned because they chose to confess. Ten others refused to do so and were sentenced to death. One of these, Dorcas Hoar, confessed at the last minute and was reprieved, another escaped from jail and fled Salem altogether.

On September 22, the remaining eight were hung. One of them, Mary Easty, sent a letter to the court before her death. "I petition your honors," she wrote, "not for my life, for I know I must die, and my appointed time is set; but…that no more innocent blood be shed." Perhaps it would have consoled her had she known that theirs would indeed be the last innocent blood spilled. In all, fourteen women and five men were executed, one man died while being tortured, and several other innocent souls perished awaiting judgment in the noxious air of prison. More than twice as many had confessed, adding their voices against the innocent.

Those who were executed were among the most courageous and self-sacrificing members of the community. They chose to live in accordance with the highest moral and spiritual principles, even though it meant bearing unjust consequences. Many of them left behind children and spouses rather than betray their conscience, their friends, or their faith. Historian Darren Staloff has called it one of the "ugliest ironies" of the entire episode that, "we can say with absolute certainty, those who were executed were most likely the most devout people in Puritan society."

Those who died accepted harsh and sometimes brutal treatment, as well as the psychological violence of false accusations, ostracism, and condemnation. They chose to die rather than commit the blasphemy that would have saved them—succumbing to earthly pressures, lying under oath, and betraying their values and faith. In the end, their steadfast willingness to stand on principle and sacrifice their lives to a higher cause was an important reason Salem's collective hysteria finally subsided, and temperance slowly returned to the city on a hill.

III

In all of us there is strength, wisdom, and a place where we may find fortitude and guidance. Whether we call it intuition, conscience, God, or our higher selves, it is always there, often beneath our awareness as we go to work, raise our families and try to live decent lives. When our routines and expectations are thrown into flux, perhaps by an illness or a death, we may find solace, confidence, and nourishment in this strength.

Some people, like Luke, rather than simply returning to this place now and then, try to make it the center of their lives. Those who do so often develop their abilities as healers, peacemakers, or humble servants of those in need. Or perhaps they find themselves struggling to be better parents, husbands, wives, sons, or daughters. Some may simply try to exude peace, or seek out quiet places away from life's clatter. Such people may also find that they face challenges they might otherwise have avoided—such as standing up against prejudice, embracing another's suffering, or making painful sacrifices for their community. For Luke it meant being a vigilant voice of protest against injustice and enduring the attacks of those who preferred silence and compliance.

Luke was captivated by the plight of the people in Salem who had refused to yield to a phalanx of adamant accusers. They embodied the moral fortitude and bottomless faith that Mima had instilled in him.

"They knew they were going to die," he said, shaking his head in admiration, "and they still stuck to their guns."

We talked about the sacrifices these people had made, how they had endured not only the humiliation of false accusations and frenzied assaults on their character, but also the painful knowledge that their families would suffer—children would grow up without mothers, husbands would be left without wives, and reputations would be ruined.

I asked Luke if he thought they had done the right thing.

"Yeah, they did."

"Wouldn't it have been better to just go along?"

"And sell your soul? No way. Then you ain't nothing but a slave."

"But their lives were turned upside down and their families suffered."

He thought about this, smiled, and threw his hands up in mock surrender, "I get it. I get it."

As silence lingered, Luke organized his thoughts. Finally, he said, "I've tried to do what's right, and I've never been a slave."

I asked if it was worth the price.

"You bet it was. You know, there's a price on the other side too. I can't imagine just going along and having to face myself in the mirror or talk to my kids about right and wrong knowing that I didn't stand up. Besides, I believe people come around sooner or later if you're doing what's right. Sometimes you're just out in front for a while, but people catch up."

By the time the last eight "witches" were hung in September 1692, the people of Salem were beginning to catch up to their friends who had stood against the shedding of innocent blood. It was becoming obvious that things had gone too far. From the beginning there had been isolated protests against the executions. People had signed petitions, defended a neighbor's innocence, or questioned the reliability of some of the accusers. Now the protestors were many.

Some pointed out that, despite the fact that twenty alleged witches had been killed, things had only gotten worse. The community was more disarrayed and divided than ever. Why had none of the confessed witches been executed? Why had so many people chosen to die proclaiming their innocence, rather than save themselves by confessing?

Many ministers continued to be troubled that the court was basing its convictions on spectral evidence. In early October, Reverend Increase Mather summarized these and other objections in an essay called, *Cases of Conscience Concerning Evil Spirits*. He warned the court of grave consequences if it persisted in such a manner. When Mather's essay was signed by fourteen other ministers and printed as a book, its impact was significant.

It was a few weeks before I saw Luke and Norma again. During that time, his physical deterioration had been rapid. Except for a few spoonfuls of pudding, he hadn't eaten anything in nearly two weeks. Recently, he'd stopped taking even miniscule amounts of fluid. His breathing was labored and he was sleeping most of the time. He was dying and Norma knew it.

Most of my visit was spent talking with her as we sat beside Luke's bed, reviewing his life and reflecting on its value. Although Luke appeared to be sleeping, he was able to hear our conversation, as was evident in various subtle facial expressions, alterations in the rhythm of his breathing, and a few barely audible sounds as we spoke. Often when people are near death, they do not have the energy or the inclination to interact much. Even when they appear to be sleeping, though, they can often hear what is being said and feel the touch of a loved one's hand.

Norma sensitively teased out the important themes of his life—commitment to family, faith in God, and fair play. She spoke to him directly to underscore a point or make sure he knew how much she appreciated and loved his gentle spirit. And like him, she refused to gloss over their hardships.

"He could be as stubborn as a bullheaded snapping turtle and bite twice as hard," she said. "And when he thought he was right, you better watch out." "After that mess in Okinawa," she remembered, "I didn't think we'd ever get back on track. But he had to stand up, and I stood up with him."

She smiled when I asked her about the personal cost of always standing up against social injustice and transgressions of principle. "The cost would have been more by not doing it." I asked her to hold Luke's hand and tell him what she meant. Slowly, with simple elegance, she reviewed one episode after another, assuring him that, "every time we had the rug pulled out from underneath us, I found something more to love about you." When I asked her to share some of those things, Luke opened his eyes.

She seemed a bit self-conscious, so I excused myself on the pretext of needing to respond to my pager. When I returned, she was crying and Luke, though his eyes were closed, was smiling. She laughed when she saw me and joked about being "a mess."

"What are you smiling at, Luke?" I asked.

Without opening his eyes he said softly, "It's all good. It's all good."

As he drifted back to sleep, Norma leaned over to one of his ears and whispered, "Mima would be proud of you."

Before I left, Norma and I discussed his impending death. Rita was due to arrive that evening and Lemeul would be over for dinner. "Maybe," she thought, it would be a "good time for everyone to have a chance to spend some quiet time alone with Luke and say what's on their mind."

I asked what she thought Luke meant when he said, "It's all good."

"When you were out of the room," she said, "I told him some of the things I loved about him and how most of those things I only realized when we were going through hard times. I told him it was all good, and the hard times were some of the best."

"Sounds like it sunk in quick," I said. "Maybe he knew it all along."

"I'm just glad he knows it now," she said.

That made two of us.

Less than two weeks after Reverend Mather's publication, Governor Phips forbade any more arrests or trials on charges of witchcraft. By then, it had become clear that a horrible tragedy had occurred. Echoing Mather's objections, he acknowledged the probability that many innocent people had been executed. "The Devill," he said, "had taken upon him the name and shape of severall persons who were doubtless innocent" and deceived the faithful into horrific misjudgments against their neighbors. By the end of October the Court of Oyer and Terminer was dissolved.

The hysteria had subsided. It would be eighteen years, however, before the General Assembly of the Massachusetts Bay annulled the verdicts and ordered compensation for the descendents of the victims. Many townspeople already recognized, however, that some of their most pious members had been sacrificed.

Although Luke had never faced death while standing up for his beliefs, he and Norma had weathered many a storm. In the end, he found sustenance in his actions, and he was able to affirm the life he had lived.

He died surrounded by his family. When I talked to Norma after the funeral, she told me he had seen his grandmother several times during the last two days of his life. "At first we thought he was just confused," she said, "but he kept on talking to her and asking us if we saw her and telling us what she was saying. After a while, we just figured old Mima really had come back, looking to take her grandson home."

"So what did she tell him?" I asked.

"She told him he did good. That he had done great things."

Chapter Five
The Voyage of the *Essex*:
On the Persistence and Healing
of Old Wounds

Nell was terrified of death. Even at ninety-three, the mere mention of the word was enough to start her on the road to a panic attack. Twice, after the subject arose, she had gone to the emergency room in the grip of anxiety so acute her breathing had become shallow and erratic. Since then, her niece Cleo had avoided mentioning anything related to the subject—especially Nell's breast cancer.

Beneath Nell's fear of death she harbored a quiet, though less visible, nervousness about loss in general. It had accompanied her throughout her life, often partially submerged, like a whale swimming just beneath the surface, breaching occasionally and diving back into the watery depths. According to Cleo, Nell had always been afraid of losing people she cared about. She had avoided relationships with men because she didn't want to get hurt when it didn't work out; she had avoided friendships because something always went wrong sooner or later; she had refused to have pets because "they only die after you start to love them." It was a soft refrain in the long song of her life: When you get close to someone, sooner or later things always fall apart. Now that she was dying—in a sense, losing her self—this refrain and the fear accompanying it had intensified to a shrill crescendo of anguish and foreboding.

In other regards Nell was self-reliant and free from anxiety. She had worked for over thirty years as a nurse in a hospital delivery room. She had been respected by colleagues who marveled at her ability to handle the pressures of a difficult job with flexibility and ease. She had lived alone until she was ninety, managing her own affairs and exercising daily. Her mind was absorbent, creative, and as sharp as a sailor's penknife. Despite describing herself as a loner, she enjoyed being around others and was lithe and engaging in conversation.

After a kitchen fire damaged her home, Nell moved in with Cleo and Cleo's husband, Sammy. They had planned for the arrangement to be temporary, but it soon became clear that Nell needed more assistance with things than she had been letting on. So, as Cleo put it, "We asked Aunt Nelly to stay past supper," and Nell moved in permanently. Shortly thereafter, she was diagnosed with cancer.

Sammy and Cleo offered to redecorate their guest room for her, but Nell preferred to live in the basement. She rarely left it and, when she did, it was usually under protest. After she learned about her illness, her little room became a tiny island where she felt safe and in control. It was only a slight exaggeration when Sammy jokingly said that, "Now that Nell's sick, you'll have to use dynamite to get her out of her corner."

Her "corner" was in the far end of the basement. It was separated from the rest of the room with partition boards and curtains. Behind these were packed a bed, chair, two tables and a television. For Nell, in her weakened condition, this was *terra firma*, the only place where she seemed to stand on solid ground. Whenever she left, she became apprehensive and eager to return.

Part of her reluctance to leave was due to the tremendous effort it took to climb the stairs. The main reason, however, was her anxiety. As her illness progressed, her nervousness became more pronounced and leaving the basement became akin to talking about death. Somehow the two combined as though conspiring to create fear, foiling her precarious efforts to find peace of mind. Whenever had to go upstairs she floundered for excuses to return to her corner. In fact, one of the reasons the family decided to use hospice was that Nell had refused to go to the doctor's office. Realizing it was unwise to push her too hard, especially since the doctor had made it clear there was no curative treatment,

Cleo and Sammy decided not to pressure her. They started bringing her meals downstairs and checking on her regularly. This helped. Within a week Nell's anxiety had abated and her mood had improved.

The afternoon I met her, she was cheerful and enjoyed talking about her life. Though apparently unfazed by her illness, she was careful not to stray from the central theme of her reminiscences, which was that her life had been happy. She had many fond memories of growing up on the coast of Massachusetts. As a child in a fishing town, she loved the water and spent as much time there as she could. The vivid detail of her recollections was astounding: the small school house with the iron furnace; the old sea captain who taught her to tie knots and etched a scrimshaw sailboat for her eighth birthday; the little boy who liked to jump out from the bushes yelling "Thar she blows" while brandishing a stick as though it were a harpoon. Although it sounded like an idyllic time, she never mentioned her family, glossing over the rest of her life with little comment.

Throughout the visit neither of us mentioned her cancer. She was eager to focus on other things and seemed nervous that I might try to steer her away from her picturesque narrative, so I did not. There would be opportunities later, as the impact of her disease accumulated, to explore any fear and sadness locked tightly beneath her stories of happy childhood.

Over the next several weeks, Nell's body was steadily abraded by her disease. It required taxing mental contortions to appear happy and convince herself that she only had the flu, or that all she needed to do to feel better was take another one of her iron supplements. Even when she lost her ability to move independently and needed a nursing assistant to bathe her, she continued to talk about getting better. She was sleeping more, eating less, and she used what little strength she had trying desperately to escape her growing fear. She told herself that if she just kept a "positive attitude" she would recover. Although she managed to push her anxiety away, it chipped away at her casual facade, emerging in the form of nightmares, fear of the dark, and occasional shortness of breath. Still, she refused to talk about anything other than what Cleo described as "happy thoughts." Death was a taboo subject even as its arrival loomed.

Despite Nell's fierce determination to hold back the emotional leviathan swimming beneath the surface, it proved impossible. I received a telephone call from Sammy one morning. He told me Nell had suffered a mild panic attack in the small hours of the night. Since then, she had been crying and withdrawn, repeating the phrase, "I don't want to die." He and Cleo had talked with the hospice nurse who had promised to consult with the doctor about a medication to reduce Nell's distress. Now, they wanted me to talk with her to see if it would do any good.

When I arrived Nell was sleeping and Cleo was reluctant to wake her. Sleep had been elusive and now that she was finally resting, Cleo worried that waking her would only plunge her back into the stormy throes of anguish. I agreed to come back later. When I did, Nell was awake. Sammy told me she had been "staring into space" for about an hour without saying a word. As I descended the stairs and approached her corner, she remained silent. When I asked if I could sit beside her she nodded her head affirmatively. Her face appeared listless and distant, like an ebbing tide. Asking questions might have overwhelmed her, so I sat silently. After several minutes, tears welled up in her eyes and, as they trickled down her cheeks, she said, "I'm dying, aren't I?"

"What do you think?" I asked gently.

She hesitated and nervously dried her eyes with the bed sheet before whispering, "I think I'm going to die."

"Have you known this for a while? Or is it just hitting you?"

Her quiet tears gave way to the voluble crying that would come throughout our conversation, like waves rolling in and out. "It's just hitting me," she said, "like a sledgehammer."

She was weak and talking required great effort. Our discussion was full of silent pauses as she struggled to find a word, thought about something, or waited for tears to subside. She knew she was dying and she was terrified. Things were complicated further in that she didn't know why she was so afraid, much less how to find some measure of peace. She had had feelings of fear throughout her life, but it was never this intense or debilitating. Now, as she approached death it was magnified and impossible to ignore. No longer able to avoid it or distract herself, she was left shaking in terror, wanting it to stop.

For someone who had gone to such great lengths to avoid talking about or even acknowledging her terror, Nell's willingness to do so now seemed rather sudden. For weeks, her efforts to hold "unhappy" thoughts and feeling at bay had taken all the energy she had. She was tired of holding it all inside. Slowly, she looked into her internal world in search of a doorway through her raw anxiety. Dredging up memories of her earlier suffering was strange and awkward at first—she was used to telling cheerful stories—but she was determined to penetrate her surface awareness for deeper insight. Hard as it was, she seemed bent on looking her fear of death in the face.

With chilling imagery, she likened her mental picture of death to a powerful bird of prey descending on a tiny rabbit, gripping it in its talons and "snapping its bones into little pieces." For as long as Nell could remember, death had always appeared in this way and it had always scared her. She had found ways to detach from such thoughts and push them into the shadows, but they had never been far away. All her life they had influenced her in subtle ways, denying her opportunities for close friendships, making anything other than happy thoughts, feelings, or behaviors unacceptable.

Trying to locate a single event at the root of such deep fear—or at the root of any persistent and pervasive emotional state—is usually a futile quest. Such things usually grow slowly over time, finding ways to survive and draw sustenance in the dimmest light and rockiest soil. In Nell's case, however, as with many types of trauma, the origin turned out to be clear. Once she set her sails into the gusts of her early pain, she found her way back to her first experience of death, the night her father was killed. Incredibly, she said that she had almost forgotten all about it.

It turned out that Nell's life had not begun in Massachusetts, nor was her childhood as idyllic as she had portrayed. She was born in the mountains of western Pennsylvania where her father worked in the coalmines. Like other mining families, she and her parents lived in a small, uninsulated shack owned by the coal company. Mining was grueling, dangerous work. The company had little concern for the safety of those who labored in the mines. Injuries and deaths were common. There were cave-ins, she said, and people died in explosions. Others died from inhaling poisonous gas or were killed by run-away coal cars.

For decades miners had tried to organize, pushing for safer conditions, shorter hours, and better pay. They had also tried to change the exploitive arrangement where families were forced to pay whatever prices the company charged for housing and basic supplies, racking up debts and further tightening the company's control over their lives.

Her father was a member of the United Mine Workers. Although such things were not discussed with children, she remembered hazy fragments of whispered stories about how he was involved in organizing for the union. As with many labor organizers, he attracted the attention of the company's goon squad. When Nell was six, they murdered her father. When the memory of that night returned, it was layered with minute detail, not just of what she saw, but also of what she heard, felt, and thought.

There were train tracks behind the shack where she and her family lived. Trains came and went at all hours, bringing supplies in and hauling coal out. It was cold that night. She remembered seeing her breath rise in frozen mist as she huddled in the corner of their little home. The events were confusing to her and she was unsure exactly what was happening. Her pregnant mother was walking back and forth on the warped floorboards, repeatedly saying, "Oh no. Oh no. Oh no." A man came to the door and talked in whispers with her mother who suddenly began screaming and wailing. Two women came in and rushed her mother out the door. The man lifted Nell into his arms and carried her to a nearby home. As they walked, she heard men's voices and the metallic sound of lanterns swinging back and forth over the railroad tracks. She remembered a voice saying, "lift him up," then the sound, very clear and distinct, of bones snapping. Later, she realized that it had been her father's bones cracking as men lifted his lifeless body from the tracks. Company thugs had placed his corpse there and driven it over with a locomotive to make his death look like an accident.

I was stunned, not only by Nell's story, but by the composure with which she recounted it. Her voice had been a trancelike monotone, as though viewing herself from far away.

"Whom have you talked with about that night?" I asked.

"No one," she said.

"Ever?"

"No one ever. Not once."

"Why not?"

"I guess," she searched for the words, "I guess I thought if I pretended it didn't happen it would just go away."

Before I could ask another question, she motioned that she didn't want to continue this particular thread of conversation. She sobbed quietly for a minute or two then blew her nose, forced a smiled and said, "I'm over 90 years old and I when I think about that night I get just as scared and worried as I was when I was a little girl."

Rather than wither away, the pain and terror of that night had remained strong, insinuating itself into her life, shifting its shape like a gray cloud able to conform to any wind, its presence strangely familiar yet never quite identifiable.

When repressed traumatic memories find their way into our awareness they can release a storm of thought and emotion that takes a long time to sort out and calm. Since Nell didn't have the luxury of much time, or the energy such assimilation requires, I was concerned that the sudden reemergence of this experience might be an emotional volcano. But it turned out she had been speaking figuratively when she said she had forgotten about that night. What she meant was that she had *tried* to forget, but she had never been able to.

We spent the rest of the visit talking about her father and her confusion surrounding his death. About how she had tried to piece things together as she and her mother left Pennsylvania for Massachusetts, where they had distant family. Taking cues from her mother, she had tried to pretend it had never happened. But the devastating pain had followed her, feeding her silent fear, constantly entangling her in its web-like rigging.

Nell was tired. She closed her eyes as she asked, "Am I crazy or something? I thought if I buried it, it would go away. I never thought it could've outlasted me like this."

"There's no expiration date on something like this," I said.

"Like those cans of beans they sold Momma at the company store," she smiled. Her capacity for humor, even in the pulse of deep pain had long been a source of strength and sanity for her.

I assured her that her struggle was a very human one. When I asked if she'd like to hear a story about someone else who had struggled with a similar experience she readily agreed. Weeks before, she had told me about a memorable whale-watching trip she had taken. It was another of her "happy memories" and she had spoken rhapsodically about her thrill at being so close to these magnificent creatures.

I told her that long ago, a young Nantucket whaler named Owen Chase had experienced a horrible trauma on a voyage to the Pacific. For much of his life he'd tried to bury it away and pretend it had not affected him, only to have it reemerge as he faced his twilight years, burying him beneath a tidal wave of anxiety.

Closing her eyes and preparing to listen to the story, she whispered, "Thar she blows."

II

If Owen Chase could have seen the future in the rippling waters of Nantucket harbor in the summer of 1819, he probably would have given up whaling and headed for Boston in search of a new vocation. Chase, however, was busy overseeing preparations for an upcoming whaling expedition and had no time for such aquatic divinations. Like most people whose lives are about to be shaken by a sudden trauma, he would be taken completely by surprise; and he would spend the rest of his life trying to sort out, or deny, its impact and meaning.

Nantucket, a small island off the coast of Massachusetts, was the center of the whaling universe. It was homeport for over sixty whaleships equipped for journeys that usually lasted two years or more. One of these ships was the *Essex*, commanded by Captain George Pollard. As whaleships went, the eighty-seven foot *Essex* was relatively small, but it had served well on prior voyages. Owen Chase was Pollard's first mate and he knew the ship in its smallest detail. Both men had recently returned on the vessel with a hold filled with huge barrels of whale oil and Chase was already eager to set out in search of more. This would be his first trip as second-in-command and, if all went well, he would soon become a captain in his own right.

Like all whaleships, the *Essex* was an industrial mill on water. Herman Melville observed that the appearance of such a craft "presents the curious anomaly of the most solid masonry joining with oak and hemp." Aboard a rolling foundation of wood propelled by canvas sail were large brick kilns, huge iron pots, and a mind-boggling array of specialized hooks, knives, and spades. The men were organized into crews so work could go on around-the-clock. Their entire focus was finding, killing, and extracting oil from as many whales as they could catch.

It was hard, monotonous work, punctuated by periods of intense excitement and danger. It was also profitable. Oil was in high demand. It was burned in lamps, lubricated machinery, and was used to make paraffin candles.

Once the ship was underway the men took turns standing in the mainmast night and day watching for signs of their quarry. Whenever whales were spotted, three twenty-five foot whaleboats were lowered into the water and six-man crews rowed feverishly in pursuit. They hunted with lances and handheld harpoons affixed to a long rope called a "whale-line." The line connected boat and whale until the men were close enough to use their lances. After a whale was killed, the massive carcass was towed back to the ship and prepared for "trying-out." The tough blubber was cut and removed in huge blanket pieces, chopped into smaller pieces, thrown into large metal try-pots and boiled to remove the oil.

Such was life aboard the *Essex* that December as it rounded the tip of South America and entered the Pacific Ocean. The crew would take Right Whales and Humpbacks if they got the chance, but the real prize was the Sperm Whale, an enormous animal named for the much coveted spermaceti oil contained in its head. It was by far the most dangerous whale to hunt. When attacked, a Sperm Whale could wield its powerful tail, snapping jaws, and steel-like brow as formidable weapons and send a whaleboat to the bottom of the ocean. Whaler Clifford Ashley recalled that, when threatened, "the Sperm Whale may stand and fight instead of running, as other whales do. His most dangerous offensive position is 'jawing back.' Rolling over on his back, with his head out of the water, he lashes out with his jaw, snapping and chewing to splinters everything within reach."

By November 20, 1820 the *Essex* had taken several whales and the barrels in its hold were filling steadily. On that day they spotted a pod of Sperm Whales. Soon all three whaleboats were being pulled through the churning water by taut lines affixed to their prey. The men in Chase's boat narrowly escaped being swamped by a flailing whale and had to return to the *Essex*. Chase, eager to rejoin the hunt, ordered his men to repair the damaged boat as quickly as they could. As they worked, a large Sperm Whale about eighty-five feet long and weighing perhaps eighty tons floated nearby as though watching them. Such behavior was unusual, but no cause for alarm. Not, that is, until the creature charged toward the ship, accelerating as it approached. As Chase remembered it, the whale, "came down upon us with full speed and struck the ship with his head, just forward of the fore-chains. He gave us such an appalling and tremendous jar as nearly threw us all on our faces."

The men on the *Essex* were dumbfounded. They surveyed the damage and found a hole in the ship's side with water pouring in. Chase ordered the men to prepare the emergency pumps, but before they could act the whale charged again. Bearing down on them with what Chase described as "tenfold fury and vengeance in his aspect," ramming its powerful brow into the ship. This time the damage was catastrophic. The *Essex* was sinking. In a matter of minutes the lives of every man aboard were changed forever.

With little alternative, Chase and his small crew lowered their hastily repaired whaleboat back into the water and jumped in. By the time Pollard and the rest of the men reached the site of the disaster, the *Essex* was a wooden corpse bobbing in the aftermath of the whale's inexplicable assault.

Although dazed and shocked, the whalers had the presence of mind to salvage what they could—fresh water, navigational instruments, some tools, a few guns, and several hundred pounds of dry biscuits. With the ship destroyed, the three whaleboats suddenly seemed flimsy and inadequate. As darkness fell, the disconsolate men circled the floating debris, preparing as best they could for the terror of that first night. According to Chase, the next morning, with the shell of the *Essex* still bobbing in the water, the whalers "wandered around in every part of the ship in a sort of vacant idleness…" hoping to find something that would help them survive the days ahead.

Although it was smashed and barely afloat, the whalers were reluctant to leave the *Essex*. It had been their home in the empty vastness of the Pacific. They had trusted its strong oak walls as they would have trusted a fortress of rock or a comfortable and familiar room; the thought of leaving the vessel behind caused deep, penetrating anxiety. Thomas Nickerson remembered how they clung to their sinking ship "as though…it were possible that she could relieve us from the fate that seemed to await us."

Reluctantly, however, they realized that remaining at the wreck site only lessened their chances of survival. If they were to reach land, they would have to move. Using cedar planks, they raised the sides of each whaleboat by about six inches. They fashioned masts from spare timber, and sails from a patchwork of canvas. There were six men in Chase's boat and seven each in Pollard's and second mate, Matthew Joy's. The men were determined to stay together. They planned to sail south for about 1,500 miles where they hoped to find friendly winds that would take them east to the distant coast of Chile. Given the vagaries of weather, limited provisions, and their reliance on dead reckoning to estimate their position, it was an optimistic plan at best.

The frightened men spent the next several days buffeted by waves and pelted with rain. Water splashed over the sides of their boats, tossing them about like splinters of driftwood. It must have seemed like a nightmare incarnate, helplessly adrift in tiny lightweight craft amid the darkness and thunder of a powerful storm. In danger of capsizing or being separated from their companions, the men bailed until their arms burned, then they bailed some more.

When the storm subsided, the men in Chase's boat were dismayed to find that part of their bread supply had been drenched with saltwater. With the daily allowance of sea biscuits for each man a scant six ounces, they had no choice but to eat it anyway. With the water ration a half pint per man, they quickly learned, as Chase put it, that the "violence of raving thirst has no parallel in the catalogue of human calamities."

By the end of November, thirst and hunger were constant. The sun bore down and reflected off the water as though the boats were floating in a giant solar oven. Nickerson, traveling with Owen Chase, later wrote, "having no way of screening ourselves from [the sun's] piercing rays...our suffering became most intolerable as our short allowance of water was barely enough to support life."

On December 8, the storms returned. That night the wind, according to Chase, "increased to a perfect gale, with heavy showers of rain." As the tempest grew "The sea rose to a fearful height, and every wave that came looked as if it must be the last that would be necessary for our destruction." Although they were all sea-faring men, none had ever faced a storm like this in such small vessels, nor had any ever been as thoroughly exhausted. Death seemed to howl in the wind.

Amazingly, the leaky whaleboats weathered the crisis and remained in sight of one another. For a short time the men even enjoyed an amicable breeze that lifted their sails and moved them forward. By December 11, however, they were stalled by a predicament as harrowing as any gale-force wind—no wind at all. They remained stuck by a calm that lasted almost a week, as if their tiny boats were glued to the surface. It was an agonizing time. Baked by the sun, too weak to row, depleting what little supplies remained and not moving any closer toward the distant sanctuary of Chile, the men were pushed to the limits of their endurance. It was not the way of these hard-bitten New Englanders to voice despair to their fellows, but each must have wondered if he would ever see home again. "Our suffering during these calm days," Chase later recalled, "almost exceeded human belief."

By the time the wind resumed, the men were nearly

dead. They were hundreds of miles from land and their water was almost gone. Physically and emotionally they were crushed beneath the pitiless accretions of trauma and privation. Writer Nathaniel Philbrick captured their unenviable state:

> Their physical torments had reached a terrible crescendo. It was almost as if they were being poisoned by the combined effects of thirst and hunger. A glutinous and bitter saliva collected in their mouths that was "intolerable beyond expression." Their hair was falling out in clumps. Their skin was so burned and covered with sores that a splash of seawater felt like acid burning on their flesh. Strangest of all, as their eyes sunk into their skulls and their cheekbones projected, they all began to look alike, their identities obliterated by dehydration and starvation.

On December 20, while the dying castaways floated listlessly in silence, one of them strained to make sure he wasn't hallucinating before shouting to the others that they were approaching land. It was Henderson Island, a tiny nondescript outcropping of coral, but to the desperate whalers it looked like salvation. Looking back many years later, Nickerson wrote, "Never have my eyes rested on anything so pleasingly beautiful."

After finding a place to beach their battered boats, they surveyed the island on weak and wobbly knees. They found some birds, eggs, and crabs, but no water. They decided to stay long enough for a more thorough search, an arduous task since, as Chase reported, "Our bodies had wasted away to almost skin and bone and possessed so little strength as often to require each other's assistance in performing some of its weakest functions."

They were elated when they discovered a modest spring with enough water to fill their empty casks and satisfy their intense thirst; but their bodies were far from restored. Unfortunately, there wasn't enough food on the island to sustain them. They would have to climb back into the boats and resume their agonizing journey. Three men: Seth Weeks, William Wright, and Thomas Chapple, couldn't bear the thought of returning to the rigors of the ocean and decided to stay behind, preferring the thin chance that they could survive long enough on the island's meager fare and hail a passing ship, to the rigors of the unsympathetic and ill-named Pacific.

On December 27, the determined survivors launched their boats into the oncoming waves. They found some solace in their filled water barrels and the fact that they were finally moving east, but circumstances were nearly as dire as when they had first sighted Henderson Island.

Matthew Joy was the first to die; starvation finally killed him on January 8, 1821. His death cast a pall over the men and seemed a cruel foreshadowing of what lay ahead. A few days later, the sky bristled with lightning as once again the waterlogged boats were at the mercy of a swirling storm. The whalers had little strength to fight the gale and even less to try to control their fate. Those aboard must have longed for the warm, reassuring deck of the *Essex*, or perhaps they wished they had never left Nantucket in the first place.

When the waters finally calmed, the men in Owen Chase's boat: Thomas Nickerson, Benjamin Lawrence, Isaac Cole, and Richard Peterson, had been separated from their companions, unsure whether their friends had survived the storm.

They were still over a thousand nautical miles from Chile with precious little food to sustain their flickering lives. Matthew Joy's death had shown them that starvation awaited. They desperately needed to extend their food supply but there was no way to do it other than cut their already inadequate allowance. It was a dilemma that Chase summed up as a choice to "either feed our bodies—and our hopes—a little longer or, in the agonies of hunger, to seize upon and devour our provisions and then coolly to await the approach of death." With stoic discipline and the first mate's strong hand, they decided to reduce the daily ration to less than three of ounces hardtack a day, "feeding their hope" a little longer.

On January 20, Richard Peterson died. The rest, Nickerson recalled, "were so feeble...that we could scarcely crawl about the boat upon our hands and knees." Several days later, Chase, sullen and losing hope, increased the rations, throwing himself and his men into the hands of Providence. As he put it, "Our sufferings were now drawing to a close. A terrible death appeared shortly to await us. Hunger became violent and outrageous, and we prepared for a speedy release from our troubles."

On February 8, Cole died. After agonizing throughout the following night, Chase broached the subject of eating Cole's emaciated remains. The others agreed and the hungry men somberly prepared and ate Cole's sun-scorched corpse. Whether this sustained them for the next nine days is hard to know, but on February 18, Benjamin Lawrence spotted an English merchant vessel, the *Indian*. As if awakening from a long nightmare, the three dazed survivors were soon on their way to the port of Valparaiso, Chile, traumatized and starving, but alive.

When Chase arrived back in Nantucket, he spent a short time recovering before returning to his trade. Despite what he had gone through, he was a whaler and he longed to be back on the water. He was intent on putting the *Essex* behind him and moving on. As soon as his physical condition allowed, he signed on as first mate for the *Florida*, a New Bedford whaleship. To outward appearances, his life continued on the same path it probably would have taken if the wreck never occurred. As Chase had hoped, he earned command of a whaleship and plied the waters of the Pacific searching for Sperm Whales until he retired in 1840. Appearances, however, are a poor measure of the subtle effects of trauma. Though we can only speculate, there is evidence that Chase was haunted by the disaster throughout his life. Near its end, his ability to outrun his past experiences broke down, leaving him anxious and disoriented.

Beginning immediately after the wreck Chase was subject to merciless headaches. These plagued him the rest of his life, becoming even more acute after he left whaling. They were often so painful and incapacitating they reduced this tough-shelled mariner to heaving sobs. It was obvious to Chase that these headaches had begun during his struggle for survival in the Pacific. Such physical complaints often grow out of the lingering anxieties and unresolved emotional pain of trauma. These symptoms can be especially fierce after protracted traumas like the one Chase endured and are apt to affect people, like Chase, whose inclination is to try to repress distressing thoughts and feelings.

It is likely that the affects of his ordeal insinuated themselves into his life in other ways as well. Despite the matter-of-fact style of his written account, Chase reported signs of post-traumatic stress disorder. He had nightmares, flashbacks, and vivid ruminations over the ill-fated events, which seized his mind and interrupted his sleep. It's impossible to know how long these symptoms persisted, but in light of what psychologists know today, it's quite possible they followed him long after he reached Chile.

Chase may also have been subject to periodic bouts of depression. Herman Melville read Chase's account of the *Essex* and was inspired to write his masterpiece, *Moby Dick*. He took an interest in gathering what information he could about the event and even spoke with Chase's son. Melville learned that, on at least one occasion, Chase was, "prey to the deepest gloom," raising the question: Was Owen Chase prone to depression? If so, was it caused or exacerbated by his experience of trauma? It is impossible to know. Whalers in the 1800s were not inclined to tease out the nuances of their long-term psychological response to crisis. We can only wonder about his inner life and speculate without certainty about the nature of his personal struggle.

When Chase was in his sixties, perhaps once again feeling the tenuous thread of his mortality, his otherwise tightly reined anxiety finally exploded into view. Neighbors began to recognize that his behavior was increasingly idiosyncratic. He developed an overwhelming obsessive fear of starving. He began hording food in his attic, squirreling away whatever he could find, convinced that without ample supplies his life was in jeopardy. Nothing could reassure him or diminish the force of his compulsive behavior. The once fiery captain was reduced to fear and panic as the haunting specter of starvation emerged like spray exploding from percussive surf.

Sadly, he was so inconsolable he was eventually judged insane. His anxiety continued until his death in 1867. Like a dormant memory awakened and revived, the horrible experiences of his youth reentered his awareness. He had tried to press it out of his mind, like oil pressed from whale blubber and hidden away in the hold of a ship. After more than four decades, however, it was very much alive and burning hot—like flames under a seasoned iron try-pot.

III

Although we often try to forget painful or traumatic experiences, they are an inextricable and important part of our stories. The more we struggle to deny them, the more creative they will become in how they influence our lives. Although we may refuse to acknowledge them, they accompany us patiently, influencing our choices and affecting us until we look at them directly and find a way to make our peace.

Shortly after Nell's father died, she had been taken away from the only place she had ever known, and probably from the only community that could have understood the challenges she and her family were facing. In Massachusetts, she was not allowed to speak about her father's death and was encouraged to pretend it had never happened. Unable to ask questions, she was isolated in her pain, left to sort out the terrible events on her own. In her confusion, she had attempted to bury the memory in a place deeper than any mineshaft had ever gone.

In some ways she was successful in her efforts. She had lived a meaningful, productive life. As a nurse she had touched many people, shared in their joy and comforted them in their despair. But try as she might, she could not erase her painful memories or the impact of early events. Ripples from her childhood ran through her life like an underground river. The fear of loss that separated her from others, her nervousness that some catastrophe was always lurking just ahead, and her insistence on banishing all but a narrow range of thoughts and feelings from her life, these were just some of the costs of her self-imposed amnesia.

As we talked further, she found that there were many other things buried along with that horrible night. Beneath her fear were deep recesses of guilt and self-blame. As a child she had believed it was her fault that her father had been killed. As an adult she was still shadowed by a gnawing sense of culpability. She wondered if she had somehow *deserved* the horrible trauma of those early years and the frustrations of her recent experience. Perhaps, she thought, God was punishing her for being a "bad person." As these revelations emerged, it was enough to give them a voice, receive reassurance, and let them drift away like crusty flecks of ancient barnacles chipped off a weathered hull and sent into the ocean's amniotic currents.

Like Nell, Owen Chase and the survivors of the *Essex* did their best to put the terrible experiences out of their minds and get on with their lives. For such men, seasoned by the ocean's constant reminders that life can be hard and unpredictable, dwelling on these things was akin to rubbing salt into an open wound. In all, there were eight survivors. George Pollard and Charles Ramsdell turned up in a second whaleboat. They had drawn straws and killed one of their friends so they could eat his flesh. The three who had stayed on Henderson Island were also rescued, but the third whaleboat was never heard from again.

In some ways these men had advantages as they

recovered from their ordeal that Nell did not enjoy. They returned to a close community of friends who cared about them. They did not have to keep their tragedy a secret; it was well known and others were interested in hearing their accounts. They could share their experiences if they chose and Chase, Nickerson, and Pollard even left written accounts of what had happened. They were also adults, having developed far more mental, emotional, and verbal sophistication for making sense of what had happened.

Despite these advantages, the subtle pull of their hellish tragedy must have remained ever beneath the surface of their lives. In Chase's case, these currents built into a powerful jet stream in his final years, pulling him into a storm beset by crippling headaches and unrelenting fears about starvation. He was left hording food; worried about death. Throughout his life this fear, however it affected him privately, had been more-or-less invisible to his neighbors. In his final years, the gathering storm clouds fused above him and began emptying torrents of rain across the sea of his life. As with Nell, the pain and fear had waited for him. Chase wrestled to stay afloat.

For Nell and Chase, their traumas were cumulative. Things that were equally challenging and destructive had followed the initial critical event. For Owen Chase, the wreck was a prelude to the savagery of starvation, exposure, and the enveloping anxiety of being lost at sea. For Nell, her father's death led to a chain of events that separated her from her friends and community, leaving her feeling confused, frightened and alone.

In the last weeks of her life, Nell's fear of death never entirely left her. Talking about dying, however, was not as frightening as she had expected and, to her surprise, it lightened the burden of her longstanding psychic pain. Just as when she was a child, she had been afraid to ask questions and had assumed that her impending death would be physically painful. She envisioned herself gasping for air as though being drawn underwater. Once she began talking openly, she realized her fears were unwarranted. Her pain would be controlled, her breathing unobstructed. Death, which had once seemed like a rapacious bird of prey, though still frightening, lost its bloodthirsty visage. Tentatively, Nell was able to view it as the natural culmination of a long and meaningful life, rather than as a violent, intrusive assailant.

She never had another panic attack. Even the nightmares disappeared as her anxiety abated. Paradoxically, when she stopped trying to elude her past, it lost much of its influence over her. It stopped being a foe that drew strength from her resistance, and became simply a part of her journey. It was a heartbreaking and tumultuous part, of course, and one that affected her in many mysterious ways, but it also reflected her spirit, resilience, and courage.

Inspired by Chase's account of the *Essex*, Herman Melville painted a vivid picture in *Moby Dick* of the way unresolved trauma can take hold of our lives and destroy us. Melville's protagonist, Captain Ahab, is a whaling man whose life has been shattered by a clash with the whale, Moby Dick. Initially, the trauma drives Ahab into madness. As he appears to recover, Melville cautions us that, "Human madness is a feline and most cunning thing. When you think it fled, it may but have become transfigured into some still subtler form." Beneath Ahab's apparent composure remains a furious and obsessive thirst for revenge. In the end, his choice to probe the seas hunting for Moby Dick, rather than probe his mind and heart hunting for equanimity, destroys him and most of his crew.

If Nell had chosen a different path during her last weeks, she may have died beneath a tempest of panic and terror like Chase, or in a desperate attempt to hide her anxiety behind "happy thoughts" in the same way Ahab attempted to hide behind his anger. Instead, her death was peaceful and her final days free from distraction. She focused only on saying goodbye. When she died, she was no longer under the influence of submerged, unresolved pain. By exploring the depths of her fear she was able to find peace, before drifting away like a cloud in a gentle breeze.

Chapter Six
The Battle of Horseshoe Bend:
When Defenses Become a Trap

There were two things Paul made sure you knew. The first was that he was brilliant. The second was that he was an alcoholic. He was aware of the apparent contradiction, but another thing you quickly learned about Paul was that he loved contradictions. He reveled in them, referring to himself as a walking paradox. As if to prove his point, he often vacillated from one extreme to another with little predictability or apparent cause. Against the backdrop of his approaching death, deep psychological tensions that had long plagued him, and which he had always casually dismissed as merely quirky contradictions, were preparing to erupt in all their furious intensity, leaving him confused and struggling for equilibrium.

Paul *was* a paradox. He was unusually sensitive and able to feel empathy for others, but often behaved aggressively, intimidating those around him. He was full of bravado and assertions of his own importance, but harbored a lingering fear that whatever he might have accomplished was of no real or lasting value. Although he was eager to inform you he was unconcerned about the opinions of others, he was hungry for their acceptance and lived with a secret anxiety that he was unlikable. Gifted with tremendous mental focus and discipline, he was also capable of impulsive and destructive acts. He could be brash, loud, and competitive one minute, withdrawn and incommunicative the next, humorous and charming in the morning, sullen and combative in the afternoon. In reality, Paul only pretended to like contradictions—they had often made his life torturous and bewildering. The problem was, he had no idea how to resolve them.

He was an anthropology professor at a college in Texas, a respected scholar in his field. Throughout his career he had been interested in the social behavior of groups, particularly the ways people are made into scapegoats and pushed to the margins. He had spent decades trying to understand the lives of poor people, immigrants, and minorities, and develop strategies to make their lives better.

Paul attributed much of his concern for others to his great grandmother who had been a Tuscarora Indian. On one of my visits he told me about how the Tuscaroras were nearly wiped out by whites and Cherokees in the early eighteenth century. He was proud of the Tuscarora blood flowing in his veins as he recounted how the tenacious remnant that survived had migrated north and were taken in by the Iroquois. In honor of this fact he had named his small calico cat, Handsome Lake, after an Iroquoian spiritual leader.

He lived in a modest home near his ex-wife Janice. It was filled with books stacked from floor to ceiling and Paul had read every one of them, often having scribbled comments in the margins expressing his disdain for an author's viewpoint or the shoddiness of his or her thinking. Many years before, Janice had gotten the house after she and Paul divorced. After he'd left for Texas with little more than a suitcase, she had decided to move to a nearby apartment and rent the home to anyone who could "deal with all the books, bad art, and ragged furniture."

Despite the divorce and years filled with battles and disappointments, they had managed to remain friends, though Janice claimed she'd long ago stopped relying on him for anything other than a laugh now and then. When Paul was diagnosed with advanced cirrhosis of the liver she offered to let him move back into their former home. She knew he was dying and she stopped by nearly every day.

Paul, however, did not believe he was dying. According to him, he had only accepted Janice's offer temporarily in order to get away from the grind of academia and build his strength back. He knew his liver was damaged but he was convinced a regimen of water and milk-thistle would allow it to regenerate. Although his alcohol abuse was an open secret, none of the faculty at his college had any idea he had a terminal illness. Technically, he was on a leave of absence and Paul supposed most of his colleagues simply assumed he was taking another shot at drying himself out at some fancy rehab center. Whatever they thought, he was sure that within a year he would be back to his teaching and research, stronger then ever.

It was a sunny day in early summer when I met him. We decided to sit outside in a garden area overgrown with ivy. He was a large man with thinning gray hair, pale complexion, and bright blue eyes. He conveyed an air of amused detachment, as though our interaction had an element of gamesmanship, the rules of which he understood and I did not. He liked to laugh and talked excitedly about his work and ideas, easily avoiding questions about himself and his illness.

He informed me that his alcoholism was simply "the family disease" which warranted no further discussion. It was an incidental fact of his life, passed down for three generations like the long spidery fingers that also ran in his family. He was an alcoholic because his father had been one and that was all there was to it. When I said this seemed like a simplistic explanation coming from someone who had spent much of his life studying the psychological complexity of human experience, he laughed, looked up as if in thought, and told me a story.

He said his father had been in a special unit responsible for collecting military intelligence during World War Two. One night in June 1944, his father and a small group had secretly landed on one of the beaches in northern France. They dug themselves into the sand near the foot of massive German defensive works and waited for the invasion of Normandy. This was D-Day, the assault by American, British and Canadian forces on the Normandy Coast. During the initial wave thousands of American troops landed on the beaches and thousands fell dead or wounded.

According to Paul, his father's job was to photograph the entire landing, capturing every bloody detail as men came ashore, fought, and were killed. When his father returned from the war he rarely talked about his experiences. He began drinking heavily and was prone to paroxysms of anger and periods of moody introversion. Reflecting on what he must have seen that day, Paul acknowledged with dry humor the "theoretical possibility" that other factors may have been behind his father's drinking. As to his own, he was noncommittal.

Over the next several visits Paul frequently spoke about his deceased parents. He described his father as an honest, hardworking man, but demanding, critical, and emotionally aloof. He had always been somewhat uneasy in the world, even before the war. His mother was strong, reliable and unquestioningly loyal to family, but beneath the surface was an undercurrent of disappointment with her life and those around her. Both parents were difficult to please. Rare words of approval were always accompanied by warnings about pride and vanity as well as some countervailing criticism just so Paul wouldn't get an "inflated opinion" of himself.

He was not judgmental when talking about their lives. Time and his own personal challenges had taught him that life is a messy business, full of imperfections and unintended conflicts. From these early years he had drawn several lessons: success depends on hard work and persistence; you must improve yourself every day and never rest or become satisfied; emotions are to be controlled, not expressed. He also learned that life was hard, usually unfair, and that there were two basic groups of people: those who fail and those who succeed. Or as his father was fond of saying, those who are hammers and those who are nails.

It was a rough blueprint for a sensitive young man to follow, but it had helped him earn status and excellence in his profession. Combined with his mother's strong encouragement to live in service to others, it had helped him positively affect many lives. It had also made his exterior appear fierce at times, although inside he felt vulnerable and alone.

As our visits unfolded, Paul began to reflect on his life. Hesitatingly at first, but illness seemed to soften him toward, and steel him for, introspection. Perhaps for the first time, he began to probe beneath his twin defenses of intellectual bluster and alcoholism. He acknowledged that his competitive life-stance had always created a great deal of anxiety in him. Feelings of nervousness and vulnerability had followed him like an undisclosed secret pressed deep into the corners of his awareness, threatening to be revealed at the most inopportune times. Fear of failure, of not being good enough, or of ruining relationships with people he cared about had shadowed him, waxing and waning, but always there. Like his father, Paul was uncomfortable in the world and unsure of himself.

It was difficult for him to talk about such things. After all, he'd spent years trying to hide his fear and sadness from others and himself. For Paul, anxiety had connotations of weakness and failure. It was something to be overcome, or at very least strenuously denied.

He had learned to deny his fear by acting powerful, intimidating others, and showing them how brilliant he was. But this was no real solution. It only kept his insecurities at a slightly more comfortable psychological distance. The only time his anxiety seemed to vanish entirely was when he was numbed with alcohol. In a moment of lucid insight he realized that he drank to feel less scared. Paradoxically, as he had come to depend more on alcohol and less on himself or others like Janice, his fear had snowballed, leading him to drink even more.

Alcohol may have temporarily anesthetized his internal terror, but it grabbed hold of his life and left a trail strewn with destruction, hurt feelings and broken relationships. It squandered his potential for intimacy and peace of mind. Despite his ability to maintain a veneer of control and appear the model of a successful man of letters, his private life was like a swirling hurricane: chaotic, violent gales and crashing waves spiraling around an eye of quiet, albeit anxious, humanity.

Not surprisingly, Paul drank most heavily when his fear was threatening to break through the surface of his other defenses. Ironically, this often corresponded with times and events most people associate with joy, like the day he and Janice were married or when he accepted his first job at a university. He had missed the first three weeks of his daughter's life because he was lost in a drunken fog. Slated to accept a major academic award, Janice had to receive it on his behalf because he had disappeared. The list was long and sad.

As our conversations progressed, Paul's growing insight and his decision to express, rather than hide from, painful thoughts and feeling brought some relief, but it also brought resistance. Moving into the center of his pain was much harder than retreating behind a whiskey bottle or his ability to intimidate. When such emotional pain is unearthed, it can seem to intensify as it dashes from the psychological cages we have devised to keep it away from our awareness. This was true for Paul. He became uncertain about whether or not he wanted to continue his self-exploration. The lonely nervousness and sadness he uncovered was so great that, despite several months of sobriety, he felt a growing urge to call one of his old drinking buddies and go on a bender. We agreed to enlist the support of Janice and another friend, as well as his hospice team, to help him manage these impulses, and we lowered the intensity of our sessions for a while.

As he pondered whether to dig deeper into his life or simply let "sleeping dogs lie," he was struck by the paradox of his circumstances. He had spent his life as what he called an "activist anthropologist," not only trying to understand others, but helping them create meaningful change in their lives, yet he had remained stuck in patterns of self-destructive thoughts and behaviors that were now, literally, killing him. The more he thought about this, the more certain he was that this was one paradox he needed to resolve before he died.

As his physical strength waned and his skin became jaundiced, Paul realized he was not going to recover. He knew his illness was the result of years of drinking. Rather than deny it, he continued his quest for understanding, innervated by the sense of urgency that comes from knowing that time is short. Healing his disease was impossible, but perhaps he could find some measure of psychological and emotional healing.

With surprising energy, he renewed his reflections on his life from his earliest memories to his most recent experience. It was his interior world, his secret life, he sought to understand, not the formidable facade he had always tried to present to others. His innermost self had long ago retreated beneath the pressures and clamor of a dangerous world, hiding behind a wall of aggressive demeanor. Paul was intent on tracking his inner self, like a gentle woodsman tracking a stealthy animal afraid of being seen. His efforts paid off when he began to hear a faint though steady inner voice of calm and hopeful encouragement. He had to listen closely, though, to hear through the static of longstanding, automatic thoughts about his self-perceived limitations and the world's crass indifference.

Like the eye of a hurricane, this voice was discernible through the storm, emanating from a still, peaceful spot within the surrounding chaos. It was the part of him that had tried to accept his imperfections, the part that had desperately wanted connection. Although this voice had always been there, it had usually been drowned by relational conflicts, alcohol, and emotional defenses. Now, in the stillness of his reflections, he found that if he quieted his mind, he could hear it beckoning. He decided to call this soft low-toned emanation his "true self," and strained harder to measure its steady pulse.

This was the part of him that had always been concerned about others, motivating him to try to make the world around him more humane. It was also the part that felt afraid and vulnerable in a world of loud unpredictable events. It had hidden behind Paul's pugnacious intellectual prowess and confident assertions, as though these were planks in some impenetrable protective wall. Behind the wall, however, Paul remained unsure of himself, easily wounded by the words and actions of others, hungry for peace.

With encouragement, his true self—who he really was—became less tentative, slowly emerging from its retreat without being swept away by alcohol or Paul's bombastic pretense of self-importance. Though these twin defenses had usually subdued the pangs of the anxiety that shadowed him, they had also drowned his capacity for wisdom and equanimity.

In the last weeks of his life, Paul continued his odyssey of self-discovery despite a profound loss of energy and difficulty concentrating. Something drove him on toward greater understanding. He hunted for a larger perspective from which to view the wreckage of a life lived with much uneasiness. From this wreckage he hoped to salvage what was, and what continued to be, good and durable. He would finally, "look the dragon in the face" without running into the psychic numbness of a nearby bottle or sending those around him scurrying for cover. Most importantly, he would do it without muffling that secret voice that had always known something was wrong and had continued to hope for something better.

For Paul, there was no eureka moment of radiant clarity. There was just the cumulative momentum of his genuine attempt to glue together the fragmented shards of a complex life. He realized that his aggressiveness and his inflated ego, as well as his drinking, were merely smokescreens obscuring his deep insecurity. The world had always seemed like a scary and uncaring place and he had always secretly expected to be crushed beneath its weight unless he appeared fearless. Ultimately his intellect and success did not cure his anxiety. The greater his outward success, the more he worried. When brilliance and charm failed to protect him, alcohol succeeded, or so he had thought. If Paul were a walking paradox, here was its most fundamental expression: what he did in the belief that he was protecting himself was actually destroying him. Or as he put it, "It's like the wall I built to protect myself has become a trap that is killing me."

In the light of this awareness he blamed himself.

It would have been disingenuous to try to alleviate his guilt and anger by pretending he bore no responsibility for his choices or that he was the powerless victim of unconscious forces pushing him toward alcoholism. Yet, as guilt overwhelmed him it threatened to undermine his progress in finding a deeper truth and a more inclusive perspective from which to understand his life. It also impeded his capacity to make, at the very least, some gestures toward self-forgiveness and peace before he died.

He wasn't aware how common this particular paradox was. I told him that many others find themselves in similar circumstances.

"Give me an example," he said. He seemed to genuinely want to know he was not alone.

Rather than give him a specific example, I wondered if a story might offer him useful insight and imagery; a story about the same people Paul had spent much of his life fighting for—underdogs and those under pressure from larger cultural forces. "Have you ever heard of the Battle of Horseshoe Bend?" I asked, knowing of his affinity for Indians.

In 1814, during a war between the Creek Indians and the United States, a large body of Indians erected a strong wall on a spit of land surrounded by the Tallapoosa River in Alabama. They had placed great confidence in their wall and in the water surrounding them. They had believed any attack on their defenses could easily be repulsed and that they were safe from the threats of a world that had become scary and chaotic. But they were wrong. Their defenses became a trap. Their wall and the river were as instrumental in their destruction as the military forces arrayed against them.

"Do you want to hear the story?" I asked.

Paul was always ready for a story, especially one that spoke of contradictions and paradox.

II

By 1800, the Creek nation was in trouble. There were tensions among the tribes, and citizens of the United States were hungry for their land. It was a time of growing uncertainty. Fear floated freely through the pine trees of their homeland in Georgia and Alabama, like snow falling on weary shoulders. Decisions had to be made about how to defend themselves from the threats of a changing world. Even strong and boisterous warriors ready to fight could feel anxiety churning deep down in their bellies.

Though Americans called them Creeks, they were a loosely knit confederation of tribes such as the Tallassees, Alabamas, and Cowetas. They contained remnants of what had once been large chiefdoms like the Apalachees, and tribes such as the Yamasee that had been driven from their homeland by war. They also included blacks escaped from slavery and Indians from tribes that no longer existed such as the Timucuans and the Westos.

They had been drawn together by the force of shared experience. They had all suffered from diseases brought by Europeans and Africans—smallpox, measles, yellow fever, dysentery—and they had shared the experience of living in a land precariously located between areas claimed by the Spanish, French, British, and more recently the Americans.

Despite common experiences and similarities in their way of life, a split had emerged between the tribes known as the Upper Creek and Lower Creek. The former lived mainly in Alabama and tended to trade with the French. The latter lived in Georgia and traded with the British and Americans. This fissure was especially critical in the early 1800s. By then, French power had waned and the United States, though small, was a new power with many citizens interested in taking control of the southeastern fur trade.

The Americans also wanted land. Intruders from Georgia and South Carolina were already squatting on Creek territory and demanding more. Tension escalated and the Indians found themselves arguing about how to respond. On one side were those who believed the best way to survive was to accommodate the Americans. Others argued that the only viable course was resistance and, if necessary, war.

These groups were further polarized in the winter of 1811, when the Shawnee leader, Tecumseh, arrived. He was intent on drawing all Indians together regardless of their tribal affiliations. He envisioned a grand alliance to resist white expansion stretching from the Great Lakes to the lower Mississippi. He urged his listeners to fight the Americans and return to traditional ways.

Born to a Creek mother, Tecumseh was intelligent and eloquent. He delivered his message with angry passion. Not surprisingly, his presence was like a lightening rod that drew the war faction together, focusing it into a highly charged staff of blazing fire. When he arrived for a counsel in Tuckabatchee, an important Upper Creek town on the Tallapoosa River in Alabama, about five thousand people came to listen. Many had traveled long distances and some, like representatives of the Cherokee and Choctaws, came from other Indian nations.

Tecumseh's message of resistance was combined with a call for unity and spiritual revival. His vision was broad and inclusive. He believed all Indians shared a common bond. At Tuckabatchee he did not mince words. "Let the white race perish!" he told them. "They seize your land, they corrupt your women, they trample on the grave of your dead. Back whence they came, on a trail of blood, they must be driven. Back! Back!"

Fueling things further were the British and Spanish, whose representatives encouraged the Creeks toward war. With disputes between England and the United States rapidly leading toward the War of 1812, Tecumseh correctly assured his followers that when battle came, "Two mighty warriors across the Great Waters will send us guns, powder and lead."

In Tecumseh's wake things moved quickly. The resistance faction, composed largely of the Upper Creek, intensified its calls for battle and became known as Red Sticks—a term that may have come from the red sticks handed out by Tecumseh with which to measure the time to begin the war. Others believe it was a reference to "their vermilion war clubs, and the red sticks, supposedly magic ones, used by their shamans." Whatever the origin, in traditional Creek symbolism everyone knew red was the color of war. On July 27, 1813 Red Sticks armed with Spanish guns and powder fought a battle with soldiers at Burnt Corn Creek. The Creek War had begun.

Among the Indians there were many who simply wanted to be left alone. Were it possible, they probably would have built a sturdy wall around themselves as protection from a hostile world and hidden behind its formidable, reassuring defenses. Now they had no place to hide. War demanded they choose sides.

In August, several hundred Red Stick warriors attacked the modest palisade of Fort Mims on the Tensaw River in Alabama. By the time the fight was over the fort was burned to the ground and two hundred and fifty people inside, many of them Creeks who had sided with the Americans, were dead.

When word of the attack spread, militia from surrounding states moved into the Upper Creek heartland. About fifteen hundred Georgians and their friendly Lower Creek allies pushed west and fought two short, but bloody battles before retreating. From Mississippi and Louisiana joint militias, supported by Chickasaws and Choctaws, advanced east. After making a show of their strength, they also withdrew. From Tennessee, Andrew Jackson moved south from Nashville with twenty-five hundred volunteers and a group of Cherokee and Creeks. Heading into Red Stick country, Jackson described himself as "Determined to exterminate them..."

By early November, Jackson had won a battle at Talledega and assaulted the Creek town of Tallushatchee where his men had killed women and children as indiscriminately as they had Red Stick warriors. The Tennesseans, however, were in a precarious condition as winter closed and food became scarce. Deep inside Red Stick country with no prospect of supplies before spring, the men faced starvation. Discipline unraveled and morale plunged. Jackson demanded reinforcements from the Governor of Tennessee and dug in his heels to tough out the winter, insisting his militia do the same. But when his men's enlistments expired, they left and his force dwindled to about a hundred men.

By spring, about five thousand new militia itching for a fight had reinforced Jackson. In late March, scouts found a large Red Stick village built on a small peninsula formed by a loop in the Tallapoosa River called Horseshoe Bend. About thirteen hundred men, women, and children were living here in a hastily constructed village they called Tohopeka, or "the fort."

Though there were many stalwart warriors at Tohopeka ready for battle, others had been swept up in events and retreated to this place seeking protection after the previous autumn's cataclysm. Many were frightened and bereft, having abandoned their homes and banded together for protection on the east bank of this familiar river.

The village was protected on three sides by the river and was accessible by land only along the eastern neck of the bend. The Creeks had constructed a sturdy breastwork across this narrow gap consisting of a zigzagging wall. It was a formidable defense, unmistakably designed to withstand a frontal assault. Even Jackson, acknowledged, "It is difficult to conceive a situation more eligible for defense than the one they had chosen, or one rendered more secure by the skill with which they had erected their breastwork."

The Creeks were confident in their defenses as they watched Jackson's men prepare for attack on the morning of March 27, 1814. The Red Sticks had several hundred warriors; their shaman had assured them the Master of Breath was smiling on them. They were sure the wall they had built—and the wall of water that surrounded them—

would keep them safe. Amidst the ravages, dislocations, and heartrending grief of war, they had retreated to this place cradled by the river. They thought their walls were impregnable and they bared their teeth, ready for Jackson and his men.

The battle that followed was horrific. Jackson sent some of his militia and Indian allies to the opposite shore of the river to prevent Red Sticks from escaping. His main force attacked the wall. The breastwork, as intended, was very effective and Creeks fired through portholes, placing the attacking troops in a menacing crossfire. While the fight raged, some of Jackson's Cherokee and Creek warriors managed to swim the river and steal some canoes. Before long, others had crossed the river and attacked the preoccupied Red Sticks from behind.

Suddenly, the watery barrier looked painfully inadequate. Attacked from two sides, the Red Sticks realized too late that the wall they had built and the river they had chosen for protection were actually the jaws of a trap. Unable to fight off a two pronged attack and psychologically upended, the battle continued, but the outcome was all but certain. All directions for the Creek were blocked. Blocked by the river that had so recently reassured them, and a wall of their own making. Tohopeka was not an impregnable fort; it was a deadly trap.

Even Jackson was aware of the irony. On the day after the battle he addressed his militia and gloated that, "By their yells, they hoped to frighten us, and with their wooden fortifications to oppose us…their yells but designated their situation the more certainly; while their walls became a snare for their own destruction." In the end, their defenses proved to be their undoing.

III

While it is natural, even sensible, to seek ways to feel safe amid the uncertainties of our journey, constructing defenses is a tricky business. The best ones are porous and flexible enough to allow for growth and change, capable of nourishing rather than impeding close relationships. They expand and change as we become wiser, or simply fall away lest they impede our passage. When we cling blindly to our defenses, or when they keep us from greater awareness, compassion, and sensitivity, they have become a trap. So we must be very careful about the walls we build. Whether they are intended to protect us from external enemies or the uncomfortable presence of thoughts, feelings, or situations we would rather not experience, there is always the possibility they will collapse and leave us paralyzed beneath their weight.

As Paul and I talked about Horseshoe Bend, he wondered what it might have been like behind that zigzagging wall with the world about to cave in under a powerful and implacable foe. For Paul, being crushed had always seemed like a real possibility; fear and vulnerability were ever-present companions and he understood the impulse to build strong walls. Looking sympathetically at the plight of the Red Sticks placed the paradox of his own behavior into a larger human context. Certainly we have all built walls that have fallen on top of us or become traps. Paul smiled at the thought that he had lots of company.

Paul's hard work and methodical self-examination in the preceding weeks allowed him to see that he had built a wall out of his arrogance and ability to intimidate others. Like the waters of the Tallapoosa, he'd unknowingly allowed a river of alcohol to separate him further from others, leaving him huddled on a spare, lonely spit of earth afraid to venture out. In a sense, he was as much a prisoner as the small group of haggard Creek survivors rounded up by Jackson's men in the aftermath of the battle. Afraid of external pressures, he had guarded the edge of his prison and pushed back all who had tried to approach. Eager to ward off internal foes and banish worries from his mind, he'd succumbed to the numbness of alcohol abuse. He had run so hard trying to escape his fear that he had become disconnected from his deepest and sanest inner voice.

Paul could see that the Creeks had realized their plight too late. "Maybe I realized things too late as well," he said.

"Too late for what?" I asked.

"Too late to live in a different way, I guess."

"Is it really too late for you to live in a different way?"

"Probably."

I asked him if he thought his recent efforts at understanding himself and his situation had been a waste of time.

He said emphatically, "No."

"Why not?"

He thought about it for a few minutes and said, "I guess it's not really too late. I mean, yeah I'm going to die, but I can live the rest of my life in a different way. Even if I've just got a day left."

A day was more than most of the Red Stick Creek had after they realized their plight. By nightfall hundreds of them were dead. There were so many Creek casualties that soldiers sent out to count them decided to cut off the noses of their fallen enemies in order to arrive at an accurate number. When Jackson asked how many noses they had gathered, he was told, "Five hundred fifty-seven here at the fort, and three hundred fifty in the water, but we can't find all that are in the water."

After the battle, the Creeks were forced to cede twenty three million acres of their homeland. This was true for all Creeks, including those who had sided with the Americans. These White Sticks, as they were called, had believed the best way to defend their families was to seek friendship with the United States and cooperate with its citizens. Ironically, like their Red Stick comrades, they had contributed to their own demise by assisting Jackson at Horseshoe Bend, paving the way for the crushing demands that followed.

For two decades after the battle the Creeks saw more and more of their land taken. Finally, in 1836, the entire Creek nation was forced from their homes and pushed onto a reservation in Oklahoma. Of the approximately 14,000 who made this forced march, nearly 4,000 died along the way, or shortly thereafter. Somehow the Creeks endured and found ways to adapt, survive, and retain their traditions. Somehow they preserved what was left of their lives and history despite the convulsions and pain of many losses.

Though the battle's carnage was indescribable, not all the people who gathered at Tohopeka were killed or captured. Some escaped by crossing the Tallapoosa and vanishing into the woods. Others waited for the cover of night before stealthily slipping away. Some joined neighboring tribes or fled to Florida and blended with the Seminoles. Others were prepared to continue fighting, though after the disaster at Horseshoe Bend, resistance was essentially broken. Thus, a handful escaped Jackson's army and survived. In the long run, so did the Creek nation.

Paul knew he wouldn't survive cirrhosis. He could, however, escape his self-imposed trap and live his remaining days in a way that expressed who he really was, rather than who he had always tried to appear to be. He learned to accept that the regret and sadness he felt was not an enemy to be fought, but simply a part of his life. Not, however, the definitive part. This he discovered in the silent voice that had been barricaded behind his invisible walls. In the shadow of his dying, this voice grew stronger and gained his trust.

He learned that he could be anxious without it being a sign a weakness. He could reach out to Janice and his children despite his fear of rejection. And he could feel sadness and cry without being a failure. Most of all, he could be himself and use what energy he had with the people he loved rather than expending it pretending to be something he wasn't. This was the final paradox perhaps, that in the process of losing his life he found out who he really was. He stepped beyond his ill-conceived fortifications and, to his great surprise, found that he liked himself.

Paul remained somewhat unsure, however, whether other people would like him. He wondered if people would take him seriously without his facade of loud and quick-witted extravagance. When he could no longer get out of bed on his own and needed care around-the-clock, he worried about having to hire strangers to help out. Before such arrangements could be made, however, his condition worsened rapidly and he was moved to a residential hospice facility for his remaining two weeks. For Paul, who had always kept his own counsel and desperately wanted to be seen as independent, leaving his home for a building filled with strangers was very difficult, especially since he needed help with many private activities. "I don't like this one bit," he said, "but I'll do it for Janice. God knows it's about time I did something for her."

Paul's need for help removed any remnants of his ability to project indestructibility. Rather than causing anxiety, however, he found this a relief. "Finally I don't have to worry about people finding out I'm a wreck inside and spending all my time trying to outmaneuver them. Now they know I'm a wreck and it's alright." With a smile he added that he was starting to suspect we are all wrecks in one way or another.

With his vulnerabilities transparent, Paul was amazed to find people liked him anyway. It didn't matter that he was afraid and sad, or that he needed help or had little energy for conversation. In fact, these needs made his humanity all the more genuine and compelling. For Janice, Paul's transformation allowed them to reconnect in a way neither had thought possible.

"It's like the part of Paul that I fell in love with," she said, "the part that has been buried for so long, has come back out at the end of his life."

"What part?" I asked her.

She grabbed a tissue from a cardboard box in the hospice room where we were sitting and motioned that she needed a minute to find the words and absorb the emotions she was feeling.

"His compassion and his gentleness and humility," she finally said. "And all his crazy insecurities too. I knew he was still in there under all his bravado, but I was afraid I'd never see that part of him again."

She likened Paul to a caterpillar who had spent much of his life plodding clumsily through a thick forest, trying all the while to convince the birds and spiders hunting him that he was a rattlesnake. In the end, he'd spun a cocoon, withdrawn, and emerged shortly before his death as a beautiful butterfly.

"He may only get to fly a little while, but what a wonderful sight," she mused.

Paul died quietly in early autumn, before the first frost. Janice was sitting on the front porch of the hospice building when the nurse came out and told her he had died. "Just before that," Janice told me, "an amazing blue and black butterfly landed on the back of my rocking chair and then flew and landed on my arm." When the door opened and the nurse stepped out, "It just flew away up into the sky."

Section Three
Hold on to My Hand:
Staying Connected

Hold on to my hand
even when I have gone
far way from you.

From a Pueblo prayer

Faced with the separation of death, the importance of the connections we have with loved ones can become as clear as polished glass. Relationships and people we have taken for granted can be seen from a new perspective radiating their true value and uniqueness. Perhaps it is ironic that such a thing may happen just as a relationship seems about to be severed. But, irony aside, this awareness can also be an invitation to give thanks and deepen one's connections, even as time grows short.

For some, this is an invitation openly and enthusiastically received; each day, however hard, stressful, or frustrating, is cherished in the shadow of life's gathering sunset. Others are more ambivalent. The invitation may be accompanied by regret at having "wasted" time or opportunities. It may unearth feelings of guilt or shame at actions that cannot be undone, words that cannot be taken back, or long silences that hang like sad memories framed in the very human shades of misunderstanding, ego, and failed communication. When this happens, it is wise to simply let these winds blow—fighting them will only cause more disappointment. Even better, is to find ways to move into and even use these winds to heighten our appreciation for this final chance to do things better. Sooner or later, the gales, although they may never be stilled, will calm.

Even though a person with a terminal illness may begin to withdraw and move their focus inward, connections can strengthen. Such things are not dependant on words and shared activities; they are dependant only on love. As a person is dying, perhaps in a light coma and verbally unresponsive, the connection can continue to grow right up to the point of separation (and, in some ways, even beyond, since a relationship does not end at death, but remains in the lives of those who have shared it).

Doing our best to tend to such connections, as with tending to the prospects for growth, meaning, and healing that we explored in the preceding sections, is another of the opportunities that attends times of suffering and upheaval. In the following three chapters this theme will be illustrated and clarified. In Chapter Seven, Frances is wracked with guilt, sadness, and anger at the alienation that has grown between her and her daughter. As the time for reaching out diminishes, she has to confront these feelings, as well as an array of doubt-inducing thoughts, if she is to reconnect before she dies. In Chapter Eight, Buddy struggles to stay connected with his wife, Flora, as Alzheimer's disease pulls her away. In Chapter Nine, Diane and Sal seek to overcome the communication difficulties that have bedeviled them for decades, leaving in their wake hurt feelings and sadness.

They all hear, and in some cases initially resist, the call toward connection. As with most of us, things may not always go *exactly* as we hope, but there is always the potential for steady movement toward deeper, more meaningful relationships between people who are doing the best they can under trying circumstances.

Chapter Seven
Adams and Jefferson:
Reconciliation and Forgiveness

When she was a child, Frances's family called her "the brain." Her perceptiveness was as apparent as her dissatisfaction with superficial answers to any of the rapid questions she constantly fired at adults who wandered into range. It had begun as a playful nickname, but became the central metaphor of her life. By fifty, she'd earned two Ph.D.s and had published several scholarly books on intellectual history and political philosophy. As a university professor, she had sharpened her questions into darts and flung them at students and faculty alike. Now, at seventy-two, living alone and feeling the effects of untreatable cancer, she was flinging them at herself and piercing holes in a thin veneer of success that no longer insulated her from her deep sadness.

While strengthening her mind and climbing the academic hierarchy, she had made many sacrifices. Before her diagnosis she'd been oblivious to these, now they tormented her like a fire of regret.

Her home reflected these sacrifices as clearly as it reflected her unquenchable thirst for learning. The eggshell colored walls were full of books stacked tightly on shelves. Awards and ornate diplomas hung in spare metallic frames. Tables were cluttered with stacks of journals. There were no mementos from vacations or campy postcards from friends traveling in distant lands. No photographs of family or crayon drawings from happy grandchildren, no handwritten recipes taped to the refrigerator and stained with tomato-covered fingerprints. Fact was, she didn't take vacations, never spoke with her grandchildren, had very few friends, and considered eating an unavoidable nuisance that had to be accommodated in order to survive.

Surviving as a professor had demanded emotional control, determination, and assertiveness. This was especially true for women of her generation, for whom academic positions had been rare. Competition and the clamoring criticism of her colleagues, though often shrouded in a mask of civility, could be harsh and disparaging. Succeeding under such circumstances had taken focus and many long hours of work. This had left little time for family or friends. These relationships had withered from neglect, dispersed like dust left in the wake of missed opportunities. Her all-consuming focus had destroyed her marriage and driven a wedge between Frances and her two surviving children. This was her most ferocious regret. "It's like they just slipped away one night," she said, "while I was preparing a lecture."

She had been married nineteen years. Although she glibly described the experience as a mistake, this was only a facade to encourage people to move on to another subject without further explanation. In truth, she remembered Ted as a kind, good-hearted person who was "much better at being a father than I was at being a mother." She described most of their years together as remote and disengaged. "I was always too busy working," she said. Even when she was home, she was usually sequestered away in her study. "I spent more time with the letters of (Thomas) Jefferson or the essays of (James) Madison than I did with my husband or kids."

After the divorce, Ted moved to California. Her two sons chose to go with him, while her daughter Martha continued to live in Ohio, near Frances's home. "I thought I'd feel liberated," Frances recalled, "but I was sad when they left." Thinking she could outrun her sadness, she buried herself in her work with an intensity she described as vehement. Without her family, she became isolated. Her days became a paradox of feeling alone while surrounded by the sprawling crowd populating her university.

Martha was the only person she ever interacted with without the convenient denominator of her work. In spite of Frances's habitual resistance, they usually met a few times a month. Although she wanted to see her daughter, Frances often felt awkward during their visits. For all her mastery of the verbal arts, she was uncomfortable with simple conversation, unscripted as it were and without time for preparation. "There's a reason," she joked, "that my parents called me 'the brain' and not the social butterfly." Secretly she worried that Martha thought she was a lousy mother and would find ample corroboration amid the long pauses that invariably textured their meetings.

She stayed informed about Ted and her sons through her daughter's occasional reports. A few years after the divorce, Martha told her that Kyle, Frances's younger son, was planning a trip to visit some colleges in the area and was hoping to see her and ask her advice. Frances was elated. She phoned him that night and she and Kyle agreed on a plan for his impending trip.

Frances could hardly contain her excitement. "Truth be told," she said, "I never really knew how to talk with kids, even my own." Now that he was a young man, she was eager to assist him with his academic goals. It was something about which she was an authority; it had been a long time since any of her children had asked for help. The silences between Frances and Martha dissolved as they discussed Kyle's "grand tour."

As the time neared, Kyle telephoned to tell Frances he would arrive the following week. It was the last time she ever heard his voice. He was killed in an automobile accident a few days later.

No torture ever devised can rival the pain inflicted by the death of a child. For Frances, it was like a descent into hell. Questions exploded like searing embers landing on exposed flesh. Why had it happened? How could she continue to live after burying a son? Why hadn't she been a better mother? Why hadn't she spent more time with him? Why couldn't it have been her instead? How could God have let this happen? What was Kyle thinking when he died? Was he afraid? Was he in pain? These questions stood stark, like weathered scarecrows on a burnt and rocky land. Their bottomless unanswerability taunted her, rendering her penetrating powers of analysis useless.

Despite the wrenching intensity of her sadness, her grief was largely private. Although there were signs that something was wrong, these were camouflaged enough to allow others to avoid noticing. Her mind was dulled, like a blade blunted by heavy use. Her concentration flagged and she had little gusto for arcane debate. Her expressiveness was muted and drawn into a narrow emotional range with a frequency resonating quiet sorrow. In the department of her university, however, with its tight schedules, emphasis on matters of the intellect, and respect for personal privacy, Frances's struggle, if noticed at all, went unacknowledged.

Even Martha had no comprehension of the depth of her mother's pain. She misunderstood Frances's attempts to use work and pursuits of the intellect as distractions from her sadness. For Martha, grief was a public event to be shared with anyone who would listen. Tears flowed easily and talking about Kyle helped loosen the shackles of her despair. Frances, on the other hand, wound everything into a tightly compressed ball and swallowed it whole. Talking about Kyle only heightened her fear that it would explode like a coiled spring, tearing her to pieces. For Frances and Martha, the languages of their grief were as different as Sanskrit and Gaelic, neither knew how to translate the unfamiliar tongue of the other.

Misunderstandings ensued, compounded by the raw emotions and haunting thoughts that come like regular visitors to those who have lost a child or sibling. The more Martha searched her mother for signs of sadness, the more Frances covered them with apparent detachment. Martha yearned to know that her pain was shared and to connect with her mother in the midst of their sudden loss. Frances was afraid that if she loosened the vice-like mental contortions through which she confined her grief, she would become lost forever in the plummeting expanse of her sorrow. Eventually, they stopped meeting and telephone calls became rare.

Frances could see she had not only lost a son, but was in danger of losing her daughter as well, yet she didn't know how to bridge the widening chasm. Instead of talking with

Martha about her concerns, she once again made work the pillar around which she organized her life. She swallowed her pain and withdrew from her daughter. Looking back, she recognized her habit of retreating into the disciplined chambers of her mind during times of crisis. At the time, however, she blamed Martha, concluding that she was emotionally unstable and that it was impossible to reason with her. Furthermore, it was Martha's "job" to initiate contact, so it was Martha's fault they had grown apart.

Years passed. There were sparse words now and then. When Martha got married she sent her mother a wedding invitation. Frances toyed with going, but convinced herself she couldn't miss an important research symposium. In retrospect, she admitted feeling ashamed of her role in their relational cold war and being apprehensive about running into Ted. Occasionally a card was sent on a birthday or holiday, but the unpredictability of this only served to accentuate the long silences. Over the years their separation became a habit that both came to view as inevitable and unchangeable. Like mortar holding brick, silence hardened into a baffling wall of separation. By the time their anger had faded, fear had grown in its place; fear of reaching out and facing the possibility of rejection.

When Frances retired to North Carolina, she had sent Martha a card. After a brief exchange of cordial, though formal notes, contact had again come to a stop. Now, it had been over four years since the last letter had been sent and no one in Frances's family knew she was dying. As she saw it, she had nobody to tell.

When death arrives on the horizon to signal the beginning of the last stretch of our journey, it has a way of scouring away illusion and leaving only those things that are most meaningful. After being diagnosed with cancer, Frances realized that her family was still very important to her. Other things, such as her legacy as a respected author and educator offered some contentment, but her family was another matter. It had been nearly twenty years since she'd spoken with Ted. Her surviving son had disappeared into a netherworld of drugs, petty crime and alcoholism. She wasn't even sure whether he was dead or alive. Her break with Martha seemed irreparable. She had never even met her grandchildren, Martha's two teenage daughters.

During her failed chemotherapy, Frances began experiencing the terrifying chill of what she referred to as "absolute aloneness." The kind of aloneness that comes when the sands beneath your feet are shifting and the people who care about you are nowhere to be found. It was as if all the various alloys that harbor loneliness and sorrow were drawn into a single blade and left dangling precariously above her head. This time she had no university or scholarly pursuits to distract her.

By the time we met, regret and loneliness were so intense she had been thinking seriously about writing a letter to Martha, and possibly Ted. She had lived alone for a long time. Recently she had decided she didn't want to die alone.

"I suppose I have no right to hope for one of those deathbed reconciliations. But I'd sure like something better than this," she said as she motioned around her arid townhouse.

Frances was hardnosed enough to believe that the possibility of she and Martha coming together bathed in forgiveness, attaining seamless closure after lives spent struggling to get along, was an unattainable fantasy. Even so, it was a fantasy that drew her attention, pointing toward deeper possibilities in a fallible world. It tapped her desire to do things better before it was too late. How to begin? That was the question.

After broaching the subject of reconciliation during our visit, she retreated into barbs of dismissive sarcasm. It was too late, she thought, for a "conversion experience" ushering in a time of familial harmony. The rifts were too entrenched. She had hope, but she told herself that hope was unrealistic. There was no use belaboring things. It would be more consistent, she concluded, to die without so much as lifting a finger toward bridging the separation.

"It'd be consistent," I agreed. "But is it what you

want?"

We both knew it wasn't. She said that if she could write a script for the end of her life, it would include her daughter, son, and some type of "closure" with Teddy.

"What stops you from trying to make that happen?" I asked.

"I don't know. I really don't know."

Ferreting out the source of her resistance was like trying to catch smoke wafting into the air. She was still angry with Martha for not pursuing her more persistently. She secretly enjoyed the thought of her family receiving the news of her death out of the blue. Would they feel guilty? Would Frances's last breath be any more serene knowing she had dug her heels into the sand and died the way she had lived? Would anything have been accomplished?

She was also afraid. What if she reached out and nobody noticed? Why risk the disappointment? And if it went well, could she withstand the possibility that the years of separation might simply lash her with renewed pain and regret over the time they had wasted? What if Martha tried to take over as Frances's condition worsened? What if, in her weakened state, Frances was unable to assert her precious independence? She could control things more easily, or so she thought, in her separate world of airtight routine. Reaching out brought countless unpredictable variables, and Frances hated unpredictability. She vacillated for weeks, lost in a maze of excuses, girded by fear and fear's shadow—longstanding habit.

She was realistic enough to know that sooner or later Martha would find out. Cancer would outpace even her tenacious willpower and eventually she wouldn't be able to stay at home without help. Although she refused to give the hospice team Martha's telephone number, she knew we could find it. She also knew that when it became unsafe for her to live alone, I would locate Martha and inform her. In purely practical terms, the kind Frances was most apt to concede, it would be better to inform her daughter prior to such an emergency, but still she refused. It was her choice. She and her family would have to live, and die, with the consequences.

There was no point trying to convince Frances to do something she had decided against. Arguing with her would only have stiffened her resolve and left little room for her to change her mind as events unfolded. It was better to respect her decision and provide a safe place to explore the inner struggles that had created so much disquiet. For weeks she deliberated. As she did, her strength waned and she required more medications to manage the physical pain. Time was running out, she needed to decide.

"Have you ever read any of Thomas Jefferson's letters?" She asked one day as we were discussing her increasingly tenuous circumstances. With Frances, any conversation could quickly turn toward history or philosophy. She was thinking of a particular letter Jefferson had written in 1786. It was written in the form of a dialogue between his head and his heart. They were at war, she explained, and Jefferson was their battlefield. She quoted parts from memory and concluded by expressing deep empathy with Mr. Jefferson. She was likewise torn between her heart's longing to reconnect with her family, and her head's prudent caution. The internal strife was becoming difficult to bear. Her head told her to forget about Martha and think her way beyond the "irrationality" of painful thoughts and emotions. Her heart told her to reach out and, even if her effort came to nothing, find comfort in having tried.

We spent some time discussing this tension and searching for common ground from which she could enlist her head's assistance in pursuing the goals of her heart. She wanted to be convinced, but her mind was strong, skeptical, and full of doubt. After sputtering through several fruitless attempts to find a way for her to feel comfortable enough to pick up the telephone and call her daughter, I asked her to think of Thomas Jefferson and his complex relationship with John Adams.

Jefferson and Adams became good friends in the 1770s. Theirs was the close and affectionate bond of kindred spirits traveling through momentous times. By 1800, however, they were political enemies and the rupture was deeply personal. For years they refused to communicate. Ice-cold silence would have followed them to the grave if Adams had not had the courage to reach out. In doing so, he created a harbor of reconciliation that made the winter of their lives a time of renewed friendship and intimacy. It was a harbor in which they shared reassurances, acknowledged regrets, and found forgiveness.

Frances knew the story better than I, but she encouraged me to tell it to her anyway.

II

In the winter of 1811, John Adams was thinking about writing Thomas Jefferson a letter. The two hadn't spoken or written each other in over ten years. Now one of his nation's aging patriarchs, Adams was wondering whether the bitter conflicts that had long ago severed their friendship might be put aside. They were growing old; the time for reconciliation was slipping away. For Adams, however, swallowing his considerable pride and picking up his pen was not something he would do without pangs of ambivalence, resentment, and the belief that it was really Jefferson's job to make the first gesture. As he looked back on the events of their lives, he may have recalled the summer of 1776, when he and Jefferson had stood shoulder to shoulder. He may have felt regret that such close friends had allowed their partnership to be wrecked by cacophonous political battles and a river of unintended misunderstandings.

In June of 1776, the American Revolutionary War had completed its first bloody year. With the British army en route to New York City, John Adams and Thomas Jefferson were certain the time had come for the American colonies to declare their independence. The two men were among the delegates of a Continental Congress meeting in Philadelphia. When Richard Lee of Virginia proposed that Congress issue a resolution declaring, "these United Colonies are, and of right ought to be, free and independent States," the matter was entrusted to a small committee with Jefferson and Adams at its head.

The two had developed a quick friendship, although at first glance they were an unlikely pair. John Adams was a fiery, pugnacious New Englander. Plainspoken and often argumentative, he was at ease speaking in front of large crowds and reveled in stormy debate. He could be impulsive, quick-tempered, and inflexible. Jefferson was the consummate Virginia gentleman. He was reserved in public and controlled his emotions and impulses with the precision of a Roman stoic. He was uncomfortable speaking before groups and his words were often artfully ambiguous. Civility and self-control were his cardinal virtues.

Either could have written a stirring and eloquent Declaration of Independence. In this case, however, it was Jefferson's work that the committee submitted to Congress. Later, Adams claimed credit for pushing his friend into the limelight. As he recalled it, he gave three reasons that Jefferson should write the Declaration: "Reason first: you are a Virginian and a Virginian ought to appear at the head of this business. Reason second: I am obnoxious, suspected and unpopular. You are very much otherwise. Reason third: You can write ten times better than I can." With Adams's encouragement, his friend rose to the occasion.

During the colonial representatives' debate, Jefferson's draft was held up to great scrutiny. Delegates argued, pleaded, and admonished each other over every detail. Jefferson sat in sullen silence, offended as they sliced up his sentences and removed others from the document altogether. Later, he wrote appreciatively that John Adams had stood firm during the debate, "fighting fearlessly for every word...He was the pillar of [the Declaration's] support on the floor of Congress, its ablest advocate and defender against the multifarious assaults encountered."

On July 4, Congress finally issued the Declaration of Independence. It was Adams and Jefferson's first collaboration and they had proven a formidable team.

Adams's defense of the Declaration had solidified their bond, signing their names on it drew them even closer. Placing one's signature on such a document was a gravely serious act. At the time, England was the most powerful nation on earth with an army and navy known for its lethality. Benjamin Franklin was speaking literally when he commented that all who signed the Declaration must, "hang together, or assuredly we shall hang separately." Surely, Jefferson and Adams's necks would have been among the first to be placed in a British noose if things went wrong. The two were riveted together as if by Vulcan's hammer; events ahead would season their connection, making it even stronger.

After leaving Congress, Jefferson returned to Virginia to serve in the state's House of Burgesses, and later as governor. Adams was appointed Minister to France. While Governor Jefferson eluded British soldiers crisscrossing Virginia, Adams worked feverishly in the courts and salons of Paris to solidify a military alliance with the French.

In 1784, the Revolution a success, Jefferson joined Adams as minister to the French Court. Adams was delighted when he learned he would be reunited with his old friend. In a letter to James Warren, he wrote that Jefferson's appointment "gives me great pleasure. He is an old Friend with whom I have often had occasion to labour at many a knotty Problem, and in whose Abilities and Steadiness I have always found great Cause to confide."

For nine months they collaborated closely, relying on each other as they plied the shifting shoals of global politics. Representing the new American states to Old World powers was a delicate job. Negotiating treaties, trade agreements, and the specifics of America's massive financial debt required great tact and seamless teamwork.

Shortly after Jefferson's arrival, John Adams—already living with his son John Quincy—was joined by his wife, Abigail, and their daughter. To Jefferson, who had suffered the deaths of four of his six children, as well as that of his young wife, the Adamses became a surrogate family.

He was a regular visitor in their home and was especially close to John Quincy. Years later, the elder Adams commented to Jefferson that during this time, John Quincy "appeared to me as much your boy as mine..."

In April 1785, Adams was appointed Minister to England. As he and his family prepared to leave for London, he wrote to Richard Cranch, "I shall part with Mr. Jefferson with great regret." By then, a rich vein of genuine and warm affection nourished their mutual respect and trust. In a letter to Adams shortly after his departure, Jefferson acknowledged his sadness, writing that, "The departure of your family has left me in the dumps. My afternoons hang heavily on me." In a letter from Abigail Adams, she told the Virginian he was deeply missed and that he was, "the only person with whom [John Adams] could associate with perfect freedom, and unreserve."

The steady flow of letters between London and Paris attests the continued importance of the friendship and their on-going reliance on each other's judgment. Adams was the senior of the two, far more experienced in diplomacy and negotiation. Jefferson had a knack for synthesizing information and viewing things from a larger perspective. More than for assistance with practical matters and advice, they relied on each other for personal support as they played the tricky and very serious game of foreign diplomacy.

As their letters crossed the English Channel they discussed critical events such as the debate over whether to ratify a new constitution written during a recent Constitutional Convention. Their correspondence was also filled with reports and inquiries about family and expressions of loyalty and friendship. In the hustle and bustle of foreign courts and exciting news from their fledgling nation, Adams proclaimed to Jefferson that, "intimate Correspondence with you...is one of the most agreeable Events in my Life."

In 1788, Adams was summoned back to the United States. Sailing across the Atlantic, he professed to have no political ambitions and anticipated a quiet return to his farm in Quincy, Massachusetts. His daughter, however, reported that, "The Americans in Europe say he will be elected Vice President." His daughter was right. By the end of 1788 the constitution was ratified, George Washington was President and John Adams had been elected Vice President. Washington appointed Jefferson his Secretary of State and soon Adams's old friend was on his way across the Atlantic. When the two reunited in New York (the temporary capital), they may well have anticipated a continuation of their fruitful collaboration and a deepening of their friendship.

Such was not to be. Without the King of England to rally against in a common cause, sharp differences arose among the nation's founders regarding the scope of the constitution and the proper direction of the new nation. Adams and Jefferson had agreed on independence, but they had different visions for the nation's future. Throughout the 1790s, as this debate intensified, two views emerged: Jefferson's, which envisioned an agrarian nation with strong, independent states, and Alexander Hamilton's (Washington's Secretary of Treasury), which saw an America with a robust, centralized federal government and thriving urban centers with commercial ties to the Old World.

This debate deteriorated into attacks of a mean-spirited and personal nature. Like many, Adams and Jefferson found themselves on opposing sides. Historian Joseph Ellis captures the fractious tone of this decade and is not exaggerating when he writes that, "in terms of shrill accusatory rhetoric, flamboyant displays of ideological intransigence, intense personal rivalries, and hyperbolic claims of imminent catastrophe, [the 1790s] has no equal in American history. The political dialogue within the highest echelon of the revolutionary generation was a decade-long shouting match."

Although Adams attempted to remain above the fray, Jefferson viewed him as a mere satellite orbiting dutifully around a Hamiltonian center of gravity. In 1793, a frustrated Jefferson resigned as Secretary of State and retreated to his estate at Monticello. Despite his claims that he was through with politics, Jefferson soon took aim at John Adams and surreptitiously encouraged scathing attacks on his politics and character.

By the time Adams was elected President in 1796, conflict and misunderstanding was rapidly battering their friendship into an empty shell. Harsh words had been spoken and actions committed that made the gulf between them seem unbridgeable. As the smoke rose from a burning landscape of distrust and recrimination, their bond became a nearly lifeless casualty of repeated political and personal collisions.

Ironically, Jefferson was elected Adams's Vice President and the two were thrown into a moment of decision. Could they repair the damage to their friendship and rise above the rancor of political factions, or would this be the final note in the dirge of their dying affections? Jefferson considered approaching Adams and offering to renew their partnership, but his confidant, James Madison, talked him out of doing so. Instead of rapprochement, antagonism grew hotter. By the end of Adams's term as President, Jefferson had privately funded some of the basest personal attacks on him by one of the most unscrupulous mudslingers of the day. For his part, John Adams had signed a law allowing the government to throw his political enemies in jail if they dared publish criticism of his administration. By then, the Adams-Jefferson friendship was a memory so ancient it seemed like little more than a wistful fantasy.

When Jefferson was elected President in 1800, Adams didn't even bother to stay for the inauguration. He left Philadelphia (the second temporary capital) before dawn and headed home, disgusted with the rapid erosion of the high-minded idealism of the Revolution into backbiting political gamesmanship. When he crossed the threshold of his home in Quincy, he had every reason to believe that he would never communicate with Jefferson again.

In 1804, on hearing of the death of Jefferson's daughter, Polly, Abigail Adams sent a note of consolation to him without her husband's knowledge. If any hope of reconciliation was behind her gesture, it was quickly dispelled by the short, belligerent exchange of letters that followed. Writing on her own behalf, without informing John Adams, Abigail castigated Jefferson for severing the "Gordian knot" of their friendship. She blamed him for machinations that had ripped apart a bond that otherwise "could not be untied by all the efforts of party Spirit, by rivalship by Jealousy or any other malignant fiend." Their short correspondence ended as abruptly as it had begun, their mutually caustic pens had only reinforced the divide.

Both men were wounded, proud, and stubborn enough to believe the responsibility for the rupture rested squarely on the other's shoulders. There would be no more direct contact between either of the Adamses and Jefferson for several years. So deep were the wounds and distrust, that a sociological scavenger picking through the wreckage of their friendship would have been savvy to expect that silence would follow them to their graves, standing as just another brick in history's long wall of shattered alliances.

As time passed, silence calcified into habit. Adams busied himself on his farm and Jefferson retired to Monticello. Their worlds remained as distant as if they were living on separate planets. If either recognized the tragedy of events, neither seemed inclined to speak about it. They had stood together during troubled times, trusted and respected each other. They had protected and consoled each other in times of grief and uncertainty. They had helped forge a new country. Could such things be completely erased by the ravages of politics? In 1809, their mutual friend, Benjamin Rush, was trusting their bond was not completely dead. He hoped it could be stirred with some nimble encouragement.

Rush shared their credentials as a revolutionary. He had signed the Declaration of Independence and weathered the same political storms as his feuding friends. Somehow, he had managed to avoid taking sides in the intense discord of clashing viewpoints and remained on good terms with both men. From his home in Philadelphia, he carried on a flourishing correspondence with them, hoping to spark one to reach out to the other.

In October 1809, with feigned innocence, he told Adams about a particularly interesting dream he had had. Mr. Adams, he reported, "addressed a short letter to his friend Mr. Jefferson...This letter did great honor to Mr. Adams. It discovered a magnanimity known only to great minds. Mr. Jefferson replied to this letter and reciprocated expressions of regard and esteem. The letters were followed by a correspondence of several years." Whether this was a dream of the waking or slumbering sort is unclear. Rush was open about his hope that the men would put their animosity aside, carefully crafting his good-natured prodding to their different temperaments. Adams responded that he had "no other objection to your dream, but that it is not history." He then slyly conceded that, "It may be prophecy."

If so, it was distant prophecy. Adams refused to budge and made it clear that Jefferson, not he, would have to take the first step. However, he told Rush that if he were to receive a letter from Jefferson, he would "not fail to acknowledge and answer it." Mildly encouraged by this, Rush began working on Jefferson. "I have ardently wished," he told the Virginian, that "a friendly and epistolary intercourse might be revived between you...I am sure an advance on your side will be a cordial to the heart of Mr. Adams."

Jefferson's response was a long letter blaming the rift on Adams. Like his old friend, he would be slow to take the first step, but he encouraged Rush to continue his affable cajoling and assured him that, other than being the first to reach out, he would do whatever he could to "second [Rush's] efforts."

Both men were gingerly probing the edge of the chasm separating them, but each believed it was the other's job to be the first onto the tenuous rope bridge Rush was attempting to construct. For over two years Rush softened them to the idea of communicating. Whenever he drew kind words or lingering affections from one, he reported them to the other. He was like a human telegraph through which

Adams and Jefferson sent and received guarded expressions of respect, regret, and hope.

By December 1811, both men had been leavened with steady doses of Doctor Rush's unflappable optimism and steadfast refusal to believe their friendship was dead. They were aging, their careers were over, and many of their contemporaries were already gone. Each had seen children die and friends whisked away by illness and old age. Perhaps, as they neared the end of their lives, they saw that the window through which they could break their silence was rapidly closing.

Still, someone had to go first.

On January 1, 1812, John Adams set aside his wounds and sent a letter to his old friend at Monticello. Whether Rush's dream was prophecy or fantasy remained to be seen. However, one thing was certain, Adams would make the effort. The rest was out of his hands.

III

Bridging the gulf between ourselves and a loved one with whom we have grown apart is often no easy matter. Our minds learn to accommodate separation and transform it into something that seems normal and routine, transmuting sadness, regret, or the general sense that something is amiss, into detachment, avoidance, or blame. Sometimes the distance becomes so familiar we even fear its removal. When death approaches, however, the sadness of separation is often unmoored from its deep anchorage and floats to the surface in search of resolution.

Such was the case with Frances. She was weary from the effects of cancer and years of pulling a sad, heavy chain of silence. She knew time was running out. Although her impending death made her struggle more urgent, it also liberated her. Even if she were rejected or her efforts went badly, she reasoned, she'd be dead soon anyway, so what did she have to loose? She took the story of Adams and Jefferson to heart and during our visit she decided to contact her daughter. Before doing so, however, she intended to "look at a few" of the letters exchanged after Adams's note of January 1812.

Adams's note was the opening chapter of a fourteen-year correspondence now regarded as one of the most extraordinary in American history. Jefferson responded at length, writing an informative and carefully proper letter. He closed by assuring Adams that, "No circumstances have...suspended for one moment my sincere esteem for you; and now I salute you with unchanged affections and respect." Though the words were a masterful display of gentlemanly protocol, it would take months before the two of them hashed through old disagreements and misunderstandings. Once this had been done, the pace and scope of their letters shifted and they discussed everything under the sun; Adams in a playfully provocative, casual tone, Jefferson usually striving for elevation and erudition. Eventually, the letters recaptured an easy familiarity rooted in shared memories and the hard lessons of age. They came to understand that, even in the heat of political battle, each had been sincere in his commitment to serve the country as best he could.

Their correspondence stands not just as a record of what was, but also of what almost was not. If Adams hadn't taken the risk of picking up his pen, there would have been no revived friendship, no eloquent record of reconciliation or ambling reflections of kindred spirits; just grave-dead quiet.

Several days after my visit with Frances, I got a call from Martha. She wanted to know what was "really going on?" Her mother had called and they had had a strained conversation that left her confused and ambivalent. The questions poured out, one after another. How sick was she? Why didn't someone from the hospice team call her? Did I think she would live another week? Another month? A year? Did Frances actually expect her to drop what she was doing and come racing down to North Carolina? Why shouldn't she just let her mother die alone? What did Mom say about me? Can I tell you my side of things? Did I understand how hard it was for her to get a call like that? Did I know Frances didn't even bother to come to her wedding?

She talked fast, as if trying to absorb decades of life's raw material in a single thin day. She was angry, scared, concerned, apathetic, hopeful, cynical, relieved, ashamed, and elated. If there is such a thing as an emotional spectrum, she encompassed its full range, from infrared to ultraviolet. As she told the story of her struggles with Frances, beneath her agitation was the steady hum of lingering sadness. Whatever the storms of history and their consequences, she missed her mother and wanted to see her.

I talked to Frances the next day and she informed me Martha had called that morning and they had arranged a visit the following week. "We decided we needed to talk about practical things," she said, "like power of attorney, my will, and the insurance policies. I don't want anybody having to clean up after me." Given the circumstances, it was about as safe an agenda as could be hoped for. As the visit neared, each of them tried hard to bridle any hopeful expectations. This time, they would be prepared for disappointment.

As Jefferson and Adams grew older, writing letters became more challenging. Adams's hand trembled and his eyesight dimmed. For the last eight years of his life he had to dictate his letters to someone else. Jefferson suffered aches and pains, and he found that moving even short distances left him with "sensible fatigue." In 1817, Adams's beloved wife died. He wrote Jefferson that he found consolation in the thought that their "separation cannot be so long as twenty separations heretofore." Jefferson also thought of death and wrote his friend that, with their bodies "running for 70 or 80 years…[they] must expect that, worn as they are, here a pivot, there a wheel, now a pinion, next a spring, will be giving way, and however we may tinker with them for awhile, all will at length surcease motion."

In July 1826, as July Fourth dawned, both men were dying. As he drifted into his final sleep, John Adams's last words were, "Thomas Jefferson survives." He was unaware that his friend had died earlier that day, the fiftieth anniversary of the Declaration of Independence.

Although Martha arrived with low expectations, she wound up extending her stay and attempting to talk her mother into moving in with her family. The practical things they had planned on discussing had offered a convenient sanctuary from which to venture into the more difficult subject of the preceding years. Martha had many questions and, in the absence of an opportunity to understand Frances's experience and intentions, she had decided on some answers that were troubling her. Frances was surprised to learn that Martha had interpreted her silence regarding Kyle's death as indifference. She was equally puzzled when Martha explained that when her mother had withdrawn, she concluded Frances didn't really love her.

These were difficult conversations, but honest ones. Frances occasionally became overwhelmed and retreated into heady abstractions, but always returned, intent on "doing it right" this time. It surprised them both when they realized that each had wanted to remain connected, but layers of misunderstanding, flawed assumptions, and dramatically different styles of coping with pain had confused them.

Though these insights were accompanied by the sour taste of regret at having lost so many years, it helped Martha forgive her mother. Frances, it turned out, was never as angry with Martha as she had pretended to be. "I guess I was more angry at myself than her," she admitted. Forgiving herself would be a slower process.

When Martha left, they began calling each other several times a week. Frances learned that her other son was in prison and Ted had suffered a stroke and was confined to a wheel chair. She mulled the idea of contacting them, but settled on relaying information to Ted through her daughter (Martha did not communicate with her brother). Like Benjamin Rush, Martha became a human telegram through which Frances and Ted culled out what had been good about their relationship, and let the rest drift away.

Frances had been surprised at Martha's offer to share her home and had turned it down without contemplation. But as her condition worsened, her desire to be with family stayed in the forefront of her mind and she gave the matter more serious thought. The next time Martha offered, Frances accepted.

It was something that would have been impossible if Frances hadn't put her fear and hurt feeling aside and extended her hand. When she initially picked up the telephone, she had no guarantee things would go well. In fact, they could have gone very poorly. The important thing had been for Frances to make an effort.

Frances transferred her care to a hospice in the city were Martha lived. I lost track of them after a final telephone conversation. During that talk, Martha acknowledged she was tired and the adjustment in their lives was a challenge. She was nervous about the road ahead, but extremely pleased that her mother had moved in.

"Mama would talk with you too," she said with a laugh, "but she's getting a facial treatment [from a granddaughter who wanted to be] a fashion consultant." "You wouldn't recognize her," she said, "she looks like a whole new person."

It seemed an apt metaphor and a good note on which to end

Chapter Eight
The Mountain Man Rendezvous:
Finding Community in the
Midst of Isolation

Buddy's life revolved around his wife, Flora. For six years he had watched her deteriorate physically and mentally from the effects of Alzheimer's disease. For Flora, the worst part had been when she had known what was happening, but could do nothing to stop it. Few things are more agonizing than descending into a fog of confusion, knowing that eventually you will become lost and unable to find your way out. Now, she was constantly confused. "There were times," Buddy recalled, "when she'd try to make me promise I'd give her an overdose when she got this bad, but I always told her I'd never do it." His response had always been to assure her he would keep on loving and protecting her no matter what happened.

For Buddy, the worst part had been when she began forgetting his name. It was as though the history they shared was being stolen one memory at a time by the winnowing blade of dementia. Even now, whenever she looked at him without recognition it broke his heart. The doctor had suggested Buddy put her in a nursing home, but he had recoiled at the idea. She had nursed him back to health after three heart operations and he intended to take care of her at home until she died. "I'll do it," he said, "even if it kills me." Which was exactly what his doctor was worried about.

Mindful of his compromised health, every morning Buddy prayed for one thing: that he lived one day longer than Flora. The thought of relinquishing her into the hands of strangers was enough to bring tears to his eyes. Though he preferred to talk of other things, this prospect was an ever-present source of concern, frequently finding its way into our conversations.

Aside from Buddy's two brothers, he and Flora had no family in the area. The rest of their siblings were dead and they had no children. Years before, they had had some friends, but when Flora's mind began slipping she became self-conscious, withdrawing from everyone but her husband. According to Buddy, when conversations became awkward, their friends disappeared. "I guess they knew Flora was nervous," he said, "and I wasn't much on socializing."

The demands of caring for her never ended, even momentarily. Buddy had equipped the doors of their home with alarms a few years earlier when she had started wandering outside and getting lost. Now there were sound monitors throughout the house. If she was awake, so was he. When she got her days and nights "mixed up," Buddy spent the afternoons cooking, cleaning, and filling prescriptions, then stayed up all night keeping an eye on his wife. Even now, although Flora was completely bed-bound, he checked on her constantly, rarely sleeping more than a few hours at a time.

Despite the sadness of watching her decline and having seen her gentle demeanor become combative and oppositional at times, his love for her was unbending. He swore he loved her even more deeply as she slowly disappeared into a wilderness of dementia. As he explained it, you come to realize just how much you love someone when you see them slipping away from you.

He knew the disease was beyond his control, but felt guilty that he couldn't stop its devastations. He searched for ways to reassure her and help her stay oriented in a world that was narrowly compressed into the walls of their modest home. He scrambled to communicate with her, vigilant for any path that would lead through the crags and peaks of her confusion. Despite many small successes, he often felt helpless and frustrated.

Alzheimer's disease had trampled across their lives like a herd of buffalo sweeping across a mountain meadow. As it did, Buddy's world shrank along with his wife's. His brothers had offered to stay with Flora, but Buddy seldom left home. When he did, it was only briefly and he worried about her while he was out. There were few people with whom he could talk freely and times, he admitted, when Alzheimer's seemed like it would envelop them both.

"Some days I really and truly think I'm going crazy."

For Buddy, learning to be a caregiver had been like exploring unfamiliar terrain. He had mastered the multiple, often simultaneous, tasks through trial and error. As his and Flora's isolation had increased, Buddy had had few opportunities to gain perspective on the intense, sometimes contradictory thoughts and emotions that arose daily. With no map to measure the journey's progress, and no one with whom to compare notes, he often doubted the value of his efforts, second-guessing almost everything he did.

Whenever something went wrong, as it often did, he invariably blamed himself. If she was in pain, he blamed himself for not giving her additional medication in time. If he was unable to assuage her tears, which came spontaneously and often, he blamed himself for not knowing the right words or gestures. If she wanted something and he couldn't understand what it was, he berated himself for not comprehending. It was like a trap with springing jaws: He loved her and wanted to do everything perfectly, but her many needs and impaired ability to communicate, not to mention his limitations as her sole caregiver, made perfection unattainable. When he fell short of his lofty expectations, he felt guilty and ashamed.

When I met him, isolation and self-doubt were as much a part of his life as his boundless love for Flora. He jumped at the chance to talk about their lives before her illness. Sharing memories brought her back, if only momentarily, strengthening the final unseverable thread that still connected them. No matter the degree of her mental erosion, nothing could break their bond as long as he remembered who she was beneath the gauzy web of her disease.

They had met late in life, when any thoughts of

finding life partners had receded and each had become resigned to living alone. Buddy was driving a bakery truck that afternoon when he stopped at a country store along his route. Flora was standing at the counter. She had recently moved to the area and had stopped to ask the clerk about local churches. Buddy was instantly drawn to her smile and soft-spoken manner. Before the bread was on the shelves, he had invited her to his church and a fish fry that Friday night. "I was running early that day because I was training a new driver and there were two of us unloading that morning," he remembered. "If the new guy wasn't there, I'd have missed her. Funny the way a little thing like that can change your whole life."

He remembered how the store's florescent ceiling lights reflected off her glasses and made her eyes sparkle. In his mind, she was still the person he had met that day long ago. On particularly bad days, he liked to think about that moment and remind himself that beneath the burdens of their current circumstances, she was still with him, sparkling and radiant.

Although modest and unassuming, Flora had also been adventurous and self-possessed. Buddy had several stories he liked to tell illustrating her independence. One of these had to do with fur trapping. For years before they were married Buddy had trapped small, fur-bearing animals near a creek meandering through woods owned by one of his brothers. He sold the pelts to a friend in the mountains who made them into hats and sold them to tourists. When he and Flora got married, Buddy assumed his trapping days were over, but to his surprise and delight she insisted that he show her how to bait the traps and cure the skins.

It was one of the many stories in which he and Flora were the sole characters. Occasionally there were others, but they were always tangential. In her company, he needed nobody else. "When you saw one of us," he said, "you either saw the other or you knew they weren't far behind."

No wonder his pain was so great when she struggled to pull his name out of the well of her deepest memory.

As with many people who have a loved one with Alzheimer's disease, his grief was complex. In some ways, Flora had already left him, as she became concealed in a cloud-covered mountain of confusion. Memories they had once shared were now his alone. And yet, he had not lost her—she was still with him. Whether she remembered him or not, he was certain she knew that he loved her. Some messages have a way of getting through, even when nothing else does.

Still, Alzheimer's was a trackless wild into which Buddy and Flora had stumbled without a compass. As her condition deteriorated, he assumed more responsibilities and felt less capable of fulfilling them. He kept his thoughts and emotions to himself, rarely giving them vent. Occasionally they gathered into perplexing storms where sadness and love, helplessness and determination, guilt and courage, all blended into an internal cascade. Buddy simply rode these times out like a lonely traveler caught in a downpour.

It was different for Flora. Such storms were over. Her bouts with anger and fear had been anesthetized by pervasive disorientation. Now, her days were spent sleeping and her face was a blank page rendering her inner world all but unknowable.

Not surprisingly, Buddy continued to doubt himself. At times, his many worries seemed to bend him to his breaking point, at other times he clung to them as though they were precious stones. In a strange way, his self-doubt reflected the indestructibility of Flora's hidden spirit. The more he struggled with his shortcomings, the more he accentuated her beauty. It was as if he were saying to others that the person trapped inside Flora's emaciated frame deserved something far better than anything he could ever provide.

He dissected every thought, feeling, and behavior for signs of his inadequacy. If, in his frustration, he momentarily raised his voice, his response was not to see this as a normal, human response, but as confirmation of his ineptitude. If he had a passing hope that Flora's life would finally come to an end, he saw this as proof of his imperfect loyalty rather than as a reflection of his fatigue or his love for someone grown tired in her suffering. Attempts to gain perspective were dampened by his certainty that he was a failure as a caregiver. He was impervious to assurances that he was doing a good job. His refrain to all who tried to chip away at his doubt was that they didn't understand because they hadn't been through what he was going through. If his efforts to reassure Flora were unsuccessful, he would make sure *he* was not consoled by the efforts of others.

Underlying his belief that others could not understand his circumstances was a sense of aloneness and separation. Next to the emotional roller coaster of his daily concerns and anxieties about the future, his life seemed far removed from the mundane rhythms of "normal" life. "Sometimes," he said, "I feel like I'm living on another planet, light years away from most people." Lost in the ethereal mist of quiet alienation, he was convinced no one could comprehend what he was going through. With so many converging pressures, responsibilities, and the confusing rush of turbulent thoughts and feelings, he saw no point in trying to explain things. He was sure he would only be misunderstood.

Separated from others by such weighty concerns, Buddy kept his own council and drew his own conclusions. More often than not, his verdict was that he was deficient as a caregiver and husband. Unintentionally, he had stepped into another trap: He had no regard for the assurances of people whose lives were untouched by Alzheimer's, but he had no opportunities to talk with those who knew what it was like. As such, his tendency to expect the impossible from himself and attribute normal thoughts and frustrations to pettiness and weakness plunged him into a freezing river of guilt.

Occasionally, Buddy thought about people he had met in the waiting room at the clinic where Flora had gone in the early years of her illness. There were a couple people in particular whose spouses or parents had Alzheimer's disease with whom he had had significant conversations. Now and then he would recall something that had reassured him or helped him make sense of things. "One day," he remembered, "I was feeling real angry at God about all that was happening and I was mad at myself for not having more faith. But I was talking to a fellow in the waiting room whose wife had Alzheimer's and he said he got mad at God all the time."

"How did that feel?" I asked.

"It felt real good. Like I wasn't all alone."

"Do you remember the first thought you had?"

"Yeah," he said, "I thought, I'm not going crazy after all. Maybe I'm not such a bad guy."

I encouraged Buddy to attend a local support group for caregivers of people with dementia. He declined and the matter was put aside. Several weeks later, however, he asked about the group again. He wanted to go and talk with people who would understand, but he was nervous. He had spent a long time huddled with Flora in their home, rarely venturing out, and the thought of talking to strangers about such a delicate subject was intimidating. He wavered, as though walking a tightrope between his fear and his desire to feel less alone. As we discussed things, he warmed to the prospect of attending the group. He had been isolated for so long it hurt. "Even if I just went once," he thought, "I think it would help knowing there are others out there and I'm not as alone as I feel."

Just when it looked like Buddy was set on going to the next meeting, his fear returned and brought a panoply of excuses about why he couldn't leave the house. As we disentangled these, he grew exasperated. Seeing his frustration, I thought a story might encourage him. I reminded him about how he and Flora used to go fur trapping and asked if he had ever heard of the Mountain Man Rendezvous.

It sounded familiar, but he wasn't sure.

I explained that during the peak of the Rocky Mountain fur trade in the 1820s and 1830s men had disappeared into the lonely mountain wilderness in search of beaver. Only a handful of souls were intrepid enough to face the hardships of the Rockies and their experiences were radically different from most of their contemporaries. It was a solitary life, understood only by those who lived it. Although the mountain men rarely came together as a group, they converged each summer at the Rendezvous to sell their pelts and buy supplies. It was a time to draw together the wandering travelers dispersed throughout the gnarled rock, towering forests, and foreboding peaks; a time for mountain men to be with others who understood the hardships of their lives in a way that others could not, and, perhaps, to feel less alone.

Buddy was eager to hear more.

II

Most Americans in the 1820s never came anywhere near the Rocky Mountains. The chain loomed like a jutting wall of massive rock and earth, as if warning any would-be traveler to reconsider his or her itinerary. Aside from a handful of Indian tribes, only a few fur trappers, known as mountain men, had entered the mountains. They were looking for beaver pelts, which were in demand to make hats that adorned the heads of gentlemen back east and in Europe. Mountain men lived lives so remote and unfamiliar to people in the eastern states that it was all but incomprehensible. Only other mountain men could truly understand the challenges they faced sloshing through the frigid streams and icy lakes, or the rewards of a hard season along the steep, lonely trails.

Some trappers worked for large companies like the Hudson Bay Company or the American Fur Company. Others worked independently, selling pelts for cash. The number of independents had increased since 1825, when Saint Louis merchants William Ashley and Andrew Henry had held the first Rendezvous. That summer they had brought goods and supplies from Saint Louis and rendezvoused with trappers at a single location. Thereafter, the Rendezvous was a much-anticipated annual event of mountain life. It was here the men sold their pelts, bought supplies, and spent time with fellow trappers.

These men had been drawn to the mountains for different reasons. Some, like the Pennsylvania farm boy, Zenas Leonard, said he simply wanted to "make my living without picking up stones." Others, like Jim Beckworth, whose mother was a slave, were escaping futures that promised to be bleak and restrictive. Others had worn out their welcome elsewhere and were looking for a fresh start. Whatever the reasons, however, mountain men shared a few things in common: an ambition for profit, courage, love of adventure, and an uncompromising sense of independence. They also shared determination, an aptitude for living in isolation, and an array of survival skills without which they would have perished.

The mountains were a harsh place to live. Skills and knowledge were often gained the hard way. An accident or momentary lack of vigilance, however small, could be fatal. In addition to paralyzing snowstorms in the winter and ferocious grizzly bears the rest of the year, the mountain man's life was filled with constant physical toil and ongoing struggles to stay warm, dry, and find food. So great were their exertions that according to historian Bernard DeVoto, "Eight pounds [of meat] a day was standard ration for Hudson's Bay Company employees, but when meat was plentiful a man might eat eight pounds for dinner, then wake up a few hours later, build up the fire, and eat as much more."

DeVoto reckons these men stayed alive only by "the exercise of total skill." There were things, he points out, one needed to know as if by instinct, such as, "Why do you follow the ridges into or out of unfamiliar country? What do you do for a companion who has collapsed from want of water while crossing a desert? How do you get meat when you find yourself without gunpowder in a country barren of game? What tribe of Indians made this trail, how many were in the band, what errand were they on…what mood were they in?"

Beaver traps were set in streams and lakes that were so cold that rheumatism was accepted as a natural part of the job. One had to be wary lest frostbite or hypothermia set in. Aside from his wits, a mountain man's most important possessions were his gun, nearly always loaded and ready for use, and the five or six traps he carried. To service his rifle, he carried an array of tools and supplies, such as a bullet mold, lead, flints, percussion caps, and gunpowder. Along with his traps he carried anchor poles and castoreum (a scent used as bait taken from glands near a beaver's tail). In other respects, he traveled light, in order to move quickly and quietly.

Although mountain men often traveled in small groups, wintered together, and many married Indian wives, it was generally a solitary existence. Ever restless to find new streams and be the first to trap virgin ground, they roamed across vast stretches between the Rockies and the Pacific, rarely staying in one place more than a season before moving on. Gingerly threading their way along steep spines of earth, dwarfed by spires of countless mountains with cloud-covered peaks, it was easy to feel disconnected and lost within the endless spaces. At times, as Zenas Leonard put it, "in the desolate wilderness uninhabited by even the hardy savage or wild beast—surrounded on either side by huge mountains of snow, without one mouthful to eat save a few beaver skins— our eyes almost destroyed by the piercing wind, our bodies at times almost buried by the flakes of snow which were driven before it. Oh! How I heartily wished myself home."

Compounding their isolation was the specter of what mountain man, Joe Meeks, called "ever-ready death." Sudden, often violent deaths were common. Men died from accidents, infected cuts and diseases; they were killed by Indians, grizzly bears, rattlesnakes, and occasionally other trappers. Some drowned, others died from exposure to the elements or simply vanished. On occasion, men even starved to death and many more could relate personal stories of near starvation. Meeks was once so hungry he plunged his hands into "an anthill until they were covered with ants, then greedily licked them off."

The rigors of survival and the countless constant challenges were a unique part of mountain life. Opportunities for gathering into a larger community were rare, so when the men emerged from the shadows of the wild Rockies once a year to attend the Rendezvous, they were lured not only by cash and supplies, but the opportunity to be with their fellows. For a few weeks they were woven into a visible community, connected with others who understood what it was like to live as a wilderness trapper. It affirmed who they were and what they were doing. It allowed them to ventilate emotions tightly reined in by the mountain's demand for self-control, and fortified them for another year in the rocky streams and passes.

The Rendezvous was held in the summer, when the beaver's coat was thin and of little interest to merchants. All that was required was an open meadow, a good stand of trees for firewood, and a nearby river. During the years the gathering was held (1825 through 1840), its location rambled through the present-day states of Wyoming, Utah, and Idaho. The trappers were informed of the year's location during the preceding Rendezvous or by the "mountain telegraph" which transmitted news by word of mouth throughout the region's camps and among the Indian tribes.

Beginning sometime in July or August, men would come in from their far ranging corners. They wandered in on foot, atop mules or horses, or in axe-hewn canoes. Along with mountain men, Indians arrived eager to participate. It was common for over a thousand people to converge on an otherwise quiet meadow and create a temporary town. It was the only time during the year so many mountain men would stand in the presence of one another in a single, albeit rowdy, community.

Usually a sizable number would arrive before the wagons and mules that carried trade goods, supplies, and cash. This offered time for what Alfred Miller, an artist who attended the 1837 rendezvous, referred to as "High Jinks," which he described as "a species of Saturnalia in which feasting, drinking, and gambling form prominent parts." The peripatetic trappers found old friends and shared news. They told stories about the year's close calls and enjoyed practical jokes played at one another's expense. There was a competitive side and fights were common, as were wrestling matches and shooting contests. Old scores were settled or further inflamed and occasionally someone wound up dead.

Whatever tensions there may have been, however, were usually dissolved within the otherwise festive atmosphere as men enjoyed the rare opportunity to rest from their burdens and be with others who shared their difficult way of life. DeVoto speculates that the trappers' "solitude had given them a surpassing gift [for] friendship," something that heightened their appreciation for time spent with other mountain men. Being around those who knew their hardships and sacrifices, as well as the nature of their small triumphs, was restorative and invigorating.

After a year in the wilderness, even necessities like gunpowder and lead might be running low. Little things like tobacco, sugar, and whiskey were scarce luxuries. As such, it is not surprising that Jim Beckworth remembered, "the arrival of such a vast amount of luxuries from the East did not pass off without a general celebration. Mirth, songs, dancing, shouting, trading, running, jumping, signing, racing, target-shooting, yarns, frolic, with all sorts of extravagances that white men or Indians could invent, were freely indulged in."

The fur company, or companies, pitched tents and opened for business. They paid cash for each pelt then quickly took it back in exchange for watered-down whiskey, overpriced supplies, or the beads, fabric, and jewelry often prized by Indian women. Amid the trading and rough carnival-like air, serious matters were discussed. Men formed groups for the coming year and strengthened bonds that would bring help in times of need. They also planned explorations into new territories. Some searched among the

Indian lodges hoping to find a wife, while others sought medical help for injuries or afflictions they had been unable to cure themselves. At the 1835 Rendezvous, for example, Marcus Whitman, a missionary whose wagon company had traveled west with the trade caravan, removed an arrowhead that had been in Jim Bridger's back for almost three years.

The group of hearty trappers dispersed after two or three weeks. By then the trade goods were distributed and the companies were in possession of all the pelts and most of the money. If a trapper left the gathering broke, but adequately re-supplied and free from debt, he generally considered that he had come away more or less even. Recharged and carrying fresh supplies, most were ready to enter the mountains for another year. Some, no doubt, wished they had done so before losing a horse on a bet or making a drunken trade that seemed far less advantageous in the light of sobriety.

The summer gathering was a time of solidarity and affirmation otherwise unknown in the lean life of a mountain trapper. Their contests of strength and skill mirrored the abilities they needed to survive on the mountain frontier. The songs they sang and the stories they told related directly to who they were, how they saw themselves, and the lives they were living. From the imagery trappers used when talking, to the jokes they found funny, the two or three weeks sprawled together in the meadow reinforced their connectedness, the choices they had made, and their commitment to a unique and difficult way of life. As the fall cold returned, friendships forged at the Rendezvous might ease the occasional pangs of loneliness. In times of doubt and isolation, this awareness might temper one's uncertainty with the knowledge that there were others out there, walking the same path.

No matter how difficult our journey or how isolated we feel, we are never alone. There are always others who understand—an invisible community of kindred souls threading their way through the canyons and ridges of a common land. We may never converge on a picturesque mountain meadow to tell the stories and sing the songs of our shared journeys, but we may trust they are with us.

Buddy identified with the mountain men as a metaphor of his experience. The support group, he thought, was "probably like a Rendezvous for people taking care of a wife or husband with Alzheimer's." The opportunity to talk with them held a strong appeal, but logistical concerns and his insistence on staying with Flora made going to the group impractical. The conversation, however, left him with the consoling awareness that he was not alone. His tribe was out there and he was connected with them by virtue of their similar paths.

With this in mind, Buddy asked me to tell him what it was like for other people, especially men, caring for spouses with Alzheimer's. In a sense, he was asking me to introduce him to some of his fellow caregivers through stories of people I had met as a hospice social worker. When I offered a few (carefully protecting privacy and confidentiality) he realized that much of what he was experiencing was normal. The guilt, anger, and doubt, were common threads, as were the occasional resentments and frustrations. The complex grief, the taxing physical and psychological demands—while incomprehensible to many—were known intimately to the people of his far-flung, invisible community. Whether their loved one was at home, or, as was more often the case, in a nursing facility, there were others who understood not only his pain, but also his enduring love and commitment.

Although men engaged in mountain trapping were hardened to, and often preferred, solitude, they found solace in the occasional gathering. Among those who kept journals or wrote memoirs, many reflected on poignant memories of the people they had left behind. Such memories could flood in like melting snowcaps swelling creeks into rivers. Zenas Leonard was not the only trapper to "heartily wish" himself home. Even those who had left for the mountains without a pang of regret might soften into nostalgia for some of the people and places they had forsaken for the beaver streams. In the crux of winter, bonds long before weakened or snapped, might be recalled with renewed affection as though they were impossible to sever. On one of the occasions when Jedediah Smith was near death, his thoughts turned to home and the people he had left behind. At least a few mountain men would have understood Buddy's claim that he loved Flora even more as she was being pulled beyond his grasp.

Although some trappers placed their own interests above those of their companions, there were plentiful examples of men standing firmly beside a wounded or sick friend and acting with self-sacrifice and kindness. Sometimes these acts rattled the nerves of the toughest in their ranks. In 1822, for example, Jedediah Smith was attacked and mauled by a grizzly bear. By the time his friends were able to kill the bear, Smith was bleeding profusely and had several broken ribs. Worst of all, the bear had ripped his scalp and most of an ear completely off. After Smith struggled for a while to sew himself back together, his friend, Jim Clyman, agreed to finish the job. "I put in my needle," Clyman wrote, "stitching it through and through and over and over." With nobody else around, mountain men often had to work by trial and error in such matters, holding their breath and learning as they went. Sometimes this meant doing things they would have never otherwise chosen to do.

Shortly after my conversation with Buddy, Flora contracted a respiratory infection that caused her lungs to fill with fluid. The sound of her gasping and gurgling as she breathed caused him tremendous anxiety. Eventually, her lungs needed to be suctioned using a tube attached to a portable suction machine. "I can't do it," Buddy protested. "I just can't do it."

Buddy's trepidation was normal. It is common for people to have reservations about such things. He found he could do it, however, after some training and reassurances from the hospice nurse. It was just one more thing he never could have imagined himself doing, which he *was* able to do. It all came down to one thing: "If it'll help Flora, I'll do it." As long as he focused on that, Buddy could do anything.

Flora's worsened condition erased any possibility that Buddy might go to the support group, but he was intrigued enough by our talk to pursue more stories on his own. The next time I saw him he was enthusiastically reading a couple of books he had found. One was *The 36-Hour Day*, a well-known handbook for people with Alzheimer's disease and their families, written by Nancy Mace and Peter Rabins. The other was a personal account written by someone who had cared for a spouse who had died after a long struggle with dementia. These books helped him identify and learn from the paths others had taken. In his own way, he was connecting with those who had wandered the same peaks and valleys.

When Flora could no longer swallow liquids, Buddy knew her life was nearing its end. He called a friend on the telephone, a retired minister who lived in Delaware, to ask him if he would be willing to lead Flora's funeral. In a strange conjunction of events, he learned that his friend's wife had been diagnosed with Alzheimer's dementia two months earlier, and she had been moved to a nursing home. Without going into details, Buddy reported that, "We probably talked for an hour." They quickly established a rhythm of talking three or four times a week, finding comfort and sanity in their renewed connection.

When Flora died, Buddy offered to excuse his friend from the responsibility of attending the funeral. He was concerned that, given the circumstances, it might be too emotionally difficult for him. His friend, however, insisted on leading the funeral and extended his visit for three days in order to spend time with Buddy. At the very end of his journey with Flora, Buddy finally connected with someone who understood what it was like. In doing so, he offered insights and support to another whose road was just beginning.

By 1840, the life of the mountain man was coming to an end. The beaver that had once seemed inexhaustible were nearly "trapped out" and even the most remote streams had been depleted. In addition, the beaver hat, long a staple of aristocratic fashion, had been replaced by silk. By the late 1830s many mountain men could see their future dimming into its twilight. In 1840, so few trappers attended the Rendezvous that it passed into the dust of history.

When the trade collapsed, trappers scrambled to adjust. Some stayed in the mountains, eking out survival, disdaining the thought of living anywhere else. Some became guides for the wagon trains moving west along the Oregon Trail—the eastern part of which had been blazed by Rendezvous supply trains. Others, like Kit Carson, became scouts for the army. Some migrated into Oregon or California. Jim Bridger opened a trading post along the Oregon Trail and remained in the mountains for three more decades. In his seventies, with his health failing, Bridger relented to the pleadings of his family and moved back to Missouri. Nearly blind, he often spoke of his yearning to see his beloved mountains just one more time before he died. Perhaps in his mind's eye they were as clear and distinct as the first time he had seen them many years earlier, full of promises for the future and countless beaver.

Buddy yearned to see Flora again. Even in her advanced illness their bond had been strong. Taking care of her had been the center of his life and he missed her. Along with losing his wife, he had lost a way of life that, despite its hardships, had provided him with meaning. His days became empty and unfocused.

Finding his bearings took time. Eventually though, he wandered out of the mountains of his solitude and began doing volunteer work. A nearby hospital was piloting a program pairing people who had experienced caring for a spouse with dementia with someone currently facing the same challenges. Schooled in the demands caregivers often face, Buddy overcame his reserve, as he had the day long ago when he and Flora met, and he was one of the first to sign up. In the months ahead, as his grief waxed and waned, Buddy's presence would be a source of encouragement and strength to those struggling through the same crags and ravines he had so tenaciously survived. Even though his responsibilities caring for Flora were complete, he remained loyal to others whose struggles he understood, and whose isolation he had shared.

Chapter Nine
The U.S. Life-Saving Service and the Wreck of the *Newman*: Staying Connected in the Pitch of a Storm

No one who met Sal was surprised to learn that he had commanded a ship. Even confined to a hospital bed, unable to speak, burrowed into the corner of a small room in a nursing home, he had the air of someone used to giving orders and having them obeyed. If he could have given orders now, he would have had a pistol delivered to his cabin before sending all hands below deck. Knowing Sal, he would have smiled, wondering how long it would take the crew to fish his body out of the water after hearing a shot and a splash. He had made no attempt to conceal his desire to die by his own hand, rather than succumb to his silent enemy, cancer. He had even demanded help killing himself, but his daughter and the staff at the nursing home had made it clear they would not assist him. The crew had mutinied and the captain was not pleased.

Sal had joined the Coast Guard at seventeen over his mother's strong opposition. His father was in the Navy and, even though they rarely saw each other, Sal had grown up hearing stories of the sea and daydreaming about the strong sailors who faced its dangers and kept its many secrets. His maternal grandfather had died in an Atlantic hurricane while stoking the boiler of a merchant marine steamer. For his mother this had been one of the most painful experiences of her life, but to a young boy it was a romantic story of heroic battle between his grandfather and the furious storm—a noble death worthy of a hardened seaman.

Sal was intelligent and he had worked hard. As an

Ensign, he had mastered tasks quickly and had always been eager for new responsibilities. Driven by his ambition to command a ship, he made many sacrifices to move up the ranks. It was a family joke—in a family that rarely joked—that his idea of shore leave was to *leave shore* while most of his shipmates were still out in the taverns and restaurants near port, in order to return to the ship to do push-ups, polish his shoes, and study navigation.

Eventually, his hard work paid off and he was given command of a Coast Guard cutter. His single-minded intensity, however, extracted a heavy cost over the years. By the time he retired, his four marriages had all ended in divorce and only one of his ex-spouses was speaking to him. He had five children and only one of them, Diane, was still calling him on a regular basis. He had developed a violent temper and was often intolerant of others, especially those he deemed incompetent or not sufficiently respectful. After the Vietnam War, he had started drinking heavily and his behavior became erratic. His mood swings, long a source of anxiety for those around him, became more intense and unpredictable. Not surprisingly, he had no close friends and was almost entirely alone. On one of our visits I asked him if gaining command of a ship had been worth the price. Unable to speak because of a tracheotomy, he spelled the words "Hell no" by using a letter opener and pointing to letters on his communication board.

When he retired from the Coast Guard, Diane talked him into moving to the North Carolina shore. "I wanted him to be close enough that I could get to him fast," she explained, "but not so close that I'd have to see him a whole lot." True to form, Sal did not bother finding a doctor in his new home. Several years later, when he began experiencing symptoms of throat cancer, he ignored the pain and the coughs, continuing to smoke cheap cigars. When he finally went to a physician and was diagnosed, he told no one; it was his fight and he would go it alone. Anyway, he thought, there were few people to tell other than Diane, and it was easy to conceal his illness from her since she had learned

192

long ago not to ask too many questions.

Sal assumed he could defeat cancer the same way he had always overcome other challenges he had faced, with discipline, focus, and hard fighting. When the disease spread despite radiation treatments and chemotherapy he dug his heels in deeper, pushing his doctors for more aggressive medical treatments. By then, there was nothing else they could do. The tumor was so close to his carotid artery that surgery was too risky. The treatments had helped some, but had not stopped the cancer from growing. Believing his medical team was giving up, Sal traveled to a hospital near Diane's home hoping to receive experimental chemotherapy.

He called and left a message for her letting her know he was in town. Reflecting on this later, Diane said she "knew immediately that something was wrong because in my entire life I don't remember him ever calling me, it was always me calling him." The next day she met him at the hospital and took notes as they consulted with a specialist. By dinner, they both knew his options were exhausted. The cancer could not be stopped and he probably had less than a year to live. The next morning Sal returned to the coast, refusing Diane's repeated offers to drive him home and traveling the same way he had arrived—by cab.

Several weeks later Sal was in the hospital after forgetting to take one of his medications for several days. His physician was adamant that Sal was no longer able to live alone and needed help. After consulting with her father's medical team, Diane visited several nursing homes near her house and chose one she thought could "handle Dad's needs and temperament."

Despite her entreaties that he move, Sal refused. After two horrendous months during which he tried unsuccessfully to live alone, in spite of, as he put it, "whatever the god-damn doctor thinks," Diane gave him an ultimatum. "I told him," she laughed, "that he needed to move to the nursing home or I was going to get all his ex-wives together and we'd pay him a visit." After much angry protest he agreed to try the nursing home. Although Diane was steeled by the fact that her father needed help, she was anxious. She braced herself for his arrival, and his wrath.

A few months later Sal agreed to use hospice care. Soon thereafter, I was on my way down the hallway to meet him for the first time. His suicidal ideation was no secret and, knowing the drill, he disdainfully anticipated a visit from the social worker. As I approached his room a woman who appeared to be in her middle-fifties exited in a hurry. She looked upset, eager to get away. I followed her at a distance, unsure if she would leave the building or simply find a place of retreat where she was safe from whatever had chased her from the room. I found Diane sitting in a wicker rocking chair on the outside porch. I introduced myself and she motioned for me to sit down as she searched her purse for a lighter to spark an unlit cigarette already dangling from the corner of her mouth.

"Why do I do this to myself?" She asked, lighting the cigarette, "He's impossible to get along with."

Diane was glad to have an opportunity to talk about her predicament. It had been a rough four months since her father had arrived. Originally she had hoped that since they were near the end of his life they would be able to put the past behind them and spend less time arguing. She had learned, however, that the past is a tenacious companion and has ways of trying to become our present and our future. Her hope was disappearing fast, like jetsam tossed over the sides of a wrecked ship and pulled into an oblivious sea. She wondered if she should cast aside any thoughts of healing the wounds of their troubled relationship.

After she had refused to help him commit suicide he had become angry and accused her of wanting to get back at him. Recently he had withdrawn into angry silence, refusing to use his communication board and ignoring her whenever she visited. She had tried everything she knew to encourage him and bring out his fighting spirit, but he refused to budge. She was frustrated and angry. She struggled with feelings of guilt, regret, and alienation. She was tormented by the belief that she and Sal were wasting what little time remained. In

194

her frustration, she was even having thoughts of "walking away," but he was her father and she would not to abandon ship. She felt helpless, but was hopeful that having the help of a hospice social worker might make it easier for them to talk.

When we returned to Sal's room he stared at us without so much as a small gesture of recognition or greeting. His face was strong and forceful, as though measuring out authority and defiance. His expression remained unchanged when I asked if I could sit down. He slowly reached for his communication board and, pointing with a letter-opener shaped like a saber, spelled the words "Who cares?"

His room was filled with photographs and mementos of his days as a sailor. Diane had helped him create a space that conveyed a sense of who he was, despite the droning sameness of the nursing home. There was a photograph of the ship he had commanded, another of him shaking hands with a high-ranking Coast Guard official. Medals and officer stripes were framed in a glass-covered box hanging beside photos of three of his grandchildren. On his dresser was a wooden model of a colonial frigate, beside his bed a poster of the Cape Hatteras Lighthouse. On a table there was something that looked like a radio but which played a recording of ocean waves and sea birds.

It was difficult for Sal to use his communication board. Spelling words often took more energy than he could muster. The silence that greeted Diane and I had become standard for anyone entering his room. The effort required, combined with the pressure to spell quickly or risk being interrupted was simply too frustrating. To his satisfaction, he had discovered that silence had an unforeseen benefit: It made people uncomfortable and was a good way to chase them out of his room quickly. Sitting there without pressuring him to respond appeared to warm his icy veneer. As he listened to Diane talk with me about his life, he picked up his board and began adding things. When he saw that Diane was unhurried and happy to include him, he even smiled, albeit reluctantly.

As Sal became more engaged, our conversation moved from his past to his current circumstances.

"You've been thinking about killing yourself," I said.

"Yes." He tapped his communication board firmly as though warning me not to try to lecture him about this.

After asking him about the frequency, duration, and intensity of such thoughts, I asked if he had made a specific plan to kill himself. He had not.

"Is it that you want to *die*, or is it that you want to *stop living* like this?"

He narrowed his eyes as though thinking and remained silent for a minute or so.

"Do you understand the question Dad?" Diane asked. He glared at her, leaving no doubt that he understood and didn't need her help grasping the nuances.

Finally he spelled, "Don't want (to) live like this."

"Do you *want* to die?" I asked.

"No." Again he was emphatic.

"Is death the only way you can think of to stop living like this?" I asked.

He nodded his head yes.

Suicidal thoughts and statements are fairly common among people with terminal illnesses. For some, these thoughts occur only briefly, for others they are persistent and can even lead to plans to act on them. It is important to take such things seriously and allow people to speak honestly and openly so loved ones and professional helpers can better understand a person's experience and offer effective support. As we explored his inner life it became clear that Sal did not want to commit suicide, he wanted to stop living in a way that he saw as "useless." It begged an obvious question: How might his life continue to have meaning and purpose despite his physical limitations and limited life expectancy?

As he thought about this his face hardened, then softened. His eyes watered and he looked at Diane then spelled the words "More visits."

"More visits?" Diane was confused and she raised

her voice in exasperation. "But you get mad at me whenever I visit you. You practically threw me out less than two hours ago."

He looked at her and again spelled the words—more visits—this time motioning as if to underline them for emphasis.

Although this was something Diane wanted too, his answer frightened her. He had intimidated her since she was a child. His invisible armor had always seemed impervious to her hopes that they could have a better connection. Although his answer suggested he shared her hope, she was afraid. Afraid, she later admitted, that she might find such a connection was not possible. Looking at him with sad, earnest eyes, she promised to visit more often and he promised not to give her the silent stare when she did. They both knew time was running out and they needed to stop distracting themselves.

When people look back on their lives, they often select and amplify a handful stories or events to stand for the whole. In Diane's mind, the memories she had of her father told a story of distance and rejection: bringing home a red ribbon from field day and being told she should have won the blue; being called a baby when she was sad; and more recently, encountering silence when she walked into his room. Other memories, important ones, had been pushed into the shadows. As she thought about her relationship with Sal, she began fishing these out from the deep sea of her past as if with some psychic driftnet, appreciating them as never before.

There was no denying Sal had been hard to live with, as his four ex-wives could attest. For a child trying to gain his approval, life had often been difficult and confusing. As Diane looked back though, she gained a deeper understanding of a man who, although infinitely fallible and difficult to satisfy, had done his best to be a good father. She realized that, despite his discomfort with expressing any emotion other than anger, he had usually tried to find ways to show her he loved her. When she was a child, for example, he would bring her aboard ship and show her how to use the signal lamps and radio. They invented their own secret code so they could communicate by hand signs when she was down on the dock. When she turned ten he sent her a special birthday telegram from sea. Before she went off to college he had given her painstaking lessons on how to "physically incapacitate an attacker" so that she would be safe. These things came floating back, like yellowed messages in barnacle-covered bottles sealed for decades and finally recovered.

The gist of these messages was that, despite the struggles and hurt feelings, she and Sal had always found ways to stay connected. When his drinking had become a problem she had continued calling him despite his ill temper. When he retired, she encouraged him to move to North Carolina, enduring his complaints, and using much of her vacation time to help him find an apartment. Over the years she had developed a knack for showing up just as he was about to get into trouble and helping him avoid catastrophe.

For his part, Sal had stood by her when she had gotten divorced and during her son's hospitalization after an automobile accident. When she needed emergency surgery, Sal, she recalled, had caught a plane the next day and made sure the doctors and nurses treated her like she was their only patient. Whenever the waves broke and crashed around them, they had stood connected, as if by an unbreakable cord, each one arriving on the scene as though sensing the other's distress.

I suggested to her that the surfmen of the United States Life-Saving Service, forerunner of Sal's U.S. Coast Guard, was a metaphor of their experience. It was the Service's job to watch over ships moving up and down the coast and help them stay out of trouble—communicating with them by signal flags, flares, whistles and hand codes. If a ship foundered in a storm or grounded on a sand bar, the surf patrollers jumped into their boats, often amid enormous waves, to bring the passengers to safety. Throughout their lives, she and Sal had kept watch on each other in such a way, sometimes from shore, sometimes from the surf, when necessary rowing out into the storm to help in times of crisis.

They never spoke about it; it was a connection that expressed itself in action. Indeed, there was much they had never talked about. Not surprisingly, Diane had many questions. She decided to use their remaining visits as an opportunity to ask her father questions she had often wondered about. Did he miss her when she left home? Why did he yell at her so much when she was a child? What did he really think of her first husband? Why did he and her mother get divorced? What happened in Vietnam? At first Sal dismissed her questions, bewildered that she wanted to dredge up such things. When she persisted, he tried to give her answers as best he could. Many times, however, he did not know the answer or could not find the words with which to communicate one. Diane accepted this, it was enough that he was trying.

As his cancer grew, Sal lost his ability to use the communication board and Diane started bringing things to read to him, including a songbook full of traditional sea shanties. Overcoming her self-consciousness, she sang to him as he slept. When he drifted into a light coma she knew the end was near. With the moment of separation fast approaching, she searched for ways to stay connected. Her father's illness had opened him up and made him "more human." She had come to understand him in a way she had never believed possible. Now that he was dying she did not want to let him go. The relationship she had always secretly dreamed of having with her father seemed to be ending as soon it had finally begun to emerge. She likened it to watching him being drawn away from shore and wanting to pull him back.

There were still many things she wanted to say and things she wanted him to know. Despite assurances that he could still hear her and that she could say what she needed to even though he was in a coma, she was skeptical. In exploring this, we returned to the Life-Saving Service and focused on the image of the rescue line. The rescue line was a thin but strong line of rope fired from shore by a cannon called a Lyle gun. If aimed well, the line could be landed on the deck of a wrecked ship. Its purpose was to connect those caught in a raging storm with the surfmen on shore. It stretched across waters that were otherwise unbridgeable. It was made to hold fast in powerful winds and high spray. I suggested that in her life, and throughout their many visits, she had fixed such a line from Sal to herself. A line that would hold firm even as he was dying and allow her to say what she needed and trust that it would get through. I assured her the line would hold now.

I told her there had been times when the waves were too rough to even fire the cannon; on a few occasions patrolmen had actually entered the seething waters to bring the rescue line out by hand. I suggested that this is what she had done with Sal by standing beside him throughout his illness.

"Did people really do that?" She asked.

I told her that one such rescue had occurred in the 1890s in the same coastal waters where her father used to fish each morning. In 1896 the surfmen from Pea Island, North Carolina, saw a ship called the *Newman* wrecked on the horizon. The surf was too choppy to use their surfboat. When they could not land a rescue line they jumped into the waves trying to reach the vessel in time.

"Would you like to hear about it?" I asked.

We were sitting in Sal's room and she looked at him as he breathed slowly. She nodded her head affirmatively and said to Sal, "Dad, Scott is going to tell us a sea tale."

II

In October 1896, as Richard Etheridge and his crew of lifesavers watched the horizon through the storm, they could barely make out the *Newman* being ripped apart by the hurricane's punishing waves. There was no way the men could reach the ship with their surfboat; the breakers were just too high. They had dragged the beach cart down the shoreline hoping to fire a rescue line, but it was impossible. The beach was covered in water and there was no place to set up the Lyle gun. If they were going to get a line out to the terrified passengers on the *Newman*, there was only one way to do it——they would have to swim.

For over two decades men like Etheridge had worked for the U. S. Life-Saving Service, patrolling the Atlantic Coast and guarding its shores. Congress had created the Service in 1871 to operate stations up and down the coast. The original plan had been to build stations along the most dangerous parts of the shoreline at intervals about twelve miles apart and have crews available from December through March. As the value of the Life-Saving Service became apparent, the distance between stations was reduced and the season was extended from September through April. By the time the *Newman* found itself in trouble there were around two hundred life-saving stations along the Atlantic from Maine to Florida, as well as some on the Great Lakes and the Pacific.

In North Carolina there were eighteen stations, eleven of which, like Etheridge's, were on the Outer Banks. Station houses varied little from one place to the next. The buildings were designed with an eye toward function and practicality, two stories high with a steep wood shingled roof on which was perched an observation platform. The six-man crew slept upstairs. The station commander, or keeper, had a separate room. Much of the first floor was used as the boathouse where the men kept a surfboat, beach cart, and tools of the trade such as cork life belts and rain gear. Although some stations maintained a modest stable for a horse or mule to help pull the heavy equipment, many relied solely on the backs of their patrolmen. By the late 1880s telephones had been installed to allow better communication, but telephone lines tended to snap or get swept away in storms.

It was a dangerous job requiring men who knew the language of the surf and skies, and who were strong swimmers skilled in the use of small boats. They had to be in good physical condition, able to withstand harsh weather while working long hours. Most of all, it was a job that required people capable of acting as part of a disciplined, interdependent team.

To stay sharp, surfmen trained almost every day—hauling the beach cart, unloading and assembling the beach apparatus, firing rescue lines at targets placed offshore. They launched surfboats, honed their skills at emergency communication and learned how to treat everything from hypothermia to lacerations. The weekly schedule under Keeper Etheridge was typical:

> Mondays and Thursdays were reserved for drilling with the beach apparatus, including firing the Lyle gun. Tuesdays were for boat drills, Wednesdays for flag and signal drills, Fridays for first aid and practice "restoring the apparently drowned." Saturdays were designated general cleaning days of the station, inside and out. According to regulations, Sundays were to be days of rest, but Etheridge inspected his crew at 9 A.M. on each Sabbath, then read to them from the blue-jacket manual.

Although the schedule at Pea Island was typical, the crew was not. They were the only black crew in the entire sixth district (which included all of North Carolina and part of Virginia). Many of them, including Richard Etheridge, had been born on the Outer Banks as slaves. Etheridge had enlisted in the Union Army and fought against the Confederacy during the Civil War, which made his position as keeper quite extraordinary in the nineteenth century South.

In addition to regular training drills, surfmen kept constant watch over the six-mile stretch of coast entrusted to their keeping. Every day, from sunrise to sunset, somebody was in the observation tower looking for signs of trouble, ready to relay any important information to passing ships. At night, and on days when visibility from the tower was poor, men walked patrols along the shore. One man walked north, another south. When they returned two more headed out in their place.

An average patrol covered about six miles roundtrip. Where possible, the route included a turn-around point adjacent to that of a neighboring station, thereby covering a continuous stretch of shoreline. In such cases, two patrolmen would meet before turning around and exchange official stamps verifying that their patrols had been completed. Where this was not possible, a patrolman inserted a key into a time clock anchored in the sand that recorded his time of arrival. To ensure accountability, the keeper checked the clock regularly and kept detailed records. In the early days of the service, lives had been lost because of inefficiency and poor training. By the 1890s, nothing was taken for granted.

Unless visibility was extremely limited or aspects of the terrain made night travel hazardous, surfmen on night patrol walked in the dark without the benefit of a light. It was feared that a passing ship might mistake a lantern on shore for another ship and miscalculate its depth or proximity to the coast. A patrolman, however, usually carried an unlit lantern and some Coston flares in case of an emergency.

On stormy nights, thick darkness, the surging ocean, and wet sand often made patrols extremely difficult. At such times it was very important to stay focused on the surf. A wrecked ship might not be visible and the sounds of breaking boards or a screaming crew could be muffled by the wind. In these circumstances, floating debris or a body washed ashore might be the only sign that people were in danger.

The primary goal of watches and patrols was to steer ships away from danger and keep wrecks from happening in the first place. If a Pea Islander in the tower could warn a passing ship about shoals, currents, or a developing storm, he might prevent a catastrophe. Simply relaying longitude and latitude to a ship could help a navigator accurately fix a vessel's position and stay clear of dangerous waters.

The same held true on night patrol. If a surfman could warn a ship away from danger by using a flare, he might avert a grounding. In the spring of 1884, for example, Etheridge recorded in his weekly log that "Robert Toler [Tolar] discoverd a vessel on the morning of March 30 about 1/2 passed 4 o'clock almost on the beach. He immediately burned his Coston Light and she immediately Keept off from the beach. It is almost likely she would have struck on New Inlet Shoals had she not been warned."

Looking back on the history of the U.S. Life-Saving Service, the focus is often on the drama of crews braving storm-tossed waves to rescue those aboard sinking ships. But day in and day out, quietly and without fanfare, lifesavers watched over ships traveling near shore, connecting momentarily in order to relay information or warn of a potential hazard, before watching them pass safely out of sight.

Usually when a ship needed assistance, conditions were at their worst. Winds could knock down masts, tear up ship planks and floor boards, rip doors off hinges and lift cargo into the air, raining down a terrifying hail of splintered debris. Given the vast stretches of beach and limited ability of a small crew to cover it all, it could be hours before a sinking ship was spotted. By the time lifesavers finished pulling the thirty-six foot surfboat and thousand pound beach cart through wet sand, additional hours had often passed.

Once the surfmen were in place, there were three ways to rescue passengers. The least desirable was to fish them out of the water after they had slipped or jumped from a fragmenting vessel. Most who wound up in the ocean died, but those who made it often did so with assistance from lifesavers that had entered the raging surf along side them.

It was far better to use the surfboat, which had the advantage of allowing most or all of a ship's occupants to be removed in a single trip. Unfortunately, sometimes conditions were too rough to launch or maneuver a boat. In these cases, provided the ship was in range, the men turned to the rescue line.

This was the preferred way to reach a ship when conditions were especially dangerous. With a line, it was not necessary to put more people in the water and risk their lives in addition to those aboard ship. The rope was weighted to a grappling shot which, if landed on deck could be attached to a beam or mast. Firing it required the beach apparatus—a contraption containing ropes, wooden crossbeam, cannon, twenty-pound grappling shot and a sand anchor. Although pulling the beach cart, which contained the apparatus, through the sand was exhausting work, its contents could be unloaded and assembled in a matter of minutes. The keeper chose the place to set things up, factoring in beach conditions as well as wind velocity and distance. Two men dug a hole and buried the sand anchor. Two others unloaded the "faking box," which contained the rescue line wrapped around wooden pegs in such a way that it could be played out without getting knotted. The other men unloaded the two hundred and fifty pound Lyle gun and prepared the shot. Once the line was secured to a ship, a traveling block could be moved back and forth along the line. This block held the breeches buoy, a circular seating platform suspended above the water used to pull people to shore one at a time.

The *Newman* was a large schooner. It had been blown off course by a hurricane so powerful it kept lifesaving stations busy throughout the entire mid-Atlantic region. The ship had left Virginia heading north with a cargo of coal, but the storm blew it all the way down to Pea Island where Richard Etheridge and his crew spotted it being pulverized on the shoals just off shore.

The weather on October 11 was so bad that patrols had been canceled. Theodore Meekins had been struggling in the gales trying to stay atop the watchtower when he had seen what appeared to be a signal flare. Sylvester Gardiner, captain of the *Newman*, was unsure of his location but he knew his crew, as well as his wife and three-year-old son, Tommy, were in big trouble. The storm had damaged the ship and grounded them on a sandbar. The menacing spray had matted the air into a thick gray haze making it difficult to gauge their distance to shore, but they could see that swimming for it was out of the question. The ocean had quickly begun dismantling the vessel, washing away sails, rails, anything not battened down. Water filled with black coal spilled from the wounded hull. All they could do was wait and hope someone had seen their flare.

The Pea Islanders weren't able to let the neighboring stations at Oregon Inlet and Chicamacomico know the *Newman* was in trouble. The telephone poles had been snapped like twigs and sucked out to sea. As the rescuers harnessed themselves to the beach cart they knew they were on their own in one of the worst storms in anyone's memory. Etheridge did not even try to bring the surfboat. There was no point since launching it under such conditions would be impossible. The rescue line was the only hope, although, as the seasoned lifesavers knew, in a hurricane like this one, it was a slim hope indeed. Wright and Zoby, historians of the Pea Island station capture the situation as the men splashed their way through the surging tide of the barrier island on their way to the *Newman*:

> From the moment the keeper had begun shouting his orders, with water up to their knees and wet sand swallowing each step, not one of the men had uttered what they all knew was true: rendering any assistance under such unfavorable conditions would probably be impossible. Maybe they could help those who, still capable of bracing the surf, tried to swim to shore—those few who successfully completed the dangerous voyage. Or maybe they'd be forced to sit and watch as the shipwrecked sailors were washed out to sea, one by one, from the deck of their doomed vessel. Maybe by the time they arrived, it would already be done.

After two hours of backbreaking toil, they finally got the beach cart in range of the ship. By then, the people aboard the *Newman* had tied themselves to whatever hadn't blown away. They had seen a Coston flare and a rocket fired by the lifesavers. Now they could dimly make out the tiny crew working to set up the beach apparatus. The ship's crew shivered in the cold, waiting expectantly for the booming echo of the Lyle gun. Unfortunately, the beach was inundated. Sand melted away whenever the men attempted to dig a hole for the anchor. Firing a rescue line was not possible—there was simply no place to set up the beach apparatus.

The patrolmen were demoralized. Just off shore were people struggling in the teeth of a raging storm, wobbling on the edge of death. If only they could reach over the threatening seas perhaps they could bring assistance. What to do next? They were powerless to alter the storm or sooth the rough waters, but there was still one thing they could try. They could enter the water and carry the line themselves.

Richard Etheridge knew it was a risky idea. The main reason for using a line in the first place was to keep men out of the water under such deadly conditions. But there are times when rendering help and forging a connection, or strengthening one that already exists, requires us to enter the waves ourselves and stand by those in trouble. Etheridge knew this as he asked for volunteers.

His plan was to tie two men together with an eight-foot rope connected to a longer rope capable of stretching all the way to the ship. This line would be held by the men on shore as the two volunteers tried to reach the *Newman*. It was a bold plan. Such a thing had been tried only rarely, and never in seas as tempestuous as these. In 1878, for example, the keeper at the Jones Hill station, a powerful swimmer, had attempted to carry a line out to the steamer *Metropolis*, and had nearly drowned. No one harbored any illusions about the work at hand. Even an expert swimmer could be quickly drained of all his strength in such surf.

Theodore Meekins and Stanley Wise volunteered.

With the rope tied around their waists, they fought their way past gigantic breakers, over sand bars, and through salt water churned into chaos by mighty gales. Often they disappeared under the water as fear tightened in the stomachs of those on shore and aboard the *Newman*. Always, however, they resurfaced, sometimes closer, sometimes farther away from the disintegrating schooner. As they neared the ship they dodged splintered planks and fragments of debris flying through the air and floating in the water. Each object brought the possibility of a death-dealing blow to their unprotected heads. When they finally reached the schooner the two men quickly secured the line. Etheridge tied the other end to the beach cart linking those on board with those on the beach. They had landed the rescue line, not by firing it over the waves, but by going into them directly.

With no breeches buoy to pull the passengers and crew to safety, Meekins and Wise held the captain's son in their arms and slowly made their way back to shore, gripping the line all the way for stability and to keep from being swept away. When they finally made it back, battered but safe, they were keenly aware that they had only begun the job of rescue. If they worked quickly, and if the creaking ship held together long enough, they might be able to save at least a few more of the *Newman*'s ill fated passengers, but they would have to do it one person at a time. Etheridge shouted above the winds, asking for two more volunteers.

III

Compared to the tumultuous intensity of a hurricane, a rescue line seems a very fragile thing. Yet it can become the hinge of a connection that the most abusive waves cannot break. A connection that reminds us we are not alone, that others care about us and are trying to keep us safe and bring comfort. In the murky waters of human relationships some lines are strong and flexible, able to stretch across the highest waves, others have became weak and unable to bear much weight, easily unbraided by any gale or billow. But once a line has been set, unless we choose to sever it, it can be made to hold fast in the hour of our deepest need.

For Diane and Sal this thin tether had often been strained and frayed, but it had always held. During Sal's illness it had allowed them to speak openly and clear up old misunderstandings, forging a deeper appreciation for each other. With her father in a coma, however, Diane was afraid the line would break. As she tried to find a way to say goodbye and let him go, she slowly realized that they were still connected even as he was being pulled away by the gravity of his dying body.

In Sal's case the line couldn't pull him back to shore. There was no daring rescue to accomplish. It was his time to die and Diane knew it. In the immediacy of his last days, however, the image of a bond in the storm was helpful to Diane. She had entered the choppy waters to reach her father as surely as Etheridge and his surfmen had entered them to reach the *Newman*. She could have walked away, avoided the nursing home altogether, or she could have hidden behind her anger. Instead, she found a way to remain buoyant despite the undertow of painful thoughts and emotions. The connection was firm and held under pressure, as Sal, like his grandfather, went down in his final storm.

Sitting with him throughout the day, Diane spoke of their lives together, trusting that her words were getting through. When she saw that he was fighting to cling to life, she encouraged him to raise anchor and sail into the sunset. For a man who had once wanted to kill himself, Sal seemed to be battling mightily to hold on. He was a tenacious man. Maybe he fought out of habit, a final affirmation of who he was, but Diane sensed something else was holding him back.

Nothing could hold Theodore Meekins back. When Etheridge called for the next pair of volunteers Meekins insisted on returning to the ship. It would take eight more trips out to the vessel and back before all those aboard the *Newman* were rescued. Meekins made every one of them.

It was after midnight before the patrolmen and their

battered visitors finally got back to the station. Surfman Irving climbed the tower to watch for other vessels, the rest of the Pea Islanders went to work giving first aid for the numerous cuts and bruises suffered by Gardiner and his companions.

Outside, the storm continued to wreak havoc, pummeling the station with rain and cyclonic winds. In the midst of it, the crew at Life-Saving Station Number Seventeen had found a way to reach weary travelers whose journey had left them stranded and afraid. In his log, Keeper Etheridge ended his report by noting matter-of-factly that, "Although it seemed impossible to render assistance in such Conditions, the ship wreck crew was all safely landed."

It surprised Diane when her stepbrother, Rick, landed at the airport and called to tell her he was in town. "I told him," Diane said, "that Dad was dying, but I didn't expect him to come up from Alabama." Rick hadn't seen Sal since his father had moved to North Carolina. He was shaken when he saw his father's skeletal body and sallow face. By then, Sal's tumor was so large the nurses were concerned it might rupture his carotid artery and cause him to bleed to death. In the crest of his anguish, Rick demanded that Sal be taken to the hospital where he could "get worked on." He refused to be calmed by the nurses and staff. He only stopped his insistence after Diane pleaded with him to "Let Dad die in peace." Later, Rick admitted he was "scared like the devil at the thought of watching my Daddy bleed to death." He hadn't known what else to do.

All were shaking their heads in disbelief a few days later when Sal was still alive. His breathing was shallow and intermittent, his blood pressure almost undetectable. Still he hung on, like a sail that refused to move in the breeze.

That day one of his other daughters, Jackie, showed up at the nursing home. Diane had spoken to her but hadn't asked her to come because she didn't want to put any pressure on her. Like her father and siblings, Jackie was plainspoken. As they sat around Sal's bed sharing stories,

210

none of them glossed over the abrasive truths of a hard sailor's life. They had all felt his anger and reproof. But they had also learned to decode the messages of love he had, often clumsily, attempted to deliver. As they compared experiences, Diane learned that Sal had been there at pivotal times for Jackie and Rick just as he had for her. Clearly, there was also a vibrant and unassuming filament connecting them to their father. It had sustained them during difficult times and, as Sal lived his last hours, it drew them to his bedside and to each other.

Hearing their voices, Sal seemed to respond. His breathing accelerated at first then became very relaxed. As they sat in his room and reminisced, his struggle seemed to subside. That evening Jackie's cellular telephone rang. "It surprised me," she said later, "because I'd tried to make calls a bunch of times that afternoon from inside his room and I couldn't get the phone to work." It was her mother, Sal's first wife. When Jackie told her Sal was dying, her mother asked her to hold the phone down to his ear. "It was eerie," Rick remembered, "and we all saw it too, Daddy just calmed down and started breathing real easy and, I swear to God, less than fifteen minutes later he was gone."

Richard Etheridge died in May of 1900. He had trained his crew well and his long-time friend Benjamin Boswer had stepped in during Etheridge's final illness to act as station keeper. Browser's daily record, like his mentor's, was matter-of-fact and left no question that the Pea Island Station would continue fulfilling its duties. "Keeper Richard Etheridge," Browser wrote, "Dide at this station at 20 minutes to 7 o.c. a.m. to day. The Condition of the Telephone at the Station is good."

In 1915, the Life-Saving Service was merged with the Revenue Cutter Service to form the United States Coast Guard. By then, the powerful steamers that plied the waters of the Atlantic were making the need for rescues far less frequent than in the days owned by sailing ships. By the time the Life-Saving Stations were finally decommissioned in the

1940s and 1950s, the Lyle gun and rescue line had been replaced by motorboats and ship-to-shore radio.

It is difficult to know for sure how many lives were saved by men like Etheridge, Meekins, and Browser, or exactly how many times a rescue line found its mark and proved a harbinger of redemption for frightened travelers. But whatever the trajectory of a line or the pitch of a surfboat, the patrolmen of the Life-Saving Service were always connected to the people on ships that passed their shores, not just by their commitment to duty, but by the tensile thread of their shared humanity—something even the darkest storm could not sunder.

A few weeks after Sal died, I spoke with Jackie on the telephone. I asked if she thought there was a connection between her mother's phone call and Sal's dying shortly thereafter.

She laughed and said "I asked my mother what she said and asked her never to say anything like that to me if I get sick."

Jackie explained that Sal and her mother, Gerry, had grown up together. When they were teenagers they liked to ride canvas rafts on the waves of a nearby beach. They often spent the entire day floating just beyond the breakers, waiting for the biggest waves they could find. If they timed it right they would be lifted by the ocean and drawn all the way to shore. According to Jackie, her mother asked Sal to imagine they were back in the surf. She described what it felt like as they rolled over the waves, waiting patiently for the right one. Then she told him that very soon the perfect wave was going to come along and he didn't want to miss it. If he kept his eye on the horizon it was sure to give him a ride all the way to shore.

Section Four
Crossing the Bar:
Letting Go

Sunset and evening star,
And one clear call for me!
And may there be no moaning of the bar
When I put out to sea.
But such a tide as moving seems asleep,
Too full for sound and foam,
When that which drew from out the boundless deep
Turns again home.
Twilight and evening bell,
And after that the dark!
And may there be no sadness of farewell,
When I embark;
For tho' from out our bourne of Time and Place
The flood may bear me far,
I hope to see my Pilot face to face
When I have crossed the bar.

Alfred, Lord Tennyson

Few things are harder than saying goodbye to a loved one. Even when we know the separation is only temporary—until the next holiday or the end of the college semester—it can bring sadness. When leaving means death, most of us resist that moment of separation with all our might. Finding ways to let go of life (our own or a loved one's) and say goodbye often gets lost beneath efforts to regain one's strength, find a cure, or search for any hope, however slim, that the doctors are wrong.

Death is often pressed into the corners of our mind; sometimes because of our fear, sometimes because we want to pack as much into our final months as we can while we still feel relatively normal. Over time, however, our body has ways of telling us that it's time to prepare for our final chapter. Though many of us initially resist this, most people eventually gain some degree of acceptance that the end is near.

Hoping for a reprieve and praying for a cure may continue, but the steady grinding of illness as it erodes our strength and taxes our energy, will urge us to peer ahead, however tentatively, toward death. Although the impulse to fight or deny may continue to our final breath, most of us will gain some level of peace. Many people even welcome death as a natural culmination of a life lived as best as one could, as a place of transition, or simply as a time to rest from the burdens that have accumulated over the course of an illness.

For some though, acceptance never has the chance to walk along side of, much less replace, the will to fight. Death remains the enemy; fear and anger its shadow. Some people, like Hap in Chapter Ten, have defined themselves as warriors and left little or no room to be at peace, or to accept death. Others, such as Mort in Chapter Eleven, though they see death approaching, fight to live, driven by a desire to complete projects or resolve some longstanding concern— maybe righting a troubled relationship, seeking forgiveness, or letting go of worry about the well-being of loved ones left behind. Some, like Manuel in Chapter Twelve, hang on because they are searching for permission of sorts, some reassurance that, despite doubts and sadness, their life has been meaningful and not lived in vain.

The stories in Section Four share this theme of finding ways to let go of life.

Chapter Ten
Osceola and the Second
Seminole War: When it is
Time to Stop Fighting

Hap was no stranger to war. At eighteen he had enlisted in the army and wound up fighting in Vietnam. After three years of battle in jungle swamps he returned to North Carolina with a heroin addiction and a head filled with enough violent images to fuel the nightmares that would often wake him up in a cold sweat. After Vietnam, his life became a war between his desire to get clean and the persistent demands of his addiction. He swung between periods of hope and relative stability, and despair and homelessness. Making things worse, alcoholism became another enemy with which he battled. For fifteen years he drifted, making ends meet by doing odd jobs or talking his mother into "loans" they both knew he would never pay back.

Although he seemed savvy and confident on the outside, inwardly he was frightened. When he met his wife, Kim, he was broke, craving drugs, and about to be thrown out of the hotel where she worked as a cook. His fast-talking swagger didn't fool her; despite his attempt to con her out of some money, she saw the "good person" beneath his abrasive appearance.

On the surface they were an unlikely couple. Hap was extroverted and talked rapidly like a machine gun. He could be rigid and impulsive, and had a long memory for every slight or harsh word he had ever received. He was fiercely loyal to family, but had few friends and was generally cynical about people. He loved to tell stories from the reservoir of his unusual experiences, stories that invariably cast him in the role of outsider and warrior. As he saw it, he went against the grain, spat at convention, and was usually under attack.

Kim was more reserved. She preferred to think before acting and measured her words cautiously before speaking. She had a relaxed manner and was slow to take offense. Where Hap's stories emphasized overcoming obstacles, hers underscored attempts to live a quiet, moral life. She was an astute and sensitive observer, perceptive and adept at discerning subtleties. She saw much more complexity in the world than Hap and didn't divide the world into simple, antagonistic categories like friends versus enemies. In many ways, she was stable where he was not. She worked hard, paid her bills, didn't drink excessively and had a small community of friends she relied on for support.

They balanced each other. Kim calmed Hap's tumultuous intensity and helped him open to the spiritual dimension of his life, trusting in something beyond his ever-vigilant senses. With her, he felt safe and was less combative. From Hap, Kim drew confidence and learned to trust in her strength and resilience. His sharp and playful humor tempered her tendency to be overly serious and kept her from the brink of occasional melancholy.

By the time they were married a year or so later, Hap had joined Kim's church, entered a heroin treatment program, and was holding down a job at a nearby asphalt plant. He continued to struggle with alcohol, but was attending a support group and talking with a counselor at the Veteran's Hospital. For the first time in his life he began believing in the possibility of a better future. Maybe the smoke of battle would finally clear. Maybe he and Kim could raise a family and live happy lives together. It was a vision bolstered by Kim's optimism and faith in a larger design and purpose for their lives.

When their daughter, Alley, was born, it was the final motivation Hap needed. Within months he had "defeated" his alcoholism and emerged, as he put it, "Drier than a Baptist preacher who knows the congregation is looking." He knew he had to be on guard for a relapse, but he was sure the enemy was finally vanquished. Even Hap, whose life had been filled with disappointment, had to admit things were getting better.

Shortly after Alley's birth, Hap caught a pulmonary infection. At first he ignored it thinking it would go away, but after a couple of weeks it became so severe he wound up in the hospital. He had been working extra hours at the plant and figured he simply needed some rest. When blood tests revealed that he had human immunodeficiency virus (HIV), the infection that causes acquired immune deficiency syndrome (AIDS), he and Kim were decimated.

They insisted the tests were wrong and demanded they be redone. To placate them, the doctor ordered more tests. When the lab confirmed the initial diagnosis Kim was horrified. As she remembered it, the world took on a surreal quality that made the next days seem like a quagmire of intense overwhelming emotions, broken only by moments of numbness and confusion. Hap received the news with sullen detachment and quickly descended into wounded fury. "I blamed everyone but myself," he remembered, "I just didn't want to admit that I got it from doing heroin. I even found ways to be mad at Kim and to blame her."

Feeling under attack, his tendency was to push people away, but when he realized he might have infected Kim and Alley he was immobilized by fear. "The day they tested my family for HIV," he said, "was the worst day of my entire life. If they'd been infected, I couldn't have lived with myself." In the years ahead he would consider it a miracle that neither was infected. At the time, however, relief was short-lived as he and Kim tried to absorb the implications of Hap's disease. Once more, he found himself at war, this time against his most insidious and tenacious foe.

His impulse to withdraw was strong. Soon after returning home Hap disappeared. Kim's anger, already burning like a slow fuse, was incandescent. She was furious at him for abandoning her and Alley. She vacillated between a desire to "say good riddance," and wanting him back. After a long night of soul searching, she decided on the latter and gathered a few friends, sending them out to search Hap's old hangouts. They looked for him at bars, shelters, hotels, and police stations, but he seemed to have vanished like a stealthy old warrior blending into a dense, endless marsh.

About a week later, tearful and contrite, he called Kim on the telephone and asked if he could return home. "To this day," Hap said, "I don't know what I was thinking or why I did it. It was like I got hijacked by a voice that told me to run." After getting a few things straight, as Kim put it, she picked him up at a local bus station and drove him home. "The first thing I did," she said with a mixture of seriousness and humor, "was to let him know he'd run out of second chances. The second thing I did was make him take a shower." After he got cleaned up, they prepared to fight the war together. There would be no more melting away into the brush, and no more retreats.

One of the things they had *gotten straight* was Hap's agreement to follow his physician's instructions to the letter. He went to the hospital clinic regularly, often bringing home pamphlets with information about his disease. Inured to war and familiar with its language, he began calling the clinic his base camp and described the combination of medications he was taking as his heavy artillery. Kim, it seemed, was his drill sergeant.

Although they attempted to keep Hap's infection a secret, word leaked out. In their small community, news traveled fast and it was not long before everybody seemed to know. There was a great deal of ignorance about AIDS and the stigma was as virulent as the disease. Suddenly, they found themselves shunned by neighbors, friends and even members of their church. Despite Hap's good work record, he was fired from his job. When he asked for an explanation he was given vague statements about health-related absences and his no longer being a "good match" for the position.

Although not everyone avoided them, the ostracism seemed all-inclusive. Paradoxically, the snubs strengthened Hap's intention to beat the odds and survive long enough to see a cure. Survival became his focus and, not surprisingly,

219

he likened it to his experiences in the Vietnam War. "When you're pinned down under enemy fire," he said, "you've got to hold on as long as it takes to bring in air support." He knew it didn't always arrive on time, but the point was to keep fighting and hoping.

In the case of HIV, air support was not guaranteed. As his immune system weakened, he began experiencing a litany of opportunistic infections and stays in the hospital became common. Amid the rounds of antibiotics and blood draws, the staff at the hospital stopped calling his condition HIV and starting calling it AIDS. Although they did not talk about it, Kim and Hap noted the distinction. They were not entirely surprised when the doctor suggested they enlist the help of a local hospice. Initially they refused, mistakenly equating hospice care with giving up, afraid it would hasten his death. As Hap's condition worsened, however, the doctor broached the subject again and asked them to reconsider. They deliberated and procrastinated for weeks. By then trips to the clinic had become so onerous that their need for help was clear; they agreed to give hospice a try.

When I met Hap he was standing in the dirt yard of their small cement block home. It was a warm spring day and he was leaning on a walking stick of twisted wood that had been sanded and coated with dark brown varnish. On top of the stick were some feathers and a small turtle shell attached with thin strips of rawhide. As it turned out, he carried the stick everywhere, even inside the house and on his trips to the hospital. He told me he had visited a friend who was an Indian shaman who had purified the stick with smoke and ritual prayer, infusing it with talismanic powers. He had declared Hap to be a member of the turtle clan and said that whenever he carried the stick he would be protected.

Hap was thin and physically frail, but he still exuded such tremendous determination that his wiry frame appeared to radiate vitality. He spoke at length about the many things he needed to do. He had to plant the garden, fix the truck, rebuild the backstairs, and so on. The list was long and, as he was giving me the particulars, Kim joined us in the yard and offered Hap her enthusiastic encouragement. The unspoken message was that he had too much to do, and too many people counting on him to allow sickness to interfere.

As the weeks passed, Hap planted the garden and fixed the truck, but quickly realized he had to cut firewood and fix the barbed wire out by the henhouse. Every time he took something off the list he added something else. In addition to projects he needed to do, there were events he needed to stick around for like Alley's sixth birthday or the Fourth of July. There was always something just ahead for which he needed to remain alive, something motivating him to fight harder.

In spite of his efforts to recover, by autumn he was so weak he couldn't go outside. Kim was terrified of new infections and cleaned the house every day trying to kill the germs she imagined were lurking everywhere. Searching for something to fortify him in his fight, Hap asked his Indian friend to visit again. When I asked how this visit had gone he was evasive and said half-heartedly that it had convinced him he was "going to win this fight." According to Kim, however, his friend had suggested Hap, "ask God for help crossing the river." For a warrior like Hap, crossing the river was the last thing he intended to do.

Near the end of the year, Hap began having hallucinations and periods of confusion. To his medical team this was simply AIDS-related dementia, something common enough as to be more-or-less incidental to them, but to Hap and Kim it was like taking a trip into hell. Invariably his confusion contained elements suggestive of war. One day he saw snipers crawling on the ceiling, on another he was convinced an army of trolls was digging through the floorboards of his home, intent on killing him.

As his confusion intensified, lasting for longer durations, a disturbing theme emerged. He believed God and Satan were battling for possession of his soul and he was convinced Satan was winning. He worried that God had given up on him because of all the "bad things" he'd done.

Eventually this war filled his entire field of vision, enveloping everything and everyone around him. He was convinced his hospice nurse was trying to poison him at Satan's behest and that his doctors were spies and assassins. Everyone he met was on one side or the other; there were no neutrals.

Now Hap fought even more tenaciously for life, terrified that if he died he would go to hell. When another respiratory infection invaded his weary body, Kim brought him to the hospital where he was diagnosed with pneumonia. Given his condition, she was hesitant to start another round of antibiotics and wondered if it might be better to "let him go."

Such decisions are often agonizingly difficult, especially when a loved one has not openly discussed their wishes with family. There often comes a time when it becomes hard to know whether to keep fighting or to accept that the end is at hand. Although Hap was a fighter, he had never been this close to death. The doctors painted a grim but realistic picture of what his life would be like even if antibiotics kept him alive for a few more weeks or months.

When faced with such decisions it is easy to feel guilty no matter what one chooses. Kim pulled her hair out trying to decide what to do. After a sleepless night and much inner turmoil, she told the physician to treat the infection. Like Hap, she was unsure how to stop fighting, even though she acknowledged that, "fighting doesn't make much sense anymore."

Despite Kim's decision, while Hap was in the hospital he died—at least for a few minutes. He went into cardiac arrest and while a team worked to resuscitate him, he was dead. I visited him and Kim the next day in the intensive care unit. Despite his recent ordeal, he was alight with energy and eager to talk about what had happened in those moments of death. He recalled that, just prior to his heart attack he had seen "the devil" at the foot of his bed. The spectral visitor was chiding him for fighting so hard, trying to convince Hap that God had forsaken him. Hap remembered his heart pounding and sweat dripping down his forehead. He was afraid he was about to go to hell and, as his pulse raced, his heart had stopped.

Hap searched for words to describe what happened next. He was self-conscious about being misunderstood and chose his words with unusual care. He said he had found himself back in the dense elephant grass of Vietnam in the middle of a firefight. All the soldiers in his platoon were dead and he was pinned down by an enemy he couldn't see. He fired his gun wherever he saw hints of movement in the grass. As the battle swirled, he searched frantically for the radio so he could call the helicopters to get him out, but when he found it, it was smashed to pieces.

In the corner of his eye he caught sight of a field of rolling grass and wildflowers some distance from the battle. He tried to ignore it, but its peaceful allure was so incongruent with the violence of battle that it drew his attention like a moth drawn toward the luminescence of a full moon. Looking more closely, he saw a small wooden building at the far end of the field, which he took to be a church made of whitewashed planks. In front stood a solitary figure in a simple white robe. The man was smiling and waving for Hap to come over. It seemed like an inviting place, but Hap was a warrior and knew that any distraction could be deadly, so he turned back to the fight. As he fired, however, his desire to go to the visitor on the hill became so powerful he did something that surprised him: He threw his weapon down, stood up, and began walking toward the field, unconcerned about the enemy's bullets.

The next thing he remembered, "Some guy from the hospital was shouting at me wanting to know if I could hear him."

Hap found the experience reassuring. He was convinced the figure by the church was a "holy man." Still, he was puzzled, unsure what the experience meant. As we talked, Kim asked him, somewhat sheepishly, if "Maybe the man was telling you that you've fought long enough and it's time to stop fighting." In the pause that followed Kim looked nervous. She knew he was a fighter and didn't want to undermine his resolve or appear insensitive. As he thought about it, tears filled his eyes and he shook his head affirmatively. "That's exactly what I think," he said, "but I don't know how to stop."

He had spent his life fighting. To do anything else was tantamount to surrendering—something he resisted from his deepest psychic fiber. For him, there was no distinction between surrender and failure. This left him in a dilemma since, if, as he suspected, he had received a direct message from God or a guiding spirit, he certainly ought to pay attention. Doing so, however, required him to do something he had spent his entire life trying to avoid. There were no clear answers that day. We agreed to think about things and meet later in the week.

A few days later he was still mystified, though he acknowledged for the first time that he was tired of fighting. He was even finding himself longing to accept death as a friend, rather than fight it as an enemy. His journey had been hard and he was exhausted. Yet, even as he allowed these thoughts to enter his mind they were countered by instant judgments that he was being cowardly and that "anybody who won't fight doesn't deserve to live." He was stuck in a swamp of tension and contradiction. He had been given permission to stop fighting and had a growing desire to do so, but he couldn't overcome his psychological mandate to resist.

Talking about these things didn't seem to be helping. Hap was never very comfortable with such psychological explorations nor did he necessarily find them helpful. He had grown up steeped in tales and story images, so I thought perhaps a story might help. Many times during the preceding months, Hap had spoken of his affinity for American Indian culture. He took pride in his membership in the turtle clan and seemed to draw strength from his mystical walking stick. He saw Native Americans as the embodiment of warrior culture and admired their fighting prowess. I asked him if he had ever heard of Osceola. Hap was familiar with the

Seminole leader, but when I asked if he knew how Osceola died he wasn't sure.

"Probably," he guessed, "he died fighting somewhere."

He didn't know that near the end of his life, the fierce warrior had grown weary from a lifetime of battle. Rather than fight until his final breath, he had rested his weapons on the ground and accepted his approaching death. When he crossed the river, he did so peacefully.

When I told Hap this, he thought about it for a moment and said, with his usual mixture of humor and earthy irreverence, "Don't bullshit me. Is that really what happened?"

"Do you want to hear the story?"

"From start to finish," he said.

II

In the winter of 1835, a long, bloody war was about to erupt between the Seminole Indians of Florida and the United States. For Osceola, a leader with growing stature among the Seminoles, war was nothing new. His entire life had been spent in a boiling cauldron of conflict. As he led a small band of warriors to the outskirts of Fort King, he was well prepared for another fight.

Osceola had been born in Alabama in 1804. He was a member of the Tallassee tribe, but Americans had called him a Creek, as they did most Indians in Alabama and Georgia. Throughout his childhood he had witnessed many conflicts. He was a boy when the Creek War had torn his tribe apart. In the horrible aftermath of the Battle of Horseshoe Bend, he and his mother had fled into northern Florida.

Although the territory of Florida was claimed by Spain, Americans had continued to antagonize Osceola and his people even in the remote wilderness of this distant land. Even here, it seemed, he couldn't escape the ravages of war.

In 1817, Andrew Jackson led an army which invaded

Florida and attacked the Seminoles. The intention of his incursion was threefold: to force Spain to hand over the territory; to discourage slaves from escaping into Florida and round up those who had; and to destroy the Seminoles or drive them into the swamps. Osceola was captured during this First Seminole War, and his adopted tribe was fragmented and driven south.

When Spain ceded Florida to the United States in 1821, pressure was immediately put on the Seminoles to move to a reservation. In 1823, a few Indian leaders signed the Treaty of Moultrie Creek, which stipulated that all Seminoles would move to a reservation in Central Florida. Despite much controversy over this treaty, many Indians, including Osceola, agreed to move after they were assured they could remain in Florida and live in peace. Osceola was only a teenager but he had already seen enough war to last a long lifetime. Perhaps as he moved to the reservation he was hopeful that he might finally live without fear or the constant need to fight. Perhaps he had already grown cynical about such hopes. Whatever his thoughts, any peace he may have found on the reservation was short-lived.

The land was poor for growing crops, game was scarce, and much of the government's promised assistance never materialized. As whites claimed the surrounding land, the Seminoles had no choice but to leave the reservation in search of food. Time and again Indians and whites collided; countless small conflicts, sometimes violence, occurred. Pressure mounted to push the Indians completely out of Florida. The Florida Legislative Council, in a petition demanding the forced removal of the Seminoles, accurately summed up the situation:

> The Treaty of 1823 deprived [the Seminoles] of their cultivated fields and of a region of country fruitful of game, and has placed them in a wilderness where the earth yields no corn...They are thus left the wretched alternative of Starving within their limits, or

roaming among the whites, to prey upon their cattle. Many in the Nation, it seems, annually die of Starvation;…the much greater proportion of those who are threatened with want, leave their boundaries in pursuit of the means of subsistence, and between these and white settlers is kept up an unceasing contest.

In 1830, President Jackson signed the Indian Removal Act, which proclaimed that all Indians living in the eastern states were to be forced from their homes and relocated west of the Mississippi River. Like the rest of his people, Osceola's life was again in flux as the shadow of grief enveloped the Seminoles. Any hopes of a better future were once again dashed to splinters.

Representatives of the United States met with a handful of Seminole leaders and signed two treaties, one at Payne's Landing and another at Fort Gibson. Among the Indians there was much confusion about what these treaties meant and whether a few leaders had the authority to speak for the entire Seminole nation. Whites, however, asserted the Seminoles had agreed to move west and the United States was prepared to make them do so, even if it was at the end of a bayonet.

The Seminoles had only a few choices. They could move, attempt to stall, melt into the swamps and pine-barrens, or fight. It was a difficult decision and people were divided. During the debate, Osceola emerged as an important leader. He was an eloquent and uncompromising advocate of resistance and spoke with an unusual blend of charm, humanity, and incendiary aggression. His oratory frightened some and inspired others. As he spoke, his dark eyes drove his point home. He was a warrior and he would not move. He would fight, preferring death in battle to surrender.

He drew together a band of ardent followers consisting of family and friends, and those who shared his will to fight. These included many blacks that had escaped slavery and joined Seminole tribes or formed their own maroon communities. In fact, the existence of a large population of free blacks was a primary reason the United States was prepared to expend its energies fighting. Florida was the gateway of the southern Underground Railroad and slaves often disappeared into the state's interior. So great was the South's desire to block these escapes that when the war commenced, General Thomas Jessup wrote, "This, you may be assured, is a Negro, not an Indian war; and if it be not speedily put down, the South will feel the effects of it on their slave population before the end of the next season [1837]."

Things reached a flashpoint in December of 1835 when Osceola led a handful of Seminoles to the walls of Fort King, near present-day Ocala. Their goal was to kill the territorial Indian Agent, Wily Thompson; an act that was both symbolic and strategic. As Thompson strolled outside the walls of the fort, he and a companion were ambushed and killed. Osceola and his warriors had struck the first blow of the Second Seminole War.

Fifty miles south another fight was raging. One hundred troops led by Major Francis Dade had been crossing a seemingly innocuous stretch of pines just south of the Wahoo Swamp when they were ambushed by another group of Seminole warriors. Recalling the ambush, one of Dade's men said, "I had not time to think of the meaning of these shots, before a volley, as if from a thousand rifles, was poured in upon us from the front, and all along our left flank..." When the battle was over, all but three of the soldiers were dead and two of these quickly died from their wounds.

Osceola had helped plan the Dade attack. He had even hoped to rendezvous with his companions and take part in the battle after dispatching the Indian Agent, but conditions for the ambush had been too favorable for his companions to wait for him. Osceola had proven that in addition to being a fine orator he was a fierce fighter and shrewd strategist. Once again, his life was embroiled in war. As a child, he had seen his people killed and driven from their homes. As a young man, he had been a prisoner of war. Later, he had been confined on a barren reservation. He had tried to live in peace, but war seemed to be his lot. This time, rather than follow others into battle he would lead them.

After hearing of the Indian attacks, General Duncan Clinch swung his troops into motion, eager to lash out. He mobilized two hundred and fifty soldiers and about five hundred Florida volunteers near Fort Drane and marched south to the Withlacoochee River. When he tried to cross the river on December 31, Osceola led others in an attack that inflicted heavy casualties.

The Battle of Withlacoochee was like an alarm in the night for white Floridians. In a few days, Osceola and other headmen such as Alligator and Jumper, had killed the Indian agent, destroyed Dade's column, and sent General Clinch and his men scurrying back to Fort Drane. As Osceola's renown grew, whites panicked and fled their homes. By summer 1836, they had abandoned the interior of the state except for a few "concentration points" at Micanopy, Garney's Ferry, and Newnansville, where settlers huddled amid outbreaks of disease in "leaky, drafty shacks."

Time and again, the Seminoles confounded the army with their lightning-like ability to appear, fight, and disperse. Their knowledge of the wilderness and ability to travel quickly were formidable advantages. Whites on the other hand moved more slowly and knew little about the Florida terrain except for a thin toehold along the coast. General Jessup lamented that, "the greater portion of [Florida] was an unexplored wilderness, the interior of which we were as ignorant of as the of interior of China." To many soldiers, such as Tennessee militiaman Henry Hollingsworth, central Florida seemed "swampy, hammocky, low, excessively hot…sickly, and repulsive in all its features."

Although the initial battles of the Second Seminole War featured large groups of Indians working in concert, most of the subsequent fighting was in the form of small skirmishes and ambushes. Sometimes Indian leaders coordinated their actions, but more often they acted independently. Although Osceola was regarded as an important leader, he had no formal authority outside his group of followers. It was by virtue of his tenacity and abilities as a warrior that his influence grew.

Confronted with a guerilla style war on uncharted terrain, the army floundered. General Winfield Scott was put in command and proved ineffective. He was trained in European style drills and the tactics of massed armies. He was stymied by fighting an enemy that was able to appear and disappear quickly, fought from behind trees, and refused to come out into the open. Scott's plight was representative of other white military leaders. The boisterous Missouri senator, Thomas Hart Benton, was succinct in his observation that, by the time the war was over, the Seminoles had "baffled the exertions of several generals."

As the army groped for a better strategy, Osceola seemed to be everywhere in the western part of the state. He was there when General Gaines was pinned down for several days on the Withlacoochee River. He was there when warriors attacked Major Heilman's troops near present-day Gainesville, and he was at the ambush of Captain Maitland's men in the Battle of Welika Pond. The army's strategy may have been muddled, but Osceola's was simple. He wanted to inflict casualties on whites while minimizing his own, displace settlers and disrupt the flow of troops and supplies. Above all he intended to survive. Maybe if the Seminoles could hold out long enough the United States would grow weary of fighting and let them stay in their homes and live in peace. If only he and his people could just hold on.

In December of 1836 command of the army fell on the shoulders of General Thomas Jessup. He quickly realized that, given the nature of the fighting, the war might go on indefinitely without any decisive outcome. Voicing his frustration in a letter, Jessup wrote, "If I have at any time said aught in disparagement of the operations of others in Florida...I consider myself bound, as a man of honor, solemnly to retract it."

Despite their toughness and adaptability, after a

couple years of battle the Seminoles were bent by war's harsh burdens. To stay ahead of marauding soldiers they had had to retreat into hammocks, forests, and swamps. Many of their towns had been destroyed, which made growing food and raising livestock nearly impossible. Hunger, disease, and despair became as devastating enemies as anything Jessup could throw against them. Osceola himself was wracked by the symptoms of malaria and weakened by malnutrition. Though his fighting spirit was strong, his body was wearing down.

The Seminoles began to lose heart. Throughout 1837 small groups of Indians surrendered and were shipped west to "Indian territory." Some blacks even surrendered, preferring the brutalities of slavery to those of war. Late in the year, a weary Osceola was willing to parley and discuss peace. Under a flag of truce, he and about seventy warriors met General Joseph Hernandez at a mutually agreed upon place just south of Saint Augustine. Although they had been assured a truce would be called and treaty talks would be held in good faith, soldiers surrounded them and forced Osceola and his friends to surrender. It was a disgraceful ploy concocted by Jessup; he had used such tactics before and his desperation had driven him to do it again.

The stunned captives were marched back to Saint Augustine and imprisoned at Fort Marion. Seeing little alternative, Osceola sent word instructing the rest of his followers to come to the fort. Some fifty additional people, including two of his wives and a sister, arrived and were thrown into prison along with their friends. Two months later they were moved to Charleston, South Carolina and held at Fort Moultrie. It was deemed prudent to relocate them after Wildcat, Osceola's fellow war leader (also captured during a "truce"), escaped from Fort Marion along with several warriors.

For Osceola, however, such precautions were no longer necessary. His body was severely weakened by illness and the demoralization of his captivity further sapped his waning strength. He had been an intelligent and charismatic leader, respected by his people and intimidating to his enemies, but his body had become frail and his power was ebbing.

At Fort Moultrie he tired easily and needed assistance with things he would have preferred to do himself. In his weakened state, his immune system was unable to ward off infections. In January 1838, he caught quinsy, a virus characterized by acute inflammation in the throat. Once again Osceola was fighting for his life.

It would not have been a surprise if he had fought to his last breath, clinging to life in a final determined stand. After all, he was a fighter hardened by life's battles. He had learned to endure pain, survive at any cost, and never surrender. But by January 31, Osceola had found another way. He knew death was approaching and his journey would soon be over. The time for clinging to life had passed. Accepting death was his final struggle, and his final act of courage.

Declining the ministrations of a Seminole healer and a fort physician, the proud warrior called his wives and several friends to his side. Doctor Fredrick Weedon was present and recalled that Osceola "seemed to be sensible that he was dying." The Seminole leader was not able to speak, but using motions from his worn out hands he asked for help getting dressed in his finest clothes, complete with ostrich plumes and silver medals. He painted his face in vermilion and then, Weedon reports, he "shook hands with us all in dead silence, and with his wives and little children."

Surrounded by those who were dear to him, the archetypal warrior prepared to accept death peacefully. Frederick Weedon was the only white present and he recalled the scene in his journal:

> He made a signal for them to lower him down
> upon his bed, which was done, and he then
> slowly drew from his war-belt his scalping
> knife, which he firmly grasped in his right
> hand, laying it across the other on his breast,

and in a moment smiled away his last breath without a struggle or a groan.

For Osceola the war was over. He had not willingly surrendered to American troops, but, in the end, he surrendered himself peacefully into the hands of the Master of Breath.

III

When death approaches many people fight it with all their strength. To do so is natural and understandable. There are some who fight until the very end, never surrendering their hope for recovery. Some may struggle to regain their strength even as they exhale their final breath. Others grow tired of fighting and search for ways to accept what is happening. Knowing when it is time to stop fighting and finding a way to do so requires as much courage and strength as surviving the most thunderous battle. For those whose lives have made them warriors this can be an especially formidable challenge.

Hap listened intently to the story. When it was done he said, "I just figured he'd died fighting or that he'd disappeared into the Everglades." He was relieved at the thought of this man—a fighter like himself—laying down his weapons and relinquishing the impulse toward battle. Adversaries may remain in the form of American troops or an invisible virus, but death was not the enemy.

As he thought about Osceola, Hap speculated that the Seminole leader probably struggled with the dueling voices of acceptance and resistance long before he was able to lay down his rifle. A fighter doesn't usually lower his guard unless he or she has resolved some deep internal tensions before deciding to no longer fight a particular enemy.

"I bet he went back and forth for a long time," Hap said pensively, "before he was ready for it to be over like that."

As the physical effects of AIDS converged with the

233

countless small indignities of illness, Hap found himself wanting "a long rest," as he euphemistically put it. At the same time, he felt the impulse to fight, to survive. Like Osceola, before he could find peace he had to reconcile these inner voices.

Hap had a few days of relatively unbroken lucidity in the hospital, but shortly after he went home the hallucinations and paranoia returned. His fear of being condemned to hell intensified as did his fragile attempts to cling to life. In hours of clarity, however, he was more at peace. At these times he would return to his near death experience and find solace in his approaching end, and in the solitary figure of his vision. His life moved between wild extremes of terrifying, almost violent fear, and a calm trust that dying harbored no threat. At times the gut-wrenching swings made Kim shudder.

Once, when his mind was clear, Hap and I puzzled over Osceola's apparent acceptance of death even though his friends and loved ones were "still under fire." It was an important question since Hap agonized over not being able to protect Kim and Alley after he died. He wondered how Osceola could have relented, knowing the hardship that lay ahead for his people.

"What do you think about that?" I asked.

"I think it must've gotten so bad," Hap said, "that it was not in his hands anymore. He just had to let it go."

"What about you?"

He gave me a stern look and said, "It's still in my hands."

"And what do you need to do?"

"I'm not sure, but it'll come to me."

The Second Seminole War dragged on until 1842 and untold numbers of Indians died from battle, disease, and starvation. Eventually, even the most strident warriors like Wildcat were persuaded to leave their homes and head west. By the end of 1843 thousands of Seminoles had been forced onto reservations in Oklahoma.

The United States government was likewise exhausted. It had lost 1,500 men and wasted 30 million dollars on war. So when several hundred Seminoles disappeared into the swamps and refused to leave, the Americans did not have the stomach to hunt them down. For over a decade these Seminoles lived in the Everglades. In 1855, the holdouts were again under pressure as white surveyors—harbingers of land speculators and would-be settlers—cut paths into Seminole territory. The ensuing conflict was called the Third Seminole War. By war's end only a handful of Seminole Indians, probably no more than 300, were left. These were never defeated, never surrendered, and many of their ancestors live in Florida to this day.

There were times when it appeared to Kim that Hap would fight until his last breath. In the last days of his life he slept constantly, but it was a light, fitful sleep. His body was restless and often moved as though startled. It seemed as though battles were being fought within him and his sudden movements were shadows of the war being waged.

The morning he died was icy, the sky a threatening gray. The roads were slippery. When I reached the house, the hospice nurse had phoned to let Kim know she had been delayed because of the weather. This gave us time to talk about Hap's life and the final hours before his death.

Sometime during the night "He just kinda woke up all of a sudden," Kim said, "and was talking like his old self." Like a turtle, he had tentatively stuck his head out from under his shell. His mind was clear and alert. He told Kim he was ready to go and he was at peace.

She asked if he was afraid. Rather than answer, he asked her to forgive him for all the "things I've put you through."

"I told him I forgave him," she recalled, "and asked him to forgive me too. Then I asked him again if he was afraid."

According to Kim, he responded by asking, "Do you

know how much I love you?"

"I told him I did, and that I loved him too," Kim said. "Then I asked him one more time if he was afraid."

"No," he said, "Are you?"

She told him no.

He asked to see Alley and Kim went to the child's room and brought her to Hap's bed. For several minutes they sat together quietly, holding hands as he stroked his daughter's hair. Then he told his family he loved them and assured them that he was ready to go, before slipping into a deep, undisturbed sleep. When he finally crossed the river, he did so peacefully.

Chapter Eleven
Building the Brooklyn Bridge:
Legacy and Asking for Help

Mort was born in Brooklyn in 1911. Whenever this came up, he was likely to tell you it was the year fire swept through the Triangle Shirtwaist Factory in Manhattan, killing one hundred and forty-six women. Many of them jumped to their deaths from sweatshop windows after finding the factory doors locked and the fire escapes inoperable. In Mort's mind, the wrenching images of these poor women falling to their deaths blended with his birth to form a single, inseparable event.

Maybe this was because his father worked in the apparel business and knew some of the young women who died, or because some of their parents attended his family's synagogue. Maybe it was simply an unforgettable reference point that gave immediate context whenever he said to other New Yorkers, "I was born the year of the fire." There was, however, a psychological dimension. Throughout his life Mort had seen people who were young and strong die quickly and unexpectedly: a schoolmate trampled by a horse drawn trolley; a brother killed during the Korean War and a sister who died on an operating table during a botched mastectomy. As a marine lieutenant in the Pacific during World War Two, he had seen many young men die. The most painful loss by far was the death of his son, Mitch, who had suffered a cerebral aneurysm before his twenty-third birthday. "I was born under the death star," he said, "and its just hung there over my head my entire life."

He wasn't surprised when he was diagnosed with cancer or when surgery failed to cure him. At eighty-one, he figured he had done well to outrun the "death star" for so long anyway, and it was simply time to "face the music." He expected to deteriorate quickly, but the doctor told him his particular kind of cancer moved slowly and the surgery had slowed it down even more. With luck, he might live another four or five years. Mort was bewildered by this and found himself pondering a question: Was it better to die quickly without any warning, like so many people he had known, or slowly, fully aware of what was coming? The former offered many advantages—no anxiety about the future, no tedium from slow days of physical decline, no clutching dramas in doctors' offices. The problem was, dying quickly offered no time to prepare—to do things that are meaningful, savor time together, and tie up loose ends. In short, there was no time to plan, and for Mort, a methodical maker of master plans, this was the crux of the matter.

By the time hospice care began, nearly four years later, Mort had resolved this question, confident it was better to see death approaching. Those years had given him time to develop a game plan for the days ahead. While he was able, he and his wife, Alma, had traveled to many places. They went to New York to visit family and pay their respects at a Brooklyn cemetery. They returned to the site of a theater (now high-rise apartments), where they had met on a blind date. They visited Paris Island, South Carolina where Mort had been inducted into the marines, and spent two weeks with their daughter Ruth, and Grand-daughter, Rhea in Washington, D.C.

They even traveled to Ireland, where Mort had spent a year attending a university in Dublin. In Eastern Europe they traced family roots and visited the town where Alma's mother had been born. Everywhere they went they visited people and places that were significant to them. In the months after they returned, Mort often spoke of their "life-tour" with relish and enthusiasm. He humorously referred to it as phase one in his two-part, earthly departure plan. When I met him, about six months after the trip ended, he had already formulated phase two.

In his mind, the plan was simple: spend as much time as he could with Alma, Ruth, Rhea, and his son Nate; write his memoir; and prepare the family's complex estate, about which only he knew the details, for his death. He was certain it was a realistic blueprint and was intent on following it to the letter. Ironically, for all his planning he failed to factor in his illness. He simply had no idea how strenuous and challenging activities would become or the toll cancer would take on his mental focus.

Spending time with family was his highest priority. After Mort and Alma returned from Ireland, Nate moved in with his parents and cut back on his hours at work so he could help manage their home and assist with practical concerns related to Mort's care. During the day Mort and Alma sat together talking, watching television, or resting. They had no need for anything dramatic; it was enough just to be together. Ruth and Rhea visited regularly and Mort's days passed with a rhythm that, despite all the uncertainty, gave him some measure of comfort. Beneath the surface, however, he was having more pain, finding it harder to concentrate, and he was beginning to worry that his plan was not as realistic as he had hoped.

As his strength waned, Mort's memoir fell by the wayside. For weeks he had tried to focus, but simply remembering the details of eighty-five years, much less organizing and writing the long story of his life, grew disheartening. After gathering some old photographs and letters, the work languished. His consternation was heightened by the fact that the book he envisioned was as much a family history as a personal one. Although this made the project more daunting, it also made it more important. One of the things that kept him awake at night with worry was that his brothers and sisters were all dead and none of them had any surviving children. As he saw it, there was nobody to remember them or his parents. Mort believed it was his "sacred responsibility" to tell their stories and he agonized that the memoir was stalled, his energy was diminishing, and time was running out.

Also stalled was the estate planning. He simply did not have the stamina to sit and analyze numbers and documents. As with his memoir, there was a larger agenda being lost. For Mort, "estate plan" was synonymous with making sure Alma was protected and secure for the rest of her life. He worried about her constantly. It was causing him a great deal of anguish that he could not meet with his lawyer and disentangle the many policies and accounts. In his mind, he was letting his wife down and putting an unwieldy burden on her and his children.

On the surface, Alma didn't appear to need Mort's protection. She was perceptive, savvy, and adaptable. However, behind the veil of competence and adaptability things were more ambiguous. After they left Brooklyn in the 1950s, she had felt isolated in the rural environs of North Carolina and had become prone to depression. When Mitch died, Alma became reclusive, fearful of strangers, and dependent on Mort for support and comfort. He had long been the bedrock on which she anchored herself and he worried that when he died she would be lost.

When I met Mort, Alma had recently broken her shoulder and been transferred to a local nursing home. The doctor said she was there temporarily for rehabilitation but no one believed him. "We all knew Mom was there to stay," Ruth admitted, "but we pretended she would be able to come home before Pop died. I guess we were trying to make her and ourselves feel better." For Mort and Alma, nothing could have been more emotionally painful. They had expected to be together for the remaining months of his life and now these hopes had been shattered. Since arriving at the nursing home, Alma had spent many days crying and was sliding into depression.

Mort was also reeling under the unyielding press of dense emotional gravity. His game plan was falling apart, its very center—being with Alma—stolen in an instant. The memoir, born only in his mind, was fading and the estate plans were floundering. He was more worried than ever about his wife and felt helpless to comfort her. It was as though he was on a bridge that was crumbling beneath his feet before he had made it safely to the other side.

In the past his response to Alma's depression had always been to remain steadfastly optimistic, standing beside her like a tower over stirring waters, trusting that she would draw strength from him and the crisis would subside. This time was different. He couldn't summon the enthusiasm for life that had always been there even in times of suffering. Now *he* was becoming depressed.

For a few visits, Mort drifted in and out of deep sadness. Reflecting on things helped. When he realized his feelings were normal, rather than signs of weakness, a weight lifted and his optimism began to stir. It was not his fault his blueprint had proven unrealistic, there were just too many things he couldn't control or anticipate. What he needed was a new game plan. One made in the full light of his growing limitations. After working for years as an executive for a marketing firm, Mort knew one thing: if a plan didn't work, you tried something else.

Looking systematically at the tasks he had set for himself, he saw that he needed help—with his failing energy he could not do it all by himself. Unfortunately, for Mort, asking for help was a practice he had abandoned years before. Even saying the words 'please help me' was like speaking a language so foreign it felt almost nonsensical to him. Although he had always been willing to give assistance to others, he had typically refused it whenever it was offered to him. And he never asked for it. Even now, on the threshold of death, the thought of needing support evoked anxiety. Rationalizations spumed forth: "I don't want to bother my kids with this"; "it's my job to take care of these things"; "I just need to try harder, that's all." Beneath these protests deeper injunctions emerged—asking for help, he thought, was a sign of "poor character" and "failure." The innocent act of asking for a hand, it seemed, was embedded with irrational fears and judgments.

Ironically, his kids were eager to help. They wanted some tangible way to show their affection, but Mort had already rebuffed several offers of assistance. Nate was a mortgage broker for a regional bank. He had a logical mind and an eye for detail. He was well suited to help Mort with the nuances of their labyrinthine finances. He was already his parents' power-of-attorney and had been appointed executor of their estate, but he knew nothing about the specifics. He had asked Mort several times if he could help organize things. He had all but pleaded with his father to review the responsibilities that waited ahead but Mort always had excuses.

As for the memoirs, Ruth was an editor and a freelance writer. She excelled at organizing information and distilling it into an engaging narrative. She had already done extensive genealogical research on Alma's side of the family, but had not pursued Mort's side, in deference to her father's long-stated intention of doing it himself. In Ruth and Nate, Mort had a team that was ideal to help him implement his plan and carry it through, even after he was gone; but there was still the problem of asking for help.

Mort refused to ask them directly. Instead, he decided to seed his conversations with hints that he needed help and wait for them to offer. When Ruth and Nate responded supportively, as he knew they would, Mort accepted. Over the next several weeks he and Nate spent time going through accounts, insurance policies, and reviewing documents. It was draining, sometimes frustrating work, but once the basics were covered Nate was able to begin sorting through the minutia on his own. Ruth came down for a week and took extensive notes as her father told stories from his life. As with Nate, she got the basics since Mort didn't have the stamina for anything more. When added to the stacks of letters, photographs, and yellowed postcards, however, it was a rich trove of family history. Certainly enough to capture the essence of Mort's life and stand as witness to the lives of his departed loved ones. Mort was relieved.

As the memoir and the estate plans slowly fell into place, Mort visited Alma regularly. Each trip, though, exacted a greater physical cost, requiring hours of rest afterward. For months Mort had maintained a rough equilibrium, declining so slowly as to be almost imperceptible, but as his cancer grew he seemed to cross a threshold beyond which things changed more rapidly. Visits with Alma suddenly ended and he rarely left his bed. Knowing he was near the end of his life, Mort asked Nate to arrange to move him to the nursing home. Being with Alma was more important than staying home, and within a few days they were together again. By then he wasn't eating and he was sleeping most of the time.

Despite his somnolence, Mort's mind was clear. In the shadow of death he vacillated between a weary acceptance of his situation and bouts of anxiety about how his family would cope with his death. Secretly, he had expected to live until Nate had a solid grasp on *all* the particulars of the estate; until Ruth had a rough draft of the emerging family history; and until Alma outran the depression that continued to bedevil her. He had even hoped to outlive his wife and spare her the renting grief he knew would come. Despite her quiet strength and resilience, he worried his death would break her spirit. When he confided his fear to his children, they assured him they would comfort her. He told himself not to worry, but he worried anyway.

Our last visit was relatively brief. He was weak and talking was difficult. Tears welled in his eyes as he described his sadness about leaving so many things incomplete. Although he trusted his children to do their best, he worried that the work they had started together would collapse when he died. He found some solace in the fact that he had crafted a blueprint for the days ahead, and he hoped that it would endure after he was gone. Still, it was work that would have to be completed without him. He would have to trust, if he could, that it would be done well. But trust, like asking for help, did not come easily and he worried everything would "go to hell in a hand basket."

Talking about things seemed to help, but in some ways his concerns were beyond the capacity of language to soothe. I wondered if a story might help him pull the various threads of his experience together and offer some insight or encouragement. On one of our visits, Mort had told me about his Uncle Saul taking him onto the promenade of the Brooklyn Bridge when Mort was a child. The bridge had been born in the mind of John Roebling. He had crafted the blueprints and worked out the details. He planned on building it too, but when he died from an acute infection the project was left incomplete and the task fell to his son. When the younger Roebling's health deteriorated, he too had to accept the assistance of others in order to complete the work laid out in his father's blueprint. It took over a decade to build the bridge and by the time it was done the project had been passed through many hands. Seeing that Mort was fatigued and needed to rest, I asked if I could tell him the story of the building of the bridge.

Still able to muster a little dry humor, he said in a low and fading voice, "Of course you can my boy, but make it good. It may be the last story I ever hear."

II

In 1869 John Roebling was at the peak of his career. Regarded as one of the great engineers of his day, he possessed tremendous physical and mental energy as well as creative vision and the practical skills to make his visions into reality. Now he was focused on building a bridge across the East River in New York—between Brooklyn and Manhattan—and when Roebling focused on something it was all but impossible to distract him. His formal plan for its construction had already been approved by the Brooklyn Bridge Company and work was about to begin. With his blueprints in hand, it would have been inconceivable to Roebling that he would have to relinquish the project to others, but that is exactly what was about to happen.

It was an ambitious undertaking, beyond the scope of any bridge ever constructed. It would be a suspension bridge, a relatively new design never employed on this scale before. Roebling's plans were exacting and comprehensive. He anticipated being involved in all aspects of construction. As he saw it, the Brooklyn Bridge would be his *magnum opus*, a masterwork perfectly fusing science and art. It would also be a thing of durable practicality and unadorned beauty. He claimed that "The completed work, when constructed in accordance with my designs, will not only be the greatest bridge in existence, but it will be the greatest engineering work of the continent, and of the age."

The magnitude of Roebling's plan was immense and would require flawless execution. To create a firm foundation for the two massive towers that would support the bridge, he intended to sink giant caissons atop the river's bedrock and fill them with cement. The use of caissons was relatively novel and still controversial, but Roebling had done the math and was convinced it would work.

Roebling turned to his son, Washington, to assist with the project. They had built bridges together in Ohio and New York and the younger Roebling was a talented engineer in his own right. As a Colonel in the Union army during the Civil War, Washington had overseen the construction of bridges at Fredericksburg and Harper's Ferry. Others may have doubted the viability of Roebling's plan, but he knew his son harbored no such doubts. Together, they would prove the skeptics wrong.

In the summer of 1869, as politicians—including the infamous William "Boss" Tweed—squabbled over the bridge's financing, the Roebling's were completing surveys on the Brooklyn side of the river. They were meticulously calculating the location of one of the towers, as well as the placement of a massive anchorage that would be built on shore. Their work was interrupted when John Roebling severely injured his right foot. It was crushed between a beam and some wooden pilings when a ferry docked against the pier where he was standing.

The wound was serious, but Roebling figured he would be back at work in a month or so, less if things went his way. Unfortunately, he developed a tetanus infection. Suddenly, his dynamic, indefatigable frame was crippled by illness and he was fighting to stay alive. Despite his strong will, the infection spread. In the throes of fever and seizures, Roebling fought hard to live; he had a bridge to build. For three agonizing weeks he clung to life, but the tetanus couldn't be cured. His mind and body were stretched to the breaking point. Whether or not he realized he was dying and that his blueprint would have to be handed over to someone else is hard to know. He died on July 22, just hours after mentally working out the design for a contraption to lift his depleted body out of bed.

The visionary behind the bridge was gone before a single block of limestone had been laid. He had left nothing but plans for a bridge many thought could never be built. An editorial in the Brooklyn *Eagle* painted the tragedy in heroic terms and proclaimed that "Henceforth we look on the great project of the Brooklyn Bridge as being baptized and hallowed by the life blood of its distinguished and lamented author." Though the *Eagle's* editor remained confident despite the death of the architect, many assumed the colossal project had died along with John Roebling.

He had drafted his designs in excruciating detail, covering everything from cost projections and time frame to the type of masonry and cable wire to use. The members of the bridge company turned to Washington Roebling to take up the blueprint and begin construction. Thomas Kinsella, editor of the *Eagle* and a member of the board, again used the paper to boost the project and give his seal of approval to the young engineer. "Not long since, before the accident which led to his death," Kinsella wrote:

> Mr. Roebling remarked to us that he had enough of money and reputation. And he scarce knew why, at his age, he was undertaking to build another and still greater bridge. His son, he added, ought to build this Brooklyn bridge—was as competent as himself in all respects to design and supervise it; had thought and worked with him, and in short was as good an engineer as his father.

Whether true or not, Kinsella captured the spirit of those interested in moving forward. Washington had worked with his father since the 1840s. He was already involved in the Brooklyn project and was one of the world's rare authorities on suspension bridges and caissons. Just as importantly, no one was more motivated to build this bridge and bring his father's dream to fruition. Without delay, Colonel Washington Roebling was made chief engineer and John Roebling's vision, and his painstakingly crafted plans, were placed officially in his hands.

The first order of business was to construct the enormous caisson on which the Brooklyn tower would stand. Essentially, the caisson was a "huge diving bell that would be built of wood and iron, shaped like a gigantic box, with a heavy roof, strong sides, and no bottom." Roebling intended to fill it with compressed air and sink it into the riverbed. Men would enter the caisson's multiple chambers to dig out the rock and sediment until they reached bedrock. As they dug, huge blocks of limestone and granite would be piled on top, sinking the caisson as the tower grew. When they reached a firm foundation the entire caisson would be filled with cement. Given the novelty and magnitude of the job, the shipbuilders making the caisson demanded money up front and refused to guarantee their work.

By May 1870, the six million pound behemoth was ready. It was floated to the site of the Brooklyn tower where a limestone block weighing about six thousand pounds was muscled into place on top of it. As more stone was piled on, the caisson began its descent and soon pressed into a layer of mud and rock. Crews cleared enough of the riverbed to make an initial survey. Roebling quickly concluded that the material "was of a very formidable nature, and could only be removed by slow, tedious, and persistent efforts." There were huge boulders that would require a lot of work to remove. Digging all the way to bedrock was going to be an arduous and time-consuming task.

Crews worked around-the-clock breaking boulders into manageable chunks and hauling them away along with huge buckets of mud. They worked in dank air lighted by calcium lamps. Day after day they hammered and scraped while temperatures climbed into the eighties and nineties. Despite their labors, some weeks the caisson descended less than six inches.

As the caisson sank deeper, the men began complaining of an array of unexplainable symptoms including headaches, joint pain, dizziness, and nausea. Something about working in the caisson was making them sick but no one knew what it was. Roebling was down in the compressed air more than anyone, inspecting things and solving problems. By December, with the caisson sunk to forty feet and the tower climbing ever higher above the water's surface, conditions in the structure were beginning to affect him. One night Roebling collapsed while surveying the work. By the time he was driven home in a carriage, he was completely paralyzed. His doctor was called in and, after a few anxious hours, the paralysis subsided and he was able to move about. It was clear, however, that his health was eroding.

Undeterred, Roebling returned to his grueling schedule. In March of 1871, the caisson finally reached bedrock at forty-five feet. By September, work was underway on the Manhattan tower; masonry going up as the caisson went down. The terrain on the Manhattan side of the river was mostly sand and gravel. Without boulders to contend with, the structure sank more quickly. On the other hand, borings had made it clear that this tower would have to descend much deeper before reaching bedrock.

Greater depth meant greater air pressure for those inside the caisson. Every time the structure sank two feet the atmospheric pressure rose one pound. By the time it reached forty-four feet, the workers were once again experiencing the same symptoms that had afflicted them on the Brooklyn tower. As the tower sank deeper more workers were affected and the symptoms became more frequent and acute. In addition to joint pain and vomiting, they experienced profuse sweating, paralysis, fatigue, and lack of mental focus. In an attempt to protect his workers, Roebling shortened the workday and hired physician, Andrew Smith, as a fulltime member of the staff. Despite Doctor Smith's conscientious attempts to treat the men and understand the mysterious illness, his efforts were largely ineffective. By April 1872, two men were dead from what people had begun calling "caisson's disease."

Caisson's disease is known today as the bends. It is a condition caused by rapid changes in compression like those experienced by workers whenever they entered or left the caisson. Over time, repeated exposures can be debilitating, even fatal. There was no diagram or calculation in John Roebling's plans with which to address this problem. He had measured every beam of steel and every pound of mortar, but there was no logarithm factoring in the frailty of the human body or the limitations of medicine.

Since his first episode of paralysis, Washington Roebling had continued going down into the caisson daily and his health had further deteriorated. As he struggled with mounting symptoms and contemplated the fact that two men were already dead, he made a startling decision. Even though they had not reached bedrock, he halted the digging at seventy-eight feet. He reasoned that, at that depth the sand was so compact as to be "good enough to found upon, or at any rate nearly as good as any concrete that could be put in place of it."

Shortly thereafter, Roebling was seized by an incapacitating attack of the bends. For months, he had pushed discomfort aside, but now it burst on him like a tsunami, leaving him in excruciating pain, paralyzed, near death. It looked as though his fate would mirror his father's. Maybe he even wondered who would pick up the project's reins if he died. Eventually, however, he surprised everyone but himself and his wife, Emily, when he rallied his strength and returned to work.

The attacks returned as well. They usually arrived suddenly, sapping his strength and leaving him nervous and exhausted. He cut back on the time he spent at the bridge and

249

by the winter of 1872 his condition was so precarious he was spending most of his time in bed, unable to concentrate and exhausted after short conversations. Failing health gave him a keen awareness of his mortality and he worried that he would die before the bridge was finished. As he pushed himself to recover, he was haunted by fears that he would leave his work, and that of his father, incomplete.

He reluctantly requested a leave of absence in April 1873 so he and Emily could travel to Europe seeking treatments for his shattered body. They hoped that time away from the demands of the bridge would restore him, but the journey was arduous. By the time they finally returned to New York, Roebling was drained and demoralized.

His mind, however, was unaffected by the illness and his resolve to finish the bridge remained strong. He resumed his role as chief engineer, although he was too sick to visit the work site. He had taken up his father's plan for the great bridge and made it his own, now he would have to rely on others, placing in their hands responsibilities he would rather have shouldered himself. He would have to ask for help and trust that others could do the job well.

Important among these helpers were assistant engineers such as C.C. Martin and Francis Collingwood. They directly supervised the crews and executed his orders. Later, Emily Roebling would comment that completing the bridge, "could never have been accomplished but for the unselfish devotion of his assistant engineers. Each man had a certain department in charge and they worked with all their energies to have the work properly done according to Colonel Roebling's plan and wishes..."

Emily assumed a role equal to that of her husband's assistants. He relied on her to write his detailed instructions and reports, relay information, and make regular inspections of the construction. As she became familiar with the science of engineering and the art of city politics, she spoke on his behalf and kept him apprised on all facets of the building. From the winter of 1874 throughout 1875 and much of the following year, the Roeblings were at their home in Trenton,

New Jersey. They hoped that getting away from the city would allow the Colonel to rest and regain his strength. He was still very much in charge of the project, but he would have been the first to admit he couldn't have overseen things without Emily to write his voluminous letters and organize the details of the far-flung enterprise.

In addition to being indispensable to his work with the bridge, Emily provided the physical care and psychological support that sustained him through his most difficult times. Later in his life Roebling would write, with fitting imagery, "At first I thought I would succumb, but I had a strong tower to lean upon, my wife, a woman of infinite tact and wisest counsel." During his time in Trenton, Roebling was in constant pain, too weak to tolerate anyone's company but Emily's. Moving around left him fatigued and frustrated. He was easily distressed and suffered from anxiety whenever he was around others.

While the Roeblings were away the towers were completed. The next step was to string steel wire between them and draw these wires into powerful cables. Reporting on the construction of the huge suspender cables, E.F. Farrington wrote Roebling that, "I have carried out your instructions to the letter…I shall expect the cables of this bridge to equal, if they do not excel, the best that ever were made." By October 1876, the Roeblings were back in Brooklyn, having taken up residence on Brooklyn Heights. From here, with the aid of a telescope, Colonel Roebling could see the cables forming from the window of their home.

Emily's role continued to expand. She visited the bridge almost every day. The project that had been at the center of John Roebling's life, and which had become the center of her husband's as well, now was inextricable from hers. No communications reached or left Roebling without her awareness. When visitors from the site or the bridge company arrived, or when the occasional reporter stopped by, the visit was often spent entirely with Emily while her husband rested. She could answer their many questions and was skillful at asking her own on her husband's behalf.

Given that Roebling could see the bridge from his window, it is tempting to imagine him bolted to his telescope watching every trowel and rivet. According to his wife, however, this was not the case. His engineering skills were so good he could judge the progress with occasional observations. Physically, perhaps psychologically, he was a shell of his former self, but his mind was razor sharp. As steel cables slowly spidered across the skyline, he could appreciate the monumental scope of what was being accomplished. He must have wondered at times what his father would have thought. There were probably moments when he would have given much to have John Roebling look out on the river and see what was being done and to know that his blueprint had been taken seriously.

By 1880 construction was progressing steadily, though it had been six years since the chief engineer had visited the site. Despite the progress, work had been going on for ten years and critics were impatient. Some suspected corruption was behind the many delays and the chief engineer's apparent disappearance was reason enough for them to blame him. In truth, the bridge was a mammoth undertaking and early estimates for its completion turned out to be unrealistic. Simply getting enough rock, steel, and cable wire to the site required the energies and precision of a seasoned army. Perhaps inevitably though, along with the delays, there was the politics.

The mayor of Brooklyn, Seth Low, became a vociferous critic of Roebling, going so far as to refer to the bridge as the "unsubstantial fabric of a dream." As a new member of the Bridge Board, he tried to have the Colonel removed as chief engineer on the grounds that he "has been for many years, and still is, an invalid..." Emily Roebling tried to insulate her husband from the more biting aspects of the fray and spoke eloquently as his representative, but it was impossible to shield him from the controversy.

Amid the maelstrom of political posturing, scathing editorials, and factionalism among board members, the bridge continued to emerge. By 1883 it was finally finished.

Roebling's health was somewhat improved by then. In April, he was able to withstand a short carriage ride to the Brooklyn anchorage. Although he did not leave the carriage, he finally got a close-up view of the great span crossing the East River. It was six thousand feet long with titanic cables capable of supporting twenty-five million pounds. It had taken much more time and money to build than anyone had imagined. At least twenty men had been killed in accidents during its construction. Its architect was dead and the health of its chief engineer was wrecked, but it was done. And as John Roebling had hoped, it was a masterwork.

III

No matter what the last weeks or months of someone's life holds, there are often things that are incomplete. Unrealized hopes, unfulfilled intentions, and unfinished projects are common. Throughout his illness Mort had many such things to attract his attention. Maybe this was a tribute to his ability to hold fast to meaning amid suffering and nourish his relationships even as he moved toward the moment of separation. Like many of us, there were bound to have been things left undone and plans left incomplete no matter how long he lived.

Entrusting one's plans, hopes, and important projects to others can be difficult. Letting go of such things can cause anxiety, shame, or a host of other thoughts and feelings. At times, there may be no one to whom such things can be passed. Sometimes doing so is too difficult or time is too short. In these instances, we must do our best to lay things aside and accept that they are unfinished. There are even some for whom the thought of such things dying with them is actually comforting, as though the incompleteness stands as a testament to their labors. Mort was not one to be comforted by this, and he was fortunate Ruth and Nate wanted to help. They understood the importance of his projects and the apprehension he had in placing them into their hands.

Mort was nearly asleep when I finished telling him about the bridge. With his eyes closed, he smiled and said, "Uncle Saul must've taken me across that bridge fifty times when I was a kid." Before drifting off to sleep he squeezed my hand and asked me to tell the story to his family after he died.

A few days later, I got a call from Ruth who was concerned that Alma wasn't "taking things well." The night before, Ruth said, Alma had asked Nate why Mort wasn't in the hospital where he could get a feeding tube and be artificially hydrated. Although Mort had been very clear about his desire not to have this done and Alma had agreed, now that he was near the end of his life Alma was afraid and she desperately wanted to keep him alive.

Conversations, such as the ones Mort had had with his family about his wishes at the end of his life are profoundly important. They can relieve families of the pressure and responsibility of making difficult decisions quickly under duress. Mort had thought long and hard about what he wanted and had decided to pursue, as he put it, "quality of life over quantity." He had written a living will expressing his desire to forgo artificial nutrition and hydration and had his doctor sign an order that he was not to be resuscitated. While his wishes were consistent with Alma's (she had also signed a living will) and she had supported his decisions in principle, following through on them was harder than she had ever imagined.

I visited Alma that afternoon after speaking with Ruth. When I arrived she was sitting by Mort's bed trying to wake him up so she could get him to eat some pudding.

"He has to eat," she said, "or he'll never get stronger."

"Do you think he is going to get stronger?" I asked.

"He's bounced back before."

"Do you think he'll bounce back this time?"

She was silent for a while and finally whispered, "I've got to try to get him to eat something."

As a person dies, his or her body slowly loses its need for food. Mort had reached that point, but for Alma, food and eating were filled with deep symbolism and importance. She equated eating with strength and saw feeding Mort as one of the last acts of love left to her. She worried that he was hungry since he had not eaten in days and he had "always loved food so much." It took time for her to understand that, for Mort, eating would be uncomfortable and the food would not be metabolized. Slowly she saw that *not* feeding him was also an act of love.

Despite her questions about feeding tubes and intravenous hydration, Alma knew what Mort wanted. After all, he had left a blueprint for that as well. At the heart of her anxiety was the fact that Mort had always been the anchorage to which she was grounded during hard times. Now that he needed her help, she wanted to make sure she was not letting him down. When I reassured her about this she seemed less anxious. Still the impulse to do something drastic, as she put it, remained strong as she watched over her beloved husband.

When the Brooklyn Bridge opened on May 24 1883, a newspaper reporter asked Emily Roebling if her husband was ever likely to undertake another such project. According to the reporter, "Mrs. Roebling elevated her brows and said decisively, 'Oh, no. This is his last as well as his greatest work. He will need a long rest after this is over. He needs it and he has certainly earned it.'" Throughout the construction he had leaned on her as though she were as strong as the Brooklyn anchorage. With his health compromised, he would continue to lean on her in the years ahead.

By 1902, however, Emily Roebling's own health was failing. In December, while her husband was in a New York hospital recuperating from an operation, Emily collapsed at their home in Trenton. The doctors found cancer in her stomach. Her decline was as swift as her husband's was gradual. She died several weeks later on February 28, 1903, not long after Washington had returned from New York.

Roebling did not speak openly about his grief. One can only guess at the depth of his pain. His life-partner, the person who had sheltered him from political storms and the scrutiny and demands of a host of skeptics when he was overwhelmed and exhausted, was gone.

Not long after my visit with Alma, Mort died. When I arrived at the nursing home Alma was alone in his room holding his hand and crying. Years before she had been filled with anger at God and had forsaken the synagogue, but in the midst of her pain and disbelief, what she wanted most was a Rabbi. After several telephone calls I found one who agreed to visit and managed to arrive at about the same time as Nate. Hearing familiar prayers, the same ones she had heard as a child growing up, was comforting and helped steady her. It was as though the Rabbi's words, prayers, and rituals traveled across some invisible bridge leading into a deep place of tradition and spiritual strength.

Weeks later, as Mort had requested, I told Alma the story of the bridge. It helped her, she said, accept not only the things Mort had left incomplete, but also the things she had not been able to say or do during his final days.

"I was too afraid to talk with him about death," she said, "and tell him it was okay to go. I wish I'd told him I was going to be okay."

"How does the story about the Brooklyn Bridge help you when you think about that?" I asked.

"It reminds me that we all leave things undone no matter how hard we try not to. The point is to get as much of it done as you can."

"And what about the rest?"

"I don't know?" She looked sad.

"Can you let it go? Let yourself be human?"

She paused in thought and finally said, "Yeah, I think I can."

Alma was particularly interested in how the characters in the drama died. She was surprised to learn that Emily Roebling died some twenty-three years before her husband. "I bet he expected to go first," she said. "Like I always thought I'd go first."

Washington Roebling's condition never improved, and in the years after Emily's death it worsened considerably. Alma and I pondered what it must have been like for him to lose his "strong tower," and how he went on with his life despite such hardship. She marveled at his strength and searched for it in herself.

For a while, Alma's grief sunk deep and rooted itself to her like a block of granite. There were few opportunities to talk about her sadness or her life with Mort. The routines and rhythms of the nursing home did not allow much time for anything but the most superficial interactions with staff and other residents. As such, she was relatively isolated. Moreover, the nursing staff confused her grief with depression (perhaps understandably, given her history of depression). After getting an order from her physician to increase the dose of a couple of her "nerve medicines," they considered the matter resolved.

Grieving is a laborious and consuming affair under the best circumstances. For many who grieve in an institutionalized environment the challenges are even more considerable. Although the people who worked at Alma's residence were kind, and the nursing care competent, she had little privacy or control over her surroundings. The noise was distracting and she lamented that she had no telephone with which to hear a familiar voice. Few people there had known Mort and those who had either did not want to talk about him or were too busy. She had very little space for photographs and keepsakes and she longed to return to her home just to sit in Mort's chair and breathe in the lingering cigar smoke.

With her permission, I called Nate and we discussed the possibility of taking his mother home for a visit. He was a bit nervous that it might be too emotionally difficult for her to have to go back to the nursing home afterward, but by the end of the week he had arranged a visit on a weekend when Ruth would be able to join them.

It turned out to be a longer visit than they had

expected. Rather than bringing Alma back in the afternoon, Nate called the nurse and arranged for his mother to spend the night at home. When I saw Alma a couple weeks later she was still brightening whenever she talked about the trip and Nate was planning to pick her up the next day for another one.

Over the next few months, Nate brought her home once every few weeks. Gradually Alma was able to cross the waters of her pain as she and her children spoke about Mort. Sitting in Mort's chair surrounded by things that reflected their lives together summoned her tears, but it also brought comfort and appreciation.

Initially, Nate was overwhelmed by his responsibilities with the estate. Slowly though, with the help of an accountant, a lawyer, and some computer software, he sorted things out and did a fine job despite all the Byzantine intricacies Mort had left behind. He made sure the bills were paid and that whatever Alma needed was taken care of.

Ruth completed the family history within a year. Using the Internet, her father's memoir led her on a fascinating journey into the lives of family she had not even known existed. She even talked on the telephone with Uncle Saul's granddaughter, who lived in Atlanta. Saul had died shortly after her birth and she was delighted when Ruth shared some of Mort's stories. Mort had worried that the story of his family would vanish when he died, but Ruth not only captured it, she reached across the waters of distance and time and connected it to the lives of others who would now carry the story with them as well.

Despite daily discomfort and pain, Roebling lived until 1926. He remarried in 1908 and ran the family wire business for many years. Late in his life he began having intense pain in his jaw and worried that he would die of tetanus like his father. By then, many people had forgotten which Roebling had actually built the bridge. Some did not even know there had been two of them. So intertwined had their lives become that the younger Roebling wrote to a friend that, "Long ago I ceased my endeavor to clear up the respective identities of myself and my father. Many people think I died in 1869."

Years earlier, the same reporter who had interviewed Emily on the day the bridge opened had asked Roebling if he thought he would ever build another bridge. He had responded very differently than his wife. "I don't know," he said "If I get well there is lots of big work in the world to do yet." By the time he died, Roebling wire was a staple of a rapidly modernizing America and could be found almost everywhere. It was spliced or braided, for example, into telegraph wires, elevator cables, electric lines, and it was essential for the wire ropes used on ships, to pull coal cars, and, of course, to build bridges. Although he never built another bridge, Roebling certainly had an indirect hand in the "big work" left to those who were busy using his wire to change the face of American towns and cities.

For all of his planning and attention to details, Mort neglected to leave any guidance on what to do with his cremated remains. Ruth and Nate left it to Alma to decide. She equivocated for a while before deciding that they should divide it between the three of them with each to "do with them as you like." Alma would keep hers and have them mixed with her own cremated remains after she died. Ruth and Nate planned to take theirs to New York. Ruth wanted to drop her share into the water while taking the Staten Island Ferry, where Mort had proposed to Alma decades earlier. Nate's plan was to spread them somewhere around where Ebbits Field had once stood as home to the Brooklyn Dodgers baseball team. I suggested they check with one of the city's funeral homes to familiarize themselves with any municipal restrictions, but I suspect that Mort's remains ended up where his kids had intended.

I don't know whether Mort ever completely relinquished to others the work he had started. At the very least, however, he learned to ask for help. By the time he died he had also learned to trust that Alma, Nate, and Ruth would do their best with the plans he had crafted. The rest was not in his hands.

Chapter Twelve
Black Elk at Harney Peak:
Trusting One's Inner Voice

In 1942, when Miguel was a boy living in the mountains of Chile, his uncle showed him how to use the short wave radio atop the hand-hewn planks of a table in his family's attic. His uncle had put it there and run taped-up electrical wire onto the roof where he had fashioned a gizmo Miguel remembered as more fire hazard than antenna. The attic was off limits to Miguel's three younger sisters, and they whispered about the radio as though it were a talismanic porthole through which adults passed in order to gain wisdom by traveling the skies.

The attic was hot in the summer, cold in the winter. Quivering light from the kerosene lamp made it a surreal otherworld of vibrating shadow and illumination. For a boy with Miguel's poetic sensitivity, the radio invited him to look beyond the visible world into the gauzy web of spirit that connects everything beneath. Voices arrived from across the globe, placing the cut glass of his life into the mosaic of a larger world. A world, he quickly learned, prone to spasms of violent pain.

It was here Miguel learned that a great war was being fought and the entire world was bleeding from its terrors. With no newsreels, magazines, or newspapers, he was left to draw mental pictures of soldiers from Germany, Japan, and places like London, Moscow, and Guadalcanal. Some nights, when there was enough moonlight, he would slip out of the house and traverse the slippery footpath to a ridge overlooking his village where he could see the Pacific Ocean. There he would spend hours straining to see if Japanese ships were anywhere on the horizon.

In the motionless morning hours he often felt his way

through the narrow hallway, moving past his parents' bedroom up to the attic. He liked to listen to Franklin Roosevelt's fireside chats, speeches given occasionally by the American President to encourage his citizens and inform them about developments in the war. As Miguel remembered, it was "like hearing the voice of America itself." Although he couldn't understand English, the voice soothed him. "Roosevelt had two tones," Miguel recalled, "strong, and stronger." It reassured him that the marching cadence of this man's calm, implacable voice could cut through miles of static-filled air to stir the morning quiet. Beneath the jumble of strange sounding words, Miguel was able to hear a message, as though sent in secret code directly to him: "Don't worry Miguel, I will keep you and your family safe."

Fifty-five years later, unable to move from his bed, looking back on his life, Miguel longed to have that radio by his side. "If I did," he said, "I would listen closely in the night for the voice of my homeland." He was convinced that beneath the wavy voices and popping transistor tubes, he would hear another encoded message: "Miguel, it is not well to die so far from your home."

It was a message he had been receiving in momentary mental pulsations he called "flashes"—composite memories that flared like plumes of swirling images from his life in Chile. They arrived suddenly, plunging him into a world part real, part mystical. Like the preternatural attic of his youth, these flashes connected him to distant lands and people. They came in transient collages of sensation: the sound of water splashing off pebbles as it trickled down rivulets of meandering mountain earth; the pungent smell of wet leaves hanging thick in morning fog; the clack of a wooden cowbell blending with the call of a seabird and the sound of his mother clearing her throat. They were imagistic, sensuous experiences, magically mundane. They percolated from the spring of his innermost self, connecting him to his homeland and, as he put it, drawing him closer to God.

Unfortunately, when the flashes passed he often felt a

furrow of lingering sadness. It was as though roots that had long been dormant had begun to grow once more, only to be severed by distance and lost time. "I would give anything," he said, "to see my village again."

Miguel's diagnosis was metaphorical of his circumstances. He was not dying from a single disease, but from a syndrome called Adult Failure To Thrive: an ambiguous diagnosis which meant he was dying from a combination of factors that, if taken separately, were not life threatening, but together were potent enough to be terminal. Essentially, he was worn out; like a salmon longing to return to the place of his birth only to find every stream and river blocked by walls of stone and packed sand.

He and his wife, Nica, had been happy in Chile, but when Augusto Pinochet had seized control of the country everything had changed. Pinochet was an ironhanded dictator intoxicated with delusions of his own importance. He used reckless force to murder or exile whomever he caught in the widening net of people and groups he supposed were his enemies. Miguel and Nica lived in Santiago. He was a doctor working at a pediatric clinic in a poor neighborhood. He objected to Pinochet's seizure of power and spoke openly about his belief that if the *Generalissimo* were not stopped, his reign would be a cataclysm of corruption, violence, and paranoia.

"I should have known better than to speak so freely," he said.

Before he could elaborate, Nica interrupted him with the speed and authority of an arrow released from a taut bowstring. "What you did was right Miguel. I'm proud of what you did, and so were your patients."

History is mixed when it comes to telling stories of those who stand against the cruelty of false leaders. For Miguel and Nica, it meant banishment and exile. Soldiers with machine guns kicked open the door of their apartment one night and ordered Nica to make them coffee while they ransacked the home searching for "evidence." When Miguel objected, he was told to shut up and informed that he was under suspicion of anti-government activities. Any pretense would have suited and it was a foregone conclusion that the men would find something on which to hang their outrageous charge. In Miguel's case, they found it in a book that reproduced a map of Russia. "I was surprised," Miguel said with a somber laugh, "that the soldiers knew what a book was, much less how to read one, perhaps that is why they were drawn to the pictures."

They were ordered to pack a few things and taken, along with their infant daughter, Mia, to a containment area: an antiseptic way of saying a prison. This part of the story was murky, since neither Miguel nor Nica liked to talk about it. Memories of their imprisonment were guarded, it seemed, by lingering sentinels wielding bolts of low thunder which muffled the tales of their suffering. Their narrative quickly jumped to their departure for the United States about two months later.

Although Miguel appreciated America as a refuge for his family, it was not his home. It was an inscrutable land and he was unschooled in its tacit subtleties and brawny excesses. He felt condemned to walk forever as a stranger. "It's different," Nica explained, "when you come to America because you want opportunity and you're motivated to be here. We came because we were ordered to leave a home we loved."

Nica's philosophy was that you accepted things as they were and went on with your life. She claimed she rarely thought about Chile, whereas Miguel thought about it constantly. Even after twenty-three years he could not numb the stabs of psychic pain that often visited him, reminding him of his long exile. He had been driven from his home, separated from family and friends, insulted, abused by those willing to use violence and force. Helpless to protect his wife and daughter, he had been torn from the very ground of his existence. As he put it, "I lost my past, present, and future, all in a single day." From the time Pinochet's men had arrived at his door, Miguel harbored a gnawing sense that his life had gone irreparably wrong.

263

According to Nica, he was never the same after that. He was "heavier" as though carrying burdensome thoughts. He was more anxious about the future and didn't laugh as much. Even the luminescence of his deep spiritual life dimmed for a time, flickering in the thin air of incomprehensible upheaval. Ultimately though, it was his family and his spirituality that sustained him through these difficult times. "My spirit-life," he said, "has always been the raft that has kept me from sinking."

Even as a child, Miguel had been enthusiastic in cultivating "rapport with God." Maybe it was his mother's infectious piety or an uncle who served as the village's only priest. More likely, he thought, it was his immersion in a natural world through which the undiluted voice of transcendent spirit could sing. "Walking in the hills," he said, "always reminded me that I was part of a larger world of spirit." It was a world that encouraged him to see with the discerning eyes of a mystic. His spiritual life became inextricable with his homeland. "When they separated me from my land," he said "they separated me from God."

Despite his regrets, he and Nica had done well in America. After leaving their home with little more than a suitcase, Miguel wasn't able to get a medical license and had to work odd jobs to support his family. For the rest of his life, he would feel a deep loss of purpose, denied his role as a healer and community caregiver. While they learned English, Nica worked taking care of children during the day and Miguel eventually found a job assisting with medical research. They had a son, Carlos, and by the time Miguel accepted hospice care both children were on their way to earning college degrees.

Reflecting on what they had accomplished in their lives Nica was moved to tears, "I wish you could have met Miguel before he got sick," she said. Despite his quiet sadness, he had been outgoing and affectionate with his family. "He was the wise one," she said, "always there to lean on."

As Miguel absorbed the impact of his approaching

death, thoughts of Chile swept in like a river swelled with melted snows from distant mountains. Although Pinochet continued to rule Chile, Miguel had always assumed that, at some point, he would return to his home before he died. After his diagnosis, it sunk in that he would never again look out across the hills of his childhood toward the Pacific. It was shortly thereafter that he began having his memory-flashes. In these moments he felt confident and peaceful, but he was unable to draw any lasting nourishment from them. "I wish that I could live in those moments," he said. But they arrived and disappeared like stray winds blowing through a grassy plain.

One day when I arrived for a visit, Miguel's gray eyes seemed to be looking beyond the walls of his room. He picked up a small red rock from his bed table. It was flecked with silver and black. Turning it in the light, it seemed like a prism through which he might channel Divine power if he could only learn its secrets. Carlos had asked an aunt to send something from his father's homeland and the rock had arrived recently in the mail.

"There was a remote place, a sacred place, in the hills near my village that only I knew about," Miguel said. "This piece of earth reminds me of that sacred place." Lost in thought, he talked as if in a trance. "I would go there to talk with God. And God would talk to me. I think God is trying to tell me something with these flashes. I wish I could go to that place to ask what he would have me do."

The place, he said, was a small alcove of moss-covered rock hidden in the side of a steep hill. His memory was as clear as a cloudless winter sky as he described how he had stumbled upon it while exploring an isolated region of the forest. With no paths or streams leading there, surrounded by thicket, the hill was hard to reach. For Miguel, it became his sacred mountain.

He meant it literally when he said God talked with him. He had heard God's voice as clear as a bell the first time he had visited. It frightened him and he ran away. Unnerved, he decided not to go back. Then he had a vision

265

that told him that if he returned he would be protected by God's love. Soon it had become a retreat to which he would go to feel connected to the Spirit of all things.

Sometimes he just sat there quietly, "waiting for the Spirit to send down His poetry." Other times he prayed fervently for assistance with some knotty problem or asked forgiveness for perceived transgressions. He did not make the journey to this place, which he called mini-pilgrimages, very often. It was difficult to reach, and more importantly, since it was a place where he stood in the immediate presence of God, he only went when he was unable to find guidance through more conventional channels. "I didn't want to ask God to do all the work for me," he explained.

Except for Nica and his children, he had never told anyone about this place. But now, in the disarray of a life unwinding to its end, he longed for that direct, immediate knowledge of God's presence. "If I could go there, I would ask God what happened to that little boy that he has become such a tired old man? I would ask if that spirit still lives in me, or if it died long ago."

No question so neatly encapsulated his struggle. He was tired to his very bones, yet his spirit, his life-force, was emerging in radiant flashes. It was an evocative paradox. On the one hand, he was worn down from life's sadness, disappointments, and his belief that his separation from the dark Andean soil was obstructing his ability to hear God's voice. On the other hand, his life was awash in spontaneous moments of complete peace, luminescent with evidence of his unbreakable ties with his homeland and God. Two channels had etched their way into his heart, one leading into despair, the other peace. For Miguel it had long been so, but in his final weeks these competing trickles had been cleaved into roaring cataracts sweeping him in opposite directions.

"If I could only hear that voice again." It was like a refrain.

As we talked about his experiences, he began to suspect that his memory flashes might be fragments of God's voice distorted by the static of a material world. If so, what was the message? I reminded him how he used to listen to Franklin Roosevelt's strange sounding words as they sparked and simmered from his radio. Somehow, he had intuitively decoded an important message within the tones and rhythms of the garbled sounds. What might the message be in this case? What was God trying to tell him?

He considered the question silently, finally saying, "I think that God is telling me that he is with me, even here in this barren place, and that my spirit still reaches my homeland. Maybe he is telling me that I do not need to hear his voice in the same way, if I only listen more closely."

Nica had come in during the conversation and was sitting on his bed. He looked to her for confirmation. She agreed, but thought there was something more. She reminded him that not all of his flashes had been of their lives in Chile. Some contained images from their lives in the United States, such as those involving the birth of their son or family trips to the seashore. "I think," she said, "that God also wants you to know that you have continued to walk your true path even in coming here [to the United States]." Miguel's face brightened as he thought about this. As we discussed it further, his optimism grew. Maybe Nica was right; maybe he had deciphered an important message.

The next time I saw him, his confidence about this had waned, replaced by uncertainty. As is often the case, the balm of healing insight rarely insulates us entirely from the icy fingers of doubt. In his youth, communications with God had been unambiguously clear. To rely now on messages that were transient and cryptic made him wonder if his spiritual connection had, after all, been irreparably frayed. He was afraid that unless he recaptured this mystical source of insight he would not know whether to trust himself to truly know whether he had heard God's words. He prayed for clear, unequivocal directions.

His sad longing for home fused with a sense of disconnection from Spirit, making the silence hang like a gray cloud.

No amount of earthly conversation could lessen his

doubts. I thought it might help him to think about things in the metaphorical mental pictures of a story. I knew Miguel was familiar with the history of some of the Indian tribes of North America. After he and his family were expelled from Chile, he had studied the plight of the Incas of South America during the period of Spanish conquest. Brutish and greedy invaders had destroyed the Inca's world and Miguel felt a significant kinship with them. This had led him to make an informal study of the Indians of the United States. They had also been exiled from their homes and sacred places, pushed into "containment areas" and forced to watch helplessly as their families suffered.

I asked if he knew anything about Black Elk, a Lakota holy man. He did not, but he was intrigued. Black Elk was born into a time of chaos. During his lifetime he lost many friends and family members to violence and dislocation. The land of his people, his traditions, his entire way of life, had been taken away. He was forced off his sacred Black Hills onto an impoverished reservation. Despite this, Black Elk's connection with God grew strong and he became a healer. Like Miguel, in his youth he had learned to hear the words of the Great Spirit with crisp clarity.

Even so, Black Elk questioned his understanding of God's messages and often doubted himself. His life full of hardship, he wondered if he had truly lived his life as God had asked. In old age, looking back on a time long vanished and, at times, longing for days past, Black Elk learned that if he listened closely he could still hear the soft thunder of sacred wisdom as it rolled across the western valleys. Miguel had grown into manhood hearing stories. He was eager to hear the tale of Black Elk.

II

Black Elk's people loved their country. It was as though the Great Spirit had tied them to the land using invisible cords. In the center of it all stood the Black Hills—

an earthen pillar of mountains rising from the plains like a beautiful poem. Standing Elk (a contemporary of Black Elk) remembered how the Lakota "would rove all around [the Black Hills, and] when they were in need of something they could just go in there and get it." It was plentiful with animals of all sorts. Pine trees grew straight, providing everything from firewood to tepee poles. It was also a sacred place and people climbed its peaks seeking visions and guidance from the Great Spirit. When Black Elk was born in the early 1860s, the Black Hills were the center of his universe.

He was a member of the Oglala tribe, one of the seven tribes of the Teton Lakota (also known as the Sioux). Further east were the Yankton and the Santee Lakota. By the mid-1860s, a flood of white prospectors was invading Oglala land, scrambling to reach the newly discovered goldfields in Montana. Black Elk remembered these early years of his life as being "like some fearful thing in a fog, for it was a time when everything seemed troubled and afraid."

Making matters worse, when the Santees fought a disastrous war against soldiers and settlers in the east, a wave of dispossessed Indians was pushed onto the northern plains. Though the United States was embroiled in the sprawling violence of the Civil War, the government sent nearly five thousand troops to fight the Lakota. Black Elk later recalled that, "every one was saying that the Wasichus (whites) were coming and that they were going to take our country and rub us all out and that we should all have to die fighting." For most Oglalas, losing their country and being rubbed out were synonymous. They drew strength from the land; it connected them to the Great Spirit. When the soldiers came, Black Elk's people were prepared to fight.

The epicenter of the ensuing war was the Bozeman trail, a shortcut to the Montana gold mines running through the heart of Lakota territory. Fighting for their homes, families, and future, the Lakota were a formidable foe, tenacious enough that by 1868 the United States decided to sue for peace. An Oglala leader named Red Cloud spoke for all Lakotas when he said to Federal representatives that, "The Great Spirit raised me in this land, and has raised you in another land. What I have said I mean. I mean to keep this land."

The United States agreed to abandon its forts along the Bozeman Trail and recognize Lakota ownership of their traditional homeland. The treaty that ended the hostilities also stipulated that, "No white person or persons shall be permitted to settle upon or occupy any portion of the territory, or without the consent of the Indians to pass through the same."

Although Black Elk was very young, he remembered this time clearly. It was amid his relief that the war was over that he heard the first of many voices emanating directly from God. "I was out playing alone," he remembered, "when I heard them. It was like somebody calling me, and I thought it was my mother, but there was nobody there." Although he later recognized this as the first step on his path toward becoming a holy man, at the time it puzzled him and "made me afraid, so that I ran home."

A short time later, while practicing with a bow and arrow, he spotted a bird that, to his astonishment, spoke to him. "Listen!" It said. "A voice is calling you!" When Black Elk looked up, he saw two men descending from the sky "headfirst like arrows slanting down." As they moved toward him they turned into geese and flew away. "Then they were gone, and the rain came with a big wind and a roaring." When he returned home, he told no one about what had happened. He was unsure what the vision meant. Although he was becoming increasingly porous to the realm of spirit, he was confused and frightened.

For the next few years, as Black Elk remembered it, "the voices would come back when I was out alone, like someone calling me…" As a young man, however, he was more focused on learning to hunt and becoming a warrior. He pushed his spiritual experiences into the back of his mind. When messages are sent from the Great Spirit, however, they have a way of gaining our attention no matter how we may try to avoid them.

At nine, he suddenly collapsed and could not walk. The next day, when his people moved camp, he had to be pulled atop a pony drag, his arms "swollen badly," and his face "all puffed up." Later, he drifted into a coma. For twelve days he hovered near death, at times barely taking a breath. With his parents and siblings huddled around him in worry, Black Elk experienced a sweeping vision that changed his life forever.

He was transported into the sky and taken to a place where "white clouds were piled like mountains on a wide blue plain, and in there thunder beings lived and leaped and flashed." There he stood before six "Grandfathers" whom he recognized as "the Powers of the World." They had summoned him to give him sacred powers, including the ability to heal and conduct important rituals. They encouraged him to keep a strong heart in the years ahead, predicting that his "nation on the earth will have great troubles."

The Powers told him he would be helped throughout his life by "thunder beings" that arrived with the rain, thunder, and wind. He was given prophetic visions of his people's suffering. He knew intuitively they would become sick, die in large numbers, and many would lose hope. And he knew that the bison would disappear and the Lakota nation would be ripped apart by war and starvation. As he absorbed this grave message, the Grandfathers gave him reassurance and guidance.

In a distant time, beyond the horizon of looming disaster, he was able to see a time of hope for all people. "I saw," he recalled, "that the sacred hoop of my people was one of many hoops that made one circle…and in the center grew one mighty flowering tree to shelter all the children of one mother and one father. And I saw that it was holy."

After completing this remarkable journey, he returned to the material world and awakened in his family's tepee. "I was sad," he said, "because my mother and my father didn't seem to know I had been so far away." In the days following, he felt awkward and preferred being alone. People noticed his behavior. Whirlwind Chaser, a holy man (Wichasha Wakan), said to Black Elk's father, "Your boy there is sitting in a sacred manner. I do not know what it is, but there is something special for him to do, for just as I came in I could see a power like a light all through his body."

Black Elk had experienced what the Lakota called wakan, "sacred and incomprehensible power," usually imparted through visions and dreams. Those sensitive to its low vibration were often summoned to walk the path of holy men and women. For all Lakota, the partition between the visible and invisible world was thin and insubstantial, but for those filled with wakan the spirit world infused everything and made their lives like an unending prayer. After his vision, whenever a thunderstorm approached, Black Elk "felt happy, as though somebody were coming to visit me."

The Grandfathers told the truth when they said his people would walk the "black road" of suffering. In 1874, the United States, ignoring its promises, sent a military force into the Black Hills. George Custer, who the Lakota called Long Hair, led the expedition under the pretense of conducting a survey, but the Lakota knew he was looking for gold.

When Custer found it, a frenzied herd of miners once again swept into Lakota country. Black Elk remembered that they seemed to be "flowing into the Hills and becoming rivers..." Some Indians, like Crazy Horse and Sitting Bull, wanted to fight. Others, like Red Cloud, counseled patience and accommodation. Black Elk's family joined Crazy Horse. "[M]y father told me," Black Elk recalled, "we were going back to Crazy Horse and that we were going to have to fight from then on, because there was no other way to keep our country."

By June 25 1876, several thousand Indians from all the Lakota tribes, as well as friends among the Cheyenne and Arapahoe, had gathered along the Little Bighorn River. Earlier that month, they had defeated an army led by George

Crook, sending the soldiers into a hasty retreat. Many believed no other bluecoats would be foolish enough to attack such a large number of Indians, but Black Elk had premonitions of impending catastrophe. "I thought of my vision," he said, "and suddenly I seemed to be lifted clear off the ground; and while I was that way, I knew more things than I could tell, and I felt sure something terrible was going to happen in a short time. I was frightened."

When George Custer happened upon this meandering village of tepees, he acted with his customary brashness and aggression. He split his men into two groups and attacked. When the soldiers swept down on the river, the teenage Black Elk retreated to a stand of trees. "I stayed there in the woods a little while and thought of my vision," he said, "It made me feel stronger, and it seemed that my people were all thunder-beings and that the soldiers would be rubbed out." Some of the soldiers fighting under Marcus Reno survived (as well as others under Frederick Benteen who had been sent on a reconnaissance patrol), but all those who went with Custer were killed.

Among whites, clamors for revenge arose almost immediately, stiffening the army's relentless pursuit of those Lakota not willing to move to a reservation. In the next several months, as bone-freezing winter winds stung the plains, the Lakota grew hungry and shivered beneath the constant threat of violence. Not surprisingly, many surrendered. Black Elk was confused. The traditions and cohesion of his tribe were disintegrating. Within this chaos, he doubted himself, doubted his vision. "[I]t made me very sad;" he said, "for I wondered if maybe [my vision] was only a queer dream after all."

He was living a contradiction. He had had a direct experience of God's presence and it had made him stronger. On the other hand, the lives of his people were falling apart and he was powerless to stop it. Like the splintered bones of the great bison herds beginning to litter the vast grasslands, death's lonely visage cast a shadow across his people. For Black Elk, the tension between the world of spirit and the world of men was drawn tighter than a sacred drum. Even his travels in the spirit world could not insulate him from sadness and doubt.

Eventually, even the indomitable Crazy Horse surrendered along with the remnant of his followers. A short time later a soldier murdered Crazy Horse during a scuffle at Fort Robinson and a small band of his followers, including Black Elk, broke away and headed toward Canada. They intended to join Sitting Bull who had already crossed the border, moving beyond the grasp of American soldiers forever. By then Black Elk was a young man, uncertain about his abilities as a holy man, but eager to help his people repair the broken hoop of their lives. He often wondered when his power would grow strong enough to make a difference for his suffering people.

Canada turned out to be a place of bitter exile. Although there were no bluecoats, there were conflicts with the Crow and the Blackfeet. Winters were harsh and there were fewer and fewer buffalo. They missed their relatives and longed for the familiar hills, grassland, and rivers of their country. During these years, Black Elk continued to receive guidance from the Great Spirit. Even in a land far from the sacred Black Hills, he worked to cultivate his spiritual power, deepening his understanding. He "prayed for help from the Grandfathers" and they "sent the thunder beings" to protect his people.

In 1880 Black Elk joined the growing number of Lakota returning to their homeland and surrendering to authorities of the United States. By then, he was openly pursuing the path of a healer, praying, invoking God's spirit, and mastering important rituals. His efforts focused on bringing peace to his people and sustaining them through their hardship. His connection with the spirit of storms and thunder was powerful medicine, giving him the ability to heal others.

The next years were among the hardest. "All our people," Black Elk lamented, "now were…scattered here and there across this hungry land, and around them the Wasichus had drawn a line to keep them in...The people were in despair. They seemed heavy to me, heavy and dark; so heavy that it seemed to me they could not be lifted; so dark that they could not be made to see anymore." Despite the depth of his sorrow Black Elk continued to nurture the otherworldly thread connecting him to God.

Although there were differences between the Lakota and other Indian tribes, they had all been driven from their homes and seen loved ones killed from violence, disease, and starvation. Their customs, rituals and beliefs had been profaned by the degradations of reservation life. Their bison were slaughtered, the white man's whiskey had devoured many despairing souls and steel bayonets had severed the cords that bound them to their land. Their sacred places, the graves of their ancestors, had been profaned and overrun. In the bleak trough of their grief, many longed to return to a time before everything had changed. They looked back to a time before everything had gone horribly wrong.

In 1889, word spread that a prophet had come speaking words for all Indians. Many were eager to hear his message. This prophet's name was Wavoka. He was a Paiute living on a reservation in Nevada. When the Lakota sent a small party to hear his message, they learned that Wavoka had received a vision. "I went up to heaven," he told them, "and saw the Great Spirit and all the people who had died a long time ago. The Great Spirit told me to come back and tell my people they must be good and love one another, and not fight, or steal, or lie. He gave me a dance to give to my people."

He said that if the people performed this "ghost dance," it would herald the return of all their dead relatives and all the buffalo that had been killed. The Americans would disappear and the Indians' land and traditions would be restored.

To a people whose collective grief seemed as boundless as the sky, it was a compelling prophecy. Soon Indians throughout the west were gathering to perform the ghost dance. On the Lakota reservations, nervous white officials banned the practice but the Lakota danced anyway. Ominously, they added "ghost shirts" to the ritual in the belief that these garments would protect them from enemy bullets.

Initially, Black Elk was skeptical and thought that "maybe it was only the despair that made people believe, just as a man who is starving may dream of plenty of everything good to eat." However, as his people's enthusiasm grew, he began to hope that the ghost dance was pointing the way back to the red road of peace and he joined the dancing.

When reservation officials became alarmed that Sitting Bull might throw his considerable influence behind the ghost dance, reservation police showed up at his cabin to arrest him. A fight broke out and Sitting Bull was killed. When word spread that their great leader was dead, a wave of panic and foreboding rolled through the hearts of Indians and soldiers alike. In December 1890, edgy troops massacred a band of peaceful Lakota camped along Wounded Knee Creek.

In many ways, the slaughter sounded the death knell for the traditional ways of the Lakota. The force of the United States was overwhelming and, as Wounded Knee demonstrated, it was also merciless. The war for their homes and their way of life had ended in defeat. Black Elk witnessed the carnage at Wounded Knee. Looking back on it some forty years later he said:

> I did not know then how much was ended. When I look back now from this high hill of my old age, I can still see the butchered women and children lying heaped and scattered all along the crooked gulch as plain as when I saw them with eyes still young. And I can see that something else died there in the bloody mud, and was buried in the blizzard [that followed]. A people's dream died there.

Before he had reached the middle of his life, Black Elk had seen his people's way of life destroyed. Expelled from their country, those who survived were confined on small, destitute reservations. Despite his efforts to help his people and his desire to hold fast to the power of the Great Spirit, he watched helplessly as loved ones died from diseases he could not cure. As his tribe dissolved into collective depression, holding to his great vision in such a confusing world was difficult. At times his energies waned. Although Black Elk never questioned the wisdom of the Great Spirit, he doubted himself. He wondered if he had really understood his great vision and the words God had spoken to him.

He continued praying for guidance, serving his people as best he could. He even tried to assimilate the spiritual teachings of white culture. When Jesuit missionaries arrived on the reservation he studied their religion and found that it contained much of the same wisdom and depth of his traditional ways. Seeing a common spiritual path, Black Elk blended his traditions with new insights and imagery. According to his daughter, Lucy, he often "related [Bible] Scripture passages to things around him, and he used examples from nature—making comparisons of things in the Bible with flowers, animals, and even trees."

At times, however, even the merging of these two deep rivers of faith was not enough to counter his sadness and grief. He wondered if, despite his best efforts, he had failed to walk the spirit path true to his early vision. As doubts came and went, he longed for direct affirmation and guidance. As he approached seventy, he lamented that he was "a pitiful old man who has done nothing, for the nation's hoop is broken and scattered. There is no center any longer, and the sacred tree is dead."

But it was not dead.

In 1931, after telling his story to writer, John Neihardt, Black Elk went with a small party into the Black Hills. On a clear day atop Harney Peak, in the Black Hills, he gave thanks to the Great Spirit. "Again, and maybe the last time on this earth," he said, "I recall the great vision you sent me. It may be that some little root of that sacred tree still lives. Nourish it then, that it may leaf and bloom and fill with singing birds." Neihardt recounted what happened then:

> We who listened now noted that thin clouds had gathered about us. A scant chill rain began to fall and there was low, muttering thunder without lightning. With tears running down his cheeks, the old man raised his voice to a thin high wail, and chanted: "In sorrow I am sending a feeble voice, O Six Powers of the World. Hear me in my sorrow, for I may never call again. O make my people live!"
>
> For some minutes the old man stood silent, with face uplifted, weeping in the drizzling rain.
>
> In a little while the sky was clear again.

III

There are times when the din and clatter of events can all but drown out the voice of one's intuition, higher possibilities, or God (however one conceives God). Remembering to be still, if only for a moment now and again, in order to hear this voice is important. For many of us, there are special places where we hear this voice more clearly. For Miguel it was in his homeland at his sacred place, for Black Elk it was in the Black Hills. For others it may be along the bank of a river or in the quiet of a summer morning. Others may hear the stirrings of this voice in certain situations—holding a son or daughter, listening to a familiar song, or when they are acting with compassion. We are not dependent, however, on these situations and places. No matter where we are or what we are facing, guidance is always there when we pause to listen closely.

Miguel felt a kinship with Black Elk. Like the Oglala

holy man, he had become a doctor in order to serve others and help them heal. He asked some questions about the specific diseases the Lakota holy man had encountered.

"I am sure his prayers for his patients were powerful," he said, "but without antibiotics, he must have felt deep pain. He could do nothing to stop the dying."

He asked questions about how the Indians were treated once they were in captivity, eager to discuss the dehumanizing, humiliating effects of reservation life.

"When I was held by Pinochet," he said, "they did things to me and my family that I was powerless to stop. I prayed to be given the strength to stop it, but I could not."

He looked at me solemnly, his eyes searching to make sure I understood that he was talking about something he had tried hard to forget, something about which he rarely spoke. I encouraged him to elaborate and he looked up at the ceiling as though it were drawing him back to an earlier time. "There were times in my cell when I wished I would die. The only reason I didn't was because of the lives of my wife and daughter."

He paused. "I see now that it was also God's grace that saved me, but at the time I was sure God had abandoned me. Or maybe I had lost my ability to hear his voice."

"What did it mean to you, not being able to hear God's voice?" I asked.

"It meant that I," he searched for the words. "It meant that I had lost my way and would have to survive in a world that no longer honored who I was. Everything was lost. I had to find my way in a strange land without being able to know God's reassurance."

If Chile had become a strange land during Pinochet's rule, the United States was even stranger. Miguel and his family had arrived cloaked in the anonymity of outsiders worried about what their future might hold. Always for Miguel his attempt to adjust to his new culture and find purpose in his life was coupled with grief over the loss of his traditions and the people of Chile.

"I found much in my new life to cherish," he said,

"but sadness surrounded me always like a shadow. Maybe I let sadness fill my heart so much that it drowned out God's call."

It is impossible to know what was in Black Elk's heart as he attempted to adjust to the realities of the reservation. He had grown up traveling freely across the northern plains, connected to a natural world infused with Divine energy. Now many of his friends and family were dead, his people suffering. On the reservation, whites intent on forcing him to adopt new ways assailed his traditions, rituals, and religion, as well as other aspects of his culture such as language, clothing, and family structure.

Like all the Lakota, Black Elk was faced with the challenge of trying to find meaning in this strange and hostile world. As the Lakota strained to understand what had happened to them and rebuild the sacred hoop of their lives, Black Elk's role as a healer was vitally important. He continued to serve his people as a spiritual leader, conducting prayers and rituals, visiting the sick. By combining teachings from the Christian religion with the truths of traditional Lakota beliefs, he attempted to help his people hold their balance amid the falling pieces of their lives.

When he met John Neihardt, Black Elk did not expect to live much longer. He had never spoken about the details of his vision. Doing so might have diminished its power and perhaps even trivialized its sacredness. But in the fading light of his life he wanted to find a way to honor and sustain the ways of his tribe, and share some of the core truths of the Great Spirit.

By then Black Elk was nearly blind. Images of the material world were quickly being sucked into darkness. Long before, he had learned that the material world was not real anyway. He knew that there was a "world where there is nothing but the spirit of all things. That is the real world that is behind this one, and everything we see here is something like a shadow from that world." Despite the violence and melancholy of his experience, it had not destroyed this real world from which he had always drawn strength and wisdom. Many times he had doubted himself and questioned his actions, but always he remembered what was real.

On Harney Peak, when he heard once again the responsive roll of thunder and felt the cleansing droplets of rain, he knew that he had been true to his vision. His connection with the Great Spirit was still strong, despite all the hardships he had known, and despite his doubts.

"If I could stand on my sacred mountain again," Miguel mused, "I wouldn't ask for thunder and rain, I would ask for sunlight and the sound of the ocean birds."

His voice lifted and seemed to convey a sense of inner resolution. "One of the hardest things during all my years here was that I no longer heard God speak and I wondered if he had forgotten me...But I see in these flashes I've had, that he is calling me again as I prepare to die." As he thought about this, he smiled. He realized that his connection with the world of Spirit was still strong, so many miles from the hills of his childhood.

As Black Elk neared the end of his life in 1950, he made it clear to those around him that he was ready to die. His daughter recalled that he told her "I am old, so don't take my death too hard. Do not mourn a long time, you know I will be happy. My suffering will be over, and I will have no more hurt. Pray for me as I taught you to pray in the early days."

During his long life, sudden changes or anomalies in the natural world had often been signs of the Great Spirit's presence. On the day Black Elk died, the evening sky became vibrant with the electric colors of the aurora borealis. William Siehr, a Jesuit missionary living on Pine Ridge Reservation, said that the night sky "was just one bright illumination. I never saw anything so magnificent. I've seen a number of flashes of the northern lights here in the early days, but I never saw anything quite so intense as it was that night." Even in death, Black Elk's spirit was strong.

Miguel continued to have instantaneous flashes of

281

blended memories. As he was dying, they occurred so frequently he said it felt, "like all of my life is being lived over again and I'm seeing that even the darkness of my path contained rays of light."

He was also seeing, as he put it, that "it is time for me to die, and I may do so with peace in my heart."

"Aside from God, where does that peace come from?" I asked.

"From knowing that I have done what I could, despite my shortcomings."

Beneath the harvest of images was this insight that lighted his last days. Although his life had been hard and he had often grown weary, even depressed, he had tried to live in a sacred manner—holding to his own transcendent vision and trying to keep it in the center of his thoughts and actions. In the end, the flashes conveyed a fundamental message: His life, despite all the pain, had been a good one, well worth living. His connection with God, however hard it had been for him to hear God's voice amid the distorting echoes of his suffering, had always been strong.

Section Five
What Lies Before Us:
Moving On

*What lies behind us and
what lies before us are tiny matters,
compared to what lies within us.*

Ralph Waldo Emerson

The death of a loved one, while an end of sorts, is also a beginning—the beginning of a journey into grief and adapting to a world where our loved one is no longer physically present. Even if our friend or family member had been sick for a long time and we had seen death approaching, we could not have prepared ourselves entirely for this journey. Even when we have used the time before death wisely and done everything we could to smooth the transition and say goodbye, we will not escape moments of longing to have the person back so we can say "I love you" or "I will miss you" just one more time. When we have cried and grieved for weeks or months prior to death, we will have more tears yet to shed.

Grief and bereavement is a mixed, often confusing experience. It is individual enough that there are no good road maps; much of the way ahead has to be discovered and navigated as it occurs. Family and friends, support groups and self-help books, can all be important and helpful, but the journey cannot be escaped any more than the pain it involves can be avoided.

And it can be a long journey—much longer than the week or two taken away from the office during which the "normal" routines are suspended. In fact, normality and grief often intersect each other, blending into a rhythm and balance that changes over time as we explore who we are and what the world is like without our wife, husband, parent or child. It may feel like we are getting back to normal one minute, only to be plunged back into grief the next. Sometimes emotions may seem to come "out of nowhere," or apparently conflicting emotions like sadness and joy may arrive simultaneously. Many people even wonder if something is wrong with them or if they are going crazy, mistakenly thinking that they should "be over it by now."

It is important to allow oneself time to grieve and to allow oneself to be imperfect and, at times, numb, scared or confused. As with the previous sections, this part of the journey also brings gifts and possibilities for growth and healing. Whether it be insights into one's deeper self, an awareness of one's inner-strength and courage, or an enhanced appreciation for the value of our own and our loved one's life, there are countless opportunities if we only continue on as best we can.

The final two chapters are about people on this journey. In Chapter Thirteen, Gerta is paralyzed by her fear, anger, and disbelief that Bill has died and "abandoned" her. Letting go of these strong emotions and the thoughts that sustain them is hard, but it's the only way she can regain her balance. Wes, in Chapter Fourteen, had believed that the hardest challenge would be taking care of his beloved wife as she deteriorated physically. He expected that after she died, the way ahead would be much easier. He was surprised at the intensity of his grief and his realization that the path before him would get harder before getting easier.

Chapter Thirteen
John Wesley Powell Exploring
the Grand Canyon: Letting Go of
Fear, Anger, and Mistrust

Gerta was worried about who would take care of her husband, Bill, after she died. The fact that her health was good, and that he was a hospice patient diagnosed with chronic obstructive pulmonary disease (COPD) was immaterial. She was convinced that she would die first. "I know what the doctors think," she said, "but they don't understand Bill like I do. He would never leave me behind." In her mind, Bill would fight his illness, however long it took, to spare her the pain of being left alone or, as she put it, abandoning her. After fifty years together, it was hard for her to conceive of being without him; to the extent that she could, she was terrified. She had simply made up her mind that she would die first, and that was that.

Given her certainty about this, I asked if she had been having any thoughts about killing herself. Absolutely not, she said, she was "a survivor." To illustrate the point she offered a quick tour of her childhood as evidence. She was born in Germany in 1928. By the time she was seventeen her mother was dead, her brother was missing, and one of her sisters had turned to prostitution in an attempt to survive. Her voice was like tempered steel as she culled through memories of these years, salvaging the fragments of a life broken into ruin.

World War Two had wrecked her father. He had deserted from the German army and was captured by American troops in France as he tried to find his way back from the fighting. When he finally straggled home, he spent most of his time drinking and staring listlessly at the kitchen walls, catatonic with depression. Driven by poverty and hunger, Gerta and a younger sister gathered whatever valuables they could find and piled them into canvas sacks. Straining with the weight, they hiked out into the farmlands to barter vases, candelabras and silverware, for eggs, butter and flour. "Everything I had was taken from me," she said, "except my will to survive." She *was* a survivor. The one thing she was afraid she couldn't survive was Bill's death.

They met in 1945, when he was a soldier. Their connection was instantaneous and within a month they were married, despite her father's "violent objections." As Gerta explained it, "You don't waste time when you've been through war. You learn to grab the good things while you have them, and hang on tight." After Bill was discharged, he and Gerta moved to his hometown in the mountains of North Carolina. He got a job installing air conditioners and she threw herself into refining her English and learning the customs of small town America. Once her confidence allowed, she began doing volunteer work, soon becoming the director of a shelter for abandoned dogs and cats. Her determination to find homes for these animals was so palpable that people soon began calling her the rescue lady.

A few years later, they moved to a larger town so Bill could attend school to become an electrician. She continued her rescue work by adopting and finding homes for dogs the local animal shelter was planning to euthanize. To accommodate her canine charges, Bill fenced in their backyard and built twelve doghouses. For years their home was awash in activity centered on the dogs, many of which they adopted themselves. When Bill got sick Gerta tried to cut back, but he encouraged her to continue taking the animals. He and I rarely talked, due to his difficulty breathing and the high physical cost of having conversations, but he explained his reasoning about this.

"She thinks she's saving the dogs, but when I'm dead those dog will save her."

When Gerta talked about her life she divided it into two parts: before she met Bill and after. Before Bill, her journey had been a chilling testimony to life's precariousness and the constancy of suffering. It had started well enough. Her family had been comfortable and she had lived her early years insulated from the larger political and cultural tensions leading her country into fanaticism and war. In the span of five nightmarish years, however, most of the people she loved had been killed, emotionally shattered, or had disappeared. Her country was destroyed and several of the children she had played with when her parents "weren't looking" had been sent to Nazi death camps along with their families. At seventeen, she remembered, "My life was nothing but suffering and fear. I had no hope for anything in the future except more suffering and fear. If I'd died then, it would have been a relief." When she met Bill, everything changed.

After that, her story was one of redemption and rebirth. Although she'd given up any hope of experiencing love or a better future, he awakened an incipient longing for both. Soon, she was feeling the unfamiliar stirring of new possibilities. Buoyed by her nascent hope and love for Bill, she agreed to move to the United States. "This was a big deal," she said, "since my family and friends were in Germany, and American troops had just helped the Russians destroy my country."

She had vivid recollections of their first day in America—spotting the skyline of New York from the bow of a ship, passing small towns as they traveled south by train, spending their first night in Baltimore. With Bill, her life had regained hope and purpose. As she saw it, he had saved her life; and then he had made it worth saving.

They had no children and had invested much energy in making their marriage what Gerta called a "union of spirits." She was at ease in America and had insisted on visiting as much of her adopted country as they could. Every summer for nearly forty years they had packed up their car and driven "out west." She loved to recount stories from their travels and repeated her favorite ones whenever she had an audience. She especially liked to tell about the time they visited the Grand Canyon and she talked Bill into riding mules down to the Colorado River. Afterward, they had to extend their visit because Bill was unable to sit for more than a few minutes at a time, which made driving impossible.

As Gerta reminisced about their lives, it was easy to understand why she clung so tightly to her belief that Bill wouldn't die before her. She had lost everything when she was young. He was the foundation upon which she had rebuilt her life. The thought of being alone was too much for her to contemplate.

Initially, Bill's response to his illness was to rally his strength and push himself to survive at any cost. As the ravages of his disease took a toll, however, Gerta's insistence that he get better began to feel less like encouragement, and more like pressure to do the impossible. The more he deteriorated, the more adamant she became that he fight harder. The more she demanded, the more he tried to push her away. Inadvertently, Gerta's single-minded insistence drove a wedge between them at the very time when closeness would have been the most consoling.

By the time I met them, Bill had withdrawn and Gerta's demands that he "stop giving up" were only making things worse.

"I can't talk to her," he said. "I'm going to die and instead of helping me she gets mad at me for being sick."

"Do you think it's really you she's mad at, or is it something else?" I asked.

"I don't know about the psychological stuff," he said. "All I know is it feels like she's mad at me and blaming me for getting worse."

"Can you talk with her about it?"

"No. I just don't have the energy right now to get into an argument or try to explain things when I don't think she's listening anyway."

I offered to facilitate a conversation between them but he declined.

"What can you do about it then?" I asked.

He thought about it and finally said, in a tired, gravelly voice, "At this point I just don't give a damn."

"Is that really true?"

He shook his head as though unsure and threw his hands up. "Who knows?"

When death approaches and separation is imminent, people often feel conflicting internal currents of acceptance and resistance. It can feel like a tug-of-war within one's self. On the one hand, we may know that death is near and search for ways to make the most of the time remaining, while on the other, we may protest, avoid, or hope to escape death. Ideally, the blending of these currents is accomplished in a fashion that allows a family to support one another and share this time in a way that is meaningful to them. Sometimes, however, the tug-of-war moves to the surface and leaves people who love each other pulling in separate directions. For Gerta, there was no acceptance. She resisted death with all her might, leaving no room for Bill to be tired, or sad, or for either of them to prepare for his death.

Bill had accepted that he was dying, but he didn't know how to tell Gerta this. The more she rejected the reality of his physical decline, the more eager he became to "be done with all this." Rather than spending their time looking back on their lives and finding ways to say goodbye, they engaged in an exhausting battle of wills that only depleted them further. Bill was tired, his impulse was to detach himself from the world around him. Unfortunately, Gerta's demands led him to detach from her as well.

During my conversation with Bill I offered a few thoughts on the ways fear and emotional pain can appear as demands and judgments. At such times, it can be helpful to keep what a person says or does in a larger context. Often what they are trying to communicate is buried beneath words that are poorly chosen and reflect stress and fatigue. He listened intently. Near the end of our visit I asked him again what he thought Vera was *really* trying to say when she placed such demands on him.

"I guess," he said, "she's really trying to say she loves me and she's terrified."

"Would it help to keep that in mind?"

"Yeah."

"How do you really want to spend the rest of your life?"

He scratched his head and gestured as if to indicate that he had no idea. As the room hummed with silence, he finally said, "I want to let go of my anger about this and make sure Gerta knows how much she means to me."

"How are you going to do that?"

He thought for a minute. "I guess I'll remind myself that she is scared and that I won't get another chance to do this. Once I'm gone, that's it—*hasta la vista*."

If Gerta's unbending faith in Bill could have cured his disease, he would have been restored immediately to full vigor. But his illness was terminal and progressed rapidly, impervious to her hope. Throughout his last few days, Gerta remained convinced he would bounce back. She refused to speak about the possibility of death. After he ebbed into a coma, she sat by his side and pleaded with him to wake up. When friends from the shelter realized he was dying, they began stopping by regularly and even offered to spend the night. She declined their offers, assuring them their concern was unwarranted since everything was "going to be fine."

When Bill died, Gerta was sitting by his bed. A friend was present and was surprised when Gerta seemed unfazed, calling the hospice nurse and matter-of-factly asking her to come by whenever she got a chance. When I arrived, Gerta's voice was low and laconic. Her eyes were unfocused as though she was trying to awaken from the haze of a deep sleep. She talked about her dogs and the weather, seemingly unconcerned about Bill's death. Someone happening upon the scene might have assumed he was simply sleeping in the bed beside us.

Though surprising to her friend, Gerta's reaction is a fairly common one. Shock has many handmaidens: numbness and dissociation are among them. When the people from the funeral home arrived, she discussed the details of the obituary, signed the release form, and scheduled memorial services as though in a trance. After they left, however, the psychic dam holding the reservoir of her pain suddenly broke, nearly collapsing her weary frame. As she shook with sobs, she steadied herself by placing her hands on her knees. By sheer willpower, she composed herself and moved silently through a narrow hallway into the room where Bill had died and slammed the door. After the torrent of intense feeling had subsided, she returned to the family room, apologized for her "outburst," and offered to make coffee.

The ebb and flow of early grief can be a fickle thing, controlling its tides is nearly impossible. For weeks Gerta oscillated between a numbed, muted version of "normality" and a blend of sadness, fear, and anger. She searched, almost frantically, for ways to escape the gravity of these painful emotions. She tried distracting herself by keeping busy and surrounding herself with people. She adopted several dogs and lavished them with affection, but the pain refused to subside. She even tried giving herself "pep talks" about why she shouldn't feel what she was feeling. Not surprisingly, this didn't work either. Her experience was normal; chastising herself only created guilt. Trying to distract herself or fill her aching heart with love for her dogs so quickly only brought disappointment.

I saw her a month or so after Bill's funeral. By then, her anger had overshadowed everything else. Every thought seemed leavened with rage. She was angry with Bill for "giving up." She was angry with God for "taking him from me." She was angry at hospice for "letting him die." Most of all she was angry with herself for letting him smoke all those years and not making him go to the doctor sooner. The sum of her rage boiled down to two inflexible beliefs: Bill shouldn't have died and she shouldn't have been left in the world without him.

As though rejecting what had happened, Gerta had packed all the photographs of her husband in his bedroom and locked the door. For weeks she had refused to enter. It was like a vault into which she tried to push everything—her sadness, fear, and her longing to have Bill back. Everything, that is, except her anger. To this she clung as though gripping an outcropping of rock above a precipice of despair. At times the energy of her rage and the distraction it provided seemed like the only thing keeping her from plunging into depression.

Beneath her angry exterior, she missed Bill deeply. So deeply that a couple weeks later she finally decided to unlock the door to his room and face her pain. She bolstered herself as though preparing for an exploration into an unknown land and spent the entire day going through his belongings, cleaning photographs and crying.

Once the door to her deeper feelings was opened, it nearly overwhelmed her. Anger had been less threatening than sadness and aloneness. Without its protective insulation she felt like she was "falling into a bottomless hole." When I visited her a week later, she spoke in monotones, her face vacant of expression. Grief had swept her up like a whirlpool. She had withdrawn from her friends and she continued to reject Bill's death. She told herself that, since he had left her alone he must not have really loved her. If only he had fought harder, she thought, he'd still be alive. Her beliefs were so firmly rooted they were resistant to any attempts to see things from another perspective. In her sadness, she wished that she had died instead of him.

Bill's challenge may have been dying, but Gerta's was to continue living.

On our next visit, Gerta was tired. She said she was having trouble sleeping and had been having strange dreams. On a positive note, she was trying to tell herself that Bill had fought as long as he could and it was simply his time to go. It was a good step, but deep inside she didn't really believe it and remained bewildered and disoriented at being left behind. Her voice quivered. She said she wanted to die. Whatever ballast had helped her navigate life's rapids in the past seemed to have disappeared along with her beloved partner; it was as if she was being drawn into a canyon whose walls were as oblivious to her broken heart as granite.

She'd been having a recurrent dream. At first, she

had dismissed it as the convoluted firing of overwrought nerve cells, but when she had it a second, then a third time, it got her attention. In the dream she and Bill were climbing a hill. It was a warm day and the sun was comforting as they ascended a gentle slope covered with grass and wildflowers. As they climbed, the grade became steeper and the sky grew threatening with clouds. As a storm gathered, the ground changed from grass to rocks. They began losing their footing. Eventually the hill became so steep Bill had to hold Gerta's hand to help her move toward the summit. After much exertion, they found their way blocked by a vertical wall of rock. Bill searched carefully for a toehold and finally found one on a small outcropping. He scaled the wall and lodged himself onto a ledge several feet above. He extended his hand down to Gerta and she grasped it tightly. As he pulled, she struggled to propel herself upward by moving her feet against the wall. About halfway up, one of her feet became stuck in a rock. At the same time, Bill's hand became translucent and started "turning into jelly." She was trapped, unable to move forward because of her foot, and quickly losing her hold on Bill's hand as it became more amorphous.

She squeezed with all her strength but her grip loosened further and her feet slipped from the rocks. As Bill's hand dematerialized, she realized she was dangling above a bottomless canyon. She screamed in terror while Bill smiled at her calmly and lovingly. His whole body started to glow with a radiant light. In a gentle and knowing voice he said, "It's alright Gerta. It's time to let go." Just then her grip broke and she started to fall. As things faded into darkness, she woke up feeling agitated and afraid.

She knew it meant that she had to "let him go," but she protested that she couldn't. She wasn't sure how to, and even if she could, she didn't really want to. She was puzzled by how the dream ended. Bill's assurances seemed incongruous with her falling. Was he mistaken? Or did he know something that she didn't? It was a confusing question and, given her distress, she was not inclined to trust that it would be "alright."

"What might Bill know about you or your situation that tells him you'll be alright?" I asked.

She thought about this for a minute or so and tentatively suggested that "Maybe he knows I've fallen from cliffs before, and that I am a survivor."

It was a good insight, but frustration and discomfort blocked her from exploring it further. "I don't want to talk about this anymore," she said, giving me an exaggeratedly menacing look. She wanted to continue our visit, but she needed some time to think about things.

Her dream reminded me of a story about John Wesley Powell, one that called to mind the visit she and Bill had taken to the Grand Canyon. Maybe it would give her some insight or provide some images that might help. I offered to tell her about Powell. In 1869, he was the first person to explore the Grand Canyon. Along the way, he found himself in a similar situation to the one in Gerta's dream: clinging to a sheer wall of rock, unable to move forward and afraid to let go. At this frightening crossroad Powell had a choice. He could continue clinging and remain stuck, eventually falling into the canyon below when his strength finally gave out, or he could let go despite his fear, trusting that he would be safe.

II

John Wesley Powell was a survivor. At thirty-five, he had survived the seemingly boundless slaughter of the Civil War, a painful wound at the battle of Shiloh, and the surgeon's blade that cut off his right arm. After Shiloh he returned to command his Illinois artillery battery and lived through three more years of terrible battle and punishing bloodshed. On returning to civilian life he had adjusted to the chronic, often agonizing pain emanating from his wound and the limitations of living with one arm. He was tough, and although he had seen how tenuous life could be, he was unflappably optimistic. In 1869 he was planning an expedition as dangerous as any Civil War battlefield, confident that, once again, he would live to tell about it.

He intended to travel down the Green and Colorado rivers and explore the Grand Canyon—a vast blank space on the American map that nobody had dared attempt to chart. Even John C. Fremont, whose wide-ranging explorations had earned him the nickname "pathfinder," recoiled at the prospect of such a journey. No one, Fremont said, could be found who was "bold enough... to undertake a voyage which has so certain a prospect of a fatal termination." Most people agreed. Powell, however, along with the nine intrepid men who would accompany him, begged to differ.

At the time, the sum of what was known about the upper Colorado was scant. Enough, however, was clear to make anyone think twice about such a journey. Powell knew, for example, that the altitude of Green River Station (in present-day Wyoming, where he intended to begin) was 6,100 feet above sea level. The region below the canyon, where he planned to end his trip was only 700 feet. Somewhere in between, there was a decline in elevation of about 5,400 feet. For all he knew, he and his men might encounter plunges that dwarfed Niagara Falls, which tumbled over cliffs a mere 170 feet high. He knew there were places with towering cliffs surrounded by desert that would make escape by land nearly impossible. They would have no choice but to follow the river, whatever its perils. He also knew there were no settlements in the region where they could rest, re-supply, gather information, or abort the trip. They would be entirely on their own.

The small group accompanying Powell was a mix of out-of-work mountain men and ex-Union soldiers. One of them was his brother, Walter, who had been an officer in the Union Army before being captured by Confederates. He'd survived battles as fierce as any, as well as various torments as a prisoner of war. By many accounts the experience had wrecked him. When he returned from the war he vacillated between quick-tempered, sometimes violent fits of aggression, and simmering withdrawal. Walter was along because his brother was going, the rest of the men were motivated by a combination of adventure, the notoriety that goes with being the first to explore an uncharted region, and the prospect of beaver pelts.

On May 24 1869, they launched their boats into the cool waters of the Green River. The plan was to follow the Green south until it joined with the Grand River to form the Colorado. From there, they would follow the Colorado through the Grand Canyon. The Green was a formidable river in its own right, not to be taken lightly. Although it was known to a handful of Indians and trappers, parts were unexplored. It was swift and powerful, passing through steep canyons with rocks and boulders cluttering the riverbed, forming rapids and whirlpools.

The men traveled in four boats specially built for the trip. Three were identical and measured twenty-one feet. They were built of oak reinforced for strength and durability. Powell described them as "staunch and firm." The fourth was lighter and built of pine. At 16 feet, it was designed for speed and maneuverability. Since they had no idea what they would find, Powell and two others traveled ahead in the smaller boat to scout the terrain. With the thundering sound of the river often muffling their voices, when they saw a problem or needed to relay information to the others, they communicated using signal flags and hand signs.

Although some of the men had experience on rivers, none had ever tried to paddle through currents, much less rapids, as strong as these. Not surprisingly, Powell and his men spent their first few days running aground on rocks and sandbars, losing oars, falling overboard, and being spun about in the whirlpools that formed in eddies and between rocks. After a few days grappling with the oars, Billy Hawkins wrote in his journal that the men quickly realized that they "knew nothing about a boat." If they wanted to survive, they would have to learn the hard way.

On May 30, they approached the mountainous canyons of Flaming Gorge and their first set of truly dangerous rapids. The water churned into large waves as it crashed in all directions over boulders, some of which were submerged, others piercing the surface like stone teeth. As they approached the foaming tumult, Powell recalled that, "untried as we are with such waters, the moments are filled with intense anxiety...and we thread the narrow passage with exhilarating velocity, mounting the high waves, whose foaming crests dash over us, and plunging into the troughs, until we reach the quiet water below."

As "exhilarating" as these rapids were, they were benign compared to what lay ahead. Many, like the ones they saw two days later at Red Canyon, couldn't be taken head on and the boats had to be "lined." Lining was a backbreaking job. First the boats were unloaded of about 7,000 pounds of gear and supplies. Then, each one was tied with rope and pushed into the river. As the men clung to the rope with all their strength, they worked their way down alongside the rapids to calmer waters. When the boats were safely downriver the supplies had to be hauled, usually over a slippery and uneven strip of rock-strewn earth, and repacked. It was as dangerous as it was strenuous. One slip on a wet rock or a foot caught in a crevice could mean a broken leg, a cracked skull, or a man drowned.

As testimony to their endurance, when camp was set in the afternoon, rather than rest, the men hunted, fished, repaired boats, and wrote in journals. Powell usually climbed to the highest point he could find to survey the river and do some additional exploring. For him, the most compelling reasons for the journey were discovery and knowledge. He was determined to study everything from rock formations to plant life. He rarely left camp without one of his barometers or some other piece of scientific equipment with which to take readings or measurements. He may have lost an arm, but his wiry body and unbending focus more than compensated as he scaled cliffs and balanced on ledges.

By June 8, the party had entered the gloomy Canyon of Lodore. The canyon walls reached over 2,000 feet and the Green was a menacing cauldron of crashing and cascading chaos. In his journal, George Bradley described one stretch as "the wildest rapid yet seen." In spite of Bradley's misgivings, they decided to attempt the rapids by boat. Unfortunately, the water was too rough and one of the larger boats was smashed. The three-man crew managed to pull themselves onto a rocky sand bar. Later, the expedition was able to salvage the barometers and a keg of whiskey. The rest of the boat's supplies were gone. In addition to hundreds of pounds of food, they had lost all of the maps drawn by Oramel Howland, the group's cartographer. They named the place Disaster Falls.

The loss of so much food was a serious problem. The explorers were only two weeks into a journey they expected would take ten months. Just as frustrating, more stores were in danger of spoiling because of the constant soaking from waves spilling into the boats. George Bradley noted forebodingly that, "Our rations are getting very sour from constant wetting and exposure to a hot sun." Things were complicated further by the fact that the hunters were coming back empty-handed. The problem, according to Jack Sumner, one of Powell's ablest men, was that "There is nothing in this part of the country but a few mountain sheep, and they stay where a squirrel could hardly climb." They hadn't even reached the Colorado and they were faced with a threat as potentially lethal as the river: starvation.

Through June and early July they moved forward. Sometimes their progress was quick, sometimes painfully slow. Every time they passed a creek or river emptying into the Green, it meant more water pressed into the lean channels of the canyons ahead. To the world outside, it seemed like they had fallen into a bottomless hole and disappeared. Rumors circulated that they were dead. Articles appeared in newspapers like the Chicago *Tribune*, informing readers that the expedition had perished.

On the morning of July 8, the men were camped beneath cliffs and ledges so barren that Powell was "minded to call this the Canyon of Desolation." He and Bradley set out to ascend the heights carrying one of the precious barometers. The hike started well enough. "We start up a gulch;" Powell wrote, "then pass to the left on a bench along the wall; then up again over broken rocks; then we reach more benches, along which we walk, until we find more broken rocks and crevices, by which we climb; still up, until we have ascended 600 or 800 feet, when we are met by a sheer precipice."

It was a formidable cliff, dwarfing the men. Most people would have turned back, eager to return to the banks of the river, but not Powell or Bradley. Handing the barometer to his friend, Powell reached up to a rock with his only arm, intent, as usual, on going first.

He braced his feet into narrow crevices and pulled himself up a few feet. Once he was safely perched, Bradley handed him the barometer and climbed a few feet higher than Powell before turning to retrieve the barometer. In such a manner, they slowly made their way toward the summit, passing the barometer back and forth as they inched forward. It was an arduous way to climb and, in a way, metaphorical of their entire trip. They had worked hard cautiously moving into unfamiliar territory. Their way had been punctuated by unexpected dangers and flirtations with disaster. In the end, if they survived, their reward would be increased knowledge and perspective.

Well into their ascent, Powell got stuck. He had locked his feet into the cliff and grabbed hold of an outcropping of the rock over his head. Here he found that he couldn't go forward or back. Had his right arm not been severed he could have reached up while holding on with his left and found a way to extricate himself. Without his arm though, all he could do was hang on, unable to move without releasing his grasp, unable to release his grasp, lest he fall to his death.

When Bradley understood Powell's plight, he made his way to a shelf of rock above. He looked for a tree or branch to lower to Powell but there was nothing suitable. He thought about using the barometer case but realized it wouldn't work. All the while, Powell's strength was being taxed by the necessity of supporting his entire weight on the edge of the cliff-face. His legs began to quiver and sweat poured from his body. Simply staying in place required all the strength he had. Even Powell had limits though. He couldn't remain pinned against the wall much longer before his hold broke. They had to do something or he would fall to his death.

At that moment, Bradley had an idea. Like the rest of the crew, he was wearing only long underwear. Wet clothes weighed a man down enough to drown him in a fast moving river and they had learned to dress light. In a scene that would have been comic were it not a matter of life-or-death, he removed his drawers and lowered them down. As they dangled just behind Powell's head, the expedition's commander was faced with another challenge. In order to reach the lifeline and gain his rescue, he would have to release his grip and trust that he would be able to grab the line as he reached back. If he missed, he would plunge into the canyon. It was a pivotal moment and Powell's life hinged on it. Willingly or unwillingly, he must let go. The result would be a plummeting fall or salvation.

III

Like Powell and Gerta, any of us can find ourselves dangling above our own Canyon of Desolation at one time or another in our lives. Clinging, as Gerta did, to anger, blame, or denial may keep us safe for a time, but eventually it saps our strength and leads to paralysis or despair. If we are to extricate ourselves, we have to find a way to loosen our grasp and reach toward something else. Somehow we must trust that, beyond the rocky walls, we will be safe and find our way.

Although Gerta had made progress through the winding gorges of her grief, she was stuck on a cliff afraid to let go. As we discussed the story, she was particularly struck by the image of falling into the canyon. "I know what that feels like," she said, absorbed in thought.

She realized there were two things to which she was clinging: anger and fear. Her angry ruminations converged like the point of a bayonet, insisting that Bill shouldn't have died. It had become an intractable belief and it was immobilizing her, making it impossible to move through or beyond her grief.

While anger made it hard to accept that Bill was dead, fear made it difficult to trust that she could continue living without him. Fear made it easy for her to justify withdrawing from people and the world around her. She could hide behind it and vanish into the expansive space of her grief—rather than finding a way to continue living, she fantasized about dying. Between anger and fear she was pinned against a precipice as real as any Powell and his men ever encountered. "There is a big difference between me and Powell," she said. "He had something to grab hold of, and I don't."

She was afraid that if she let go, she would surely fall. Without anger to focus on and fill her with energy, and without escapist thoughts of dying to distract her from the challenges of living, she might plunge into her underlying sadness and be swept away.

"Is there really nothing?" I asked. "Suppose you decided to let go and reach out, what do you think you might find to hold onto?"

She was silent. Rather than fill the silence with words, we let it expand like a river released from a narrow channel and freed to sweep across a large horizon. Finally, she said, "Maybe I'd find my dogs."

It was a toehold. Once she found it, she found others, such as her community of friends, prayer, writing in her journal.

Pulling himself as close to the cliff as he could, Powell let go of the rock and reached back. As his weight shifted he grasped the outstretched line and clung to it with renewed vigor, trusting in his connection with Bradley. The two men's fate merged as Powell slowly made his way forward. In the act of letting go, he was freed from the constraint of the wall and able to gain another foothold. Eventually he reached the top of the canyon.

Once he and Bradley were back in camp, the band of explorers moved forward. Paddling down the Green, they made it to the Colorado River where they braved hair-raising rapids, boulders the size of buildings and clumps of floating debris bigger than steam locomotives. They contended with hunger, anxiety, and longings to reach the end of their journey and be reunited with loved ones.

Soon they were inside the Grand Canyon with its otherworldly walls and spires reaching thousands of feet above them. By the end of August, the most treacherous looking rapid they had ever seen blocked their way. At first Powell was convinced that "To run it...would be sure destruction." Unfortunately, there was no way to portage around it. After spending an entire day surveying the river, Powell almost decided to abandon the expedition, but after intense contemplation he chose to move forward.

Three of his men, however, decided otherwise. The brothers Oramel and Seneca Howland, and their friend, Bill Dunn, had had enough. They informed Powell they would rather take their chances trying to scale the cliffs and cross the desert than face the river. Despite Powell's attempts to change their minds, they were determined to leave. Their departure was amicable and the men named the place of their parting Separation Rapids.

As ominous and impassable as the rapids ahead looked to Gerta, during our conversation she suddenly realized that they seemed vaguely familiar. As a young woman whose life was thrown into disarray by war, she had been in this place. After her town and family had been nearly destroyed, she had felt intense anger and had rejected everything that had happened. "I just kept saying to myself, over and over, this should never have happened." There were days when she secretly longed for death to come and end all the pain. Despite the bleak horizon and the uneasy rhythm of anger and fear, she had survived and gone on to live a meaningful life. She had done it before, and she could do it again.

Able to see the way ahead more clearly, Gerta gingerly put her oar in the river and began to paddle beyond her anger and anxiety. She decided to make an appointment with a bereavement counselor. It was a step that affirmed her life and openly acknowledged her separation from Bill. It was hard, but she was determined to survive and live as best she could. When the visit with the counselor went well, she scheduled regular sessions to get help charting the furious rapids and elusive eddies ahead.

Shortly thereafter, she visited Bill's grave— something she had avoided ever since the burial. Slowly, her anger faded and, despite her fear, she didn't fall into paralyzing, lonely despair. Hope began to rise, as if from a spring renewed by rains that had long been absent. Hope that her life still had purpose and that things would get better.

Two days after Powell and his men survived the monstrous rapids that sent three of their party scrambling into the desert, the expedition reached the end of its journey. They had been prepared to continue, but breathed with relief when they realized they were near a settlement, back in charted territory. Separation rapids turned out to be their last great challenge. The Howland brothers and Bill Dunn were not so fortunate. They were killed attempting to pass through the desert. The identity of their assailants is still the subject of debate.

A couple years later Powell returned to map more of the mysteries of the Grand Canyon. In 1872 he brought a photographer on his second expedition down the Green and Colorado rivers. Although the challenges of this journey were formidable and the dangers plentiful, never again would he, or anyone else, need to explore the Grand Canyon without at least some inkling of what lay ahead.

I called Gerta on the telephone as the anniversary of Bill's death approached. She sounded upbeat and talked about her activities at the animal shelter. She'd accepted a paying job there and was working three days a week. She spoke about Bill's death openly, without a hint of anger or anxiety. As the anniversary neared, she was finding that she was "reliving" much of what had happened the year before. This time, however, rather than crippling her, the anger and fear passed through quickly like loud unruly waves. She had made it through the year and was better prepared for the ups and downs that still lay in store. Like John Wesley Powell, she was confident she could find her way.

She had survived. She had learned to trust that she could let go of anger and not be destroyed by the pain of separation. She missed him and, at times, she was still very sad, but she had learned to accept things over which she had no control. Having reached beyond the ledge, she found she could survive the unthinkable. Her life could hold, once again, some measure of happiness. After all, she said, "It's what Bill would have wanted."

Chapter Fourteen
Lewis and Clark at Lemhi Pass:
When a Tough Journey Gets Tougher

"When I saw her that night the ice around my heart began to melt and fall away." Wes's voice rippled with emotion as he recalled how he and Shirley met. He remembered small details of that night, like water pooling on patio tables under cold margarita glasses, the smell of insect repellent, and the way Shirley's eyes radiated with vitality. He mustered his nerve, asked her to dance, and they lost track of time gliding beneath the plastic outdoor lights strung above a makeshift dance floor. "Not exactly the Waldorf," he joked, but by the end of the evening they were falling in love.

Ten years earlier, when Wes's first wife, Anne, had died, he had assumed that, except for the technicality of continuing to breathe, his life was over as well. Those intervening years before he met Shirley had been hard and he seldom spoke about them. He was unsentimental about suffering and saw no reason to talk of such things. When he did, though, he conveyed a sense of bleak, isolated anonymity, as though straining alone against the relentless current of an unfriendly river.

Although these years stood like a vast blank space, there was one experience from this time he discussed freely–his journey retracing the expedition of Meriwether Lewis and William Clark. In the early nineteenth century Lewis and Clark had explored the American West all the way to the Pacific Ocean. Wes had long been drawn by their courage and determination. He had enthusiastically studied their travels, reading their journals as though they were sacred texts. Summoning the eloquence and imagery of a master storyteller, he often spoke of his trip in their footsteps as though it were the needle of some existential compass pointing into his deepest self.

Shortly after Anne died, he decided to follow their route west. It was something he had always dreamed of, and, in the shadow of his painful loss, the idea of disappearing for a while was as compelling as his affinity for these early explorers. He began in Pittsburgh where, in 1803, Lewis had fitted out a large keelboat before heading down the Ohio River en route to a rendezvous with Clark. Wes followed their route down the Ohio, up the Mississippi, onto the Missouri River and all the way to the Rocky Mountains. Unlike Lewis and Clark's self-proclaimed "Corps of Discovery," however, he never made it to the Pacific. He stopped at Lemhi Pass in present-day Idaho, a nondescript mountain passage that marks the continental divide—the place where rivers begin running west instead of east.

It was here Lewis and Clark first saw the formidable barrier of seemingly endless mountains that awaited them. Standing at Lemhi Pass, they had realized their journey was going to be far longer and much more arduous than they had ever imagined. It was a pivotal juncture for the expedition. Wes was cryptic about why he stopped here.

"I just couldn't go any further," he said. "That was far enough."

When he returned to Chicago it no longer felt like home. The bustle and energy of the city had offered excitement when Anne was alive, but now it caused pain. She seemed to peer out of every store window and arrive with each breeze, especially those carrying the familiar aromas of a bakery down the street where she used to buy croissants every Sunday. Even the muffled thunder of the trains moving along the tracks conjured her memory out of their grimy steel and squealing brakes.

Acting decisively, he moved to a small retirement community in Florida where he settled into a routine of solitary walks, working in his flower garden, reading mystery novels, and writing poetry. On the surface it was a comfortable life, but it contrasted sharply with his years in

Chicago where, according to his daughter, Trudy, Wes had always been like a "prince at the ball." His natural gregariousness and humor receded into dormant slumber, as though he were hunkered down in the bracing winds of a long winter. He rarely spoke to anyone.

Initially his isolation was consoling. He was awkward being in the world without his wife and needed time to grieve. But as his desire for the company of others slowly returned, he found himself among strangers far from the friends he had left in his haste to escape Chicago. Eventually he forced himself to join activities and talk to some of his neighbors. "If I hadn't done that," he said, "I'd never have been at the dance where I met Shirley."

Within a year, Wes and Shirley were married. They were inseparable, as happy as either had ever been. In contrast to the preceding years, Wes's reflections on this time drew a rich picture of vibrant, flowering lives. Despite his metallic voice, Wes joined Shirley's choral group and learned to sing. Though she playfully chided him for his boyish romanticism, Shirley began reading some of Lewis and Clark's voluminous journals. "We did everything together," he said, "from dentist appointments to grocery shopping."

They spent three years enjoying every moment before Shirley was diagnosed with Amyotrophic Lateral Sclerosis (ALS), a progressive neuromuscular disease usually known as Lou Gerhig's Disease. Volcanic shock rocked them as they struggled to absorb this horrible news. Although they knew it was fatal, they pursued treatments and therapies in the hope of extending her life. Nothing worked.

Both Shirley and Wes were in their eighties and had known from the start that their time together would be relatively short, but accepting that it would end much sooner than either had foreseen was difficult. As Wes put it, "We'd just found each other and WHAM! We're faced with this." In response, they honed their focus down to each day as though it were a lifetime in itself, squeezing it hard for its full potential. As each day passed, they knew their time of

308

separation was closer. Beneath the surface, sadness and fear came and went in a steady pulse.

As Shirley weakened and began losing muscle control, she and Wes moved to North Carolina to live with her son Patrick. This was a difficult decision, but the cumulative impact of her disease made it necessary. Her physical limitations and growing need for assistance stood in contrast to her earlier life as a ballet dancer. Strength, flexibility, and creative expression had been as natural to her as breathing. They were woven tightly into the fabric of her identity, an integral part of her assumptions about the future. These assumptions were shredded by the hard realities of ALS, which left her nearly incapable of voluntary movement.

Her communication was reduced to eye blinks. One blink for *yes*, two blinks for *no*. Her once subtle and expressive face was curtained behind a quiet, unflinching flatness. Behind the curtain, however, her mind was still razor sharp and her experience of emotion and ability to reflect on her circumstances was unaffected. As Wes put it, she seemed trapped behind a wall that let her look out at, but not participate in, the world around her.

Over the next year or so Wes and Shirley found ways to stay connected. Simply being together became an end in itself. Sometimes he read her poetry or reminisced about their lives, at other times they would simply nap side by side. Eventually, as her condition deteriorated, Wes began to speak of death. He used code words and euphemisms at first but eventually spoke more directly, without any encumbering verbal facade. She responded in blinks.

By then she was dependent on an oxygen concentrator to help her breathe and was spending most of her time asleep. They both knew she would die soon.

She was sleeping the day I met Wes. Thin and fit, he conveyed immense energy as we sat at the kitchen table discussing the time he and Shirley had spent together. The effect of Parkinson's disease was apparent in his slightly quivering left hand, but seemed of little concern to him as he explained the system he used to manage both Shirley's and his own medications. When I noted that he was taking cardiac medicine, he laughed and joked that he was racing her to the finish line.

When our conversation turned to her death, however, it became clear he had no intention of crossing the finish line first. His eyes flashed with gentle intensity as he spoke of his determination to live long enough to accompany her to the end of her life. He attributed his determination to a long career as a firefighter during which he had never left a building while someone was inside. It was an axiom: however perilous the flames, you stand by those in need until they are safe. The fact that he and Shirley were in love had distilled his determination into an essential and uncompromising potency. He would be there until the end. Period.

This focus offered little opportunity for him to think about what his life might be like after she died. Intuitively, he reckoned it would be a time of quiet reflection comforted by the knowledge that he had served Shirley devotedly. Twice during our initial visit he made allusions to doing his "grieving in advance." He expected that when she was gone he would feel relief at having done a difficult job well and at seeing Shirley's deep suffering finally come to an end.

As for the time before her death, Wes had already drawn a mental map of the terrain. On it he had charted many of the challenges he expected would emerge as he cared for Shirley in her last weeks. He saw himself rising to every challenge, foregoing his own comforts without complaint and tending to her as she breathed her last breath. He envisioned the time after her death as a sudden release from his anguish, as though the terrain were suddenly smooth, the slopes gentle and the winds favorable. Under the circumstances, it was a nice vision, but such mental maps usually fail in one way or another as the weight of actual events bears down.

On subsequent visits Shirley made it clear she was ready to die. In fact, she wanted to die. Once, her greatest challenge had been acceptance, now it was patience. Blinking eyes revealed a spirit that was tired and worn down. Haunted by thoughts that she was a burden to Wes, and afraid that her suffering was a punishment meted out by God, she struggled to find peace. Wes's attempts to offer reassurance seemed, at times, to be futile. They paled beside the simple act of just being with her in her pain and continuing to love her.

Although her last weeks were among the most difficult, Shirley appeared to die peacefully. Her struggle along the rough and craggy summits of a slow, heavy illness was over. The dull hum of the oxygen concentrator was finally quiet. Wes sat in this strange silence as two men from the funeral home removed a body that had once danced with vitality.

At such times, many people have a tendency to move toward others and draw support and strength from close relationships, but some, like Wes, are drawn toward solitude. In the surreal and hectic days following Shirley's funeral, Wes decided to make a quick get-a-way. He found it in a remote cottage along the Atlantic Coast owned by an old friend. He and Shirley had spent several weekends there. In the days after her death it was a place of peaceful sanctuary.

I visited Wes about a month later as he was packing to go back to Florida. He had returned to North Carolina for a few days to tie up loose ends. By then, grief had established an uneasy rhythm, never far away, yet receding enough to allow him to feel almost normal from time to time. We talked about Shirley and looked at some photographs he had found while sorting through her belongings. They had been taken during a vacation they had spent on the Gulf of Mexico. We commented on Shirley's beatific smile and laughed at Wes's colorful Bermuda shorts.

Despite his sadness, Lewis and Clark were never far from his mind. We spoke of their tenacity and recalled some of his favorite parts of their journey as though we were reminiscing about old friends. He seemed to gain strength as we did this and went searching for a large book buried under a stack of papers on a writing table. Soon we were studying maps of the Missouri River and paintings of Mandan Indians.

Our conversation moved between Shirley and the expedition until they were melded together like two tinctures forming a single color. Wes was surprised at the intensity of his sadness. He had genuinely believed that when she died the hardest part would be over and things would get easier. But no easy passage had opened up and his grief was overwhelming. The relief he had anticipated was indeed present, but so was the searing aloneness of separation. Although he had prayed for her to be released from her struggle, he yearned to have her back. The two years of her illness that had once seemed to move so slowly now seemed like a mere instant. Wrestling with sadness and fatigue, Wes looked at the ground and shook his head.

"I just didn't expect to hurt this bad. I really thought it would be easy from here."

We both swallowed hard, allowing the silence to lengthen unadorned by words or gestures.

I finally said, "Maybe you're standing at Lemhi Pass again."

His eyes watered briefly and he nodded his head in understanding. "Yep. That's it. I'm back at Lemhi Pass."

II

In 1803, the United States ended at the Mississippi River. The vast region from there to the Pacific Ocean was the subject of heated dispute. Much of it was claimed by European powers such as France, Britain, and Spain. Even Russia was eying parts of the Oregon Territory with its thriving otter skin trade. Further complicating things was the fact that the land was already inhabited by various Indian nations and some of them, like the Lakota and the Blackfeet, were powerful and determined to pursue their own interests. When President Thomas Jefferson sent a secret message to

Congress asking for funds to launch an expedition into this region he knew it would have to be approached delicately.

Jefferson was eager to explore this territory and take as much of it as he could for his new nation. His task was made easier when Napoleon Bonaparte of France agreed to sell the United States a huge swath known as the Louisiana Territory, stretching from the western bank of the Mississippi River all the way to the Rockies.

Jefferson's highest priority was to find a navigable water route that would connect the Mississippi to the Pacific Ocean. For three centuries men had been searching for a waterway through or around the Americas in order to pursue trade and profit in the Orient. They called this imaginary shortcut the Northwest Passage and Jefferson was certain it existed. Preparing instructions for the expedition's leaders, he told them "The object of your mission is to explore the Missouri river, and such principal streams of it, as, by its course and Communications with the waters of the Pacific Ocean may offer the most direct and practicable water communication across the continent for the purposes of commerce…"

To command the venture Jefferson chose Meriwether Lewis, a twenty-eight year old fellow Virginian. Lewis was an army officer with plentiful experience as a woodsman and formidable survival skills. He was also Jefferson's personal secretary. For two years the President had been grooming him for this journey, giving him regular lessons in cartography, botany, geography, Indian diplomacy, and steadfastly encouraging the young man's growing enthusiasm for the daunting task ahead.

With Jefferson's approval, Lewis offered joint command of the enterprise to William Clark, a tough, even-tempered woodsman who had ample experience with Indians and a knack for leadership. The two had met while serving in the army and had become close friends. Clark jumped at the chance to participate and the two made plans to rendezvous at Clarksville on the north bank of the Ohio River.

They understood their most important objective was

to discover, map, and lay claim to the Northwest Passage. Despite the fact that very little was known about the land they were planning to enter, both were confident they would find the passage by following the Missouri River. A few years earlier, American ships had charted the location of the Columbia River where it empties into the Pacific in present-day Oregon. They believed that the Columbia, when linked by a short portage from the headwaters of the Missouri, would provide the western flowing waterway to the ocean. They were sure that the hardest part of the journey would be moving against the onrushing Missouri River and ascending the mountains. After that, it would be much easier as the westerly currents of the Columbia River pulled them effortlessly down the gentle mountain slopes, landing them on the shores of the nearby Pacific. They had drawn a map in their mind as clear as any on paper, based almost entirely on "the geography of hope."

By July of 1803, Lewis was in Pittsburgh awaiting the completion of a fifty-five foot keelboat and eager to begin down the river. On August 31 he got his chance and, along with seven soldiers and a few recruits, he headed out onto the Ohio River. The Ohio was low. Progress was slow and required a tremendous amount of effort. When the keelboat couldn't be rowed or poled, it had to be pulled with ropes or pushed by men standing in the water. Writer, Don Holm captures the experience, noting that it "was hot and humid that autumn. The thermometer in the cabin often reached the high eighties. Days were filled with strenuous exertions, dragging the boats over the shallow riffles and bars and rowing through water stagnant with scum and fallen leaves of buckeye, gum, and red sassafras. Frequent stops were made at river settlements, hiring and firing crew members, buying supplies, engaging teams of oxen from farmers. There was little time for sleep..." Even after a grueling day's work, sleep was not an option until gear was packed or unpacked, camp prepared, meals made, watch set, and journal entries completed.

By the middle of October the group had muscled its

way to Clarksville where they met Clark and his slave, York, who would accompany the expedition. Staying long enough to select a group of nine young men from a pool of would-be volunteers, the Corps of Discovery was again on its way to the confluence of the Ohio and Mississippi rivers. From there they headed north on the Mississippi toward Saint Louis. On the Mississippi they encountered something that would be a constant challenge all the way to the mountains: moving boats against the current of a strong river. They quickly realized that this was a Herculean task that required more hands so they recruited additional men from the military post at Kaskaskia.

The commanders set up winter camp just outside Saint Louis, a city built where the Mississippi meets the mighty Missouri. Lewis and Clark spent the next four months drilling the men into a crack team, leaving no doubt this would be a military expedition with strict unwavering discipline. When Lewis was not overseeing the men, buying supplies, surveying the surrounding country, or writing reports, he spent every available minute studying maps and speaking with men engaged in the fur trade, trying to get a picture of what lay ahead.

Saint Louis was the hub of the Missouri River trade so finding men who had traveled the river was not difficult. Few, however, had gone beyond the Platte River and none had gone all the way to the Rockies. One who *had* reached the Platte was James Mckay. He gave Lewis a hand drawn map of the Missouri all the way to the villages of the Mandan Indians in present-day North Dakota. He also spent time answering Lewis's questions and making recommendations about the upcoming journey. Taking what he learned from Mckay and combining it with additional maps and conversations, Lewis probably had a clearer picture of the geography of the American West than any other American at the time. Still, he knew very little. More problematic were the things he thought he knew, which were flat-out wrong.

The map ended at the Mandan villages. After this the

course of the Missouri was mere speculation. Lewis knew where the Columbia ended but not where it began or how long it ran or what rivers it intersected. But on his mental map the way was clear. The Missouri continued on to the Rockies, which he believed was a single range of mountains no higher than the Alleghenies. From there, he thought, the party would find the Columbia nearby and it would take them to the Pacific, itself only a short distance, perhaps even visible from the crest of the mountains. With confidence in this map of their imagination, the explorers, now numbering forty, departed Saint Louis in the spring of 1804.

The swift current of the Missouri was fed by melting snow. Progress was slow and at times dangerous. Uprooted trees bore down on them like battering rams, combining into clumps to form floating walls that threatened to damage or capsize the boats. Moving forward was backbreaking work. With the river's constant twists and turns, a day's labor often found them little distant from where they had begun when the sun had come up. Much time was spent in the water, pushing the keelboat and pulling on ropes. The mosquitoes were torturous; dysentery and painful boils plagued the men. Even walking along shore was dangerous as large chunks of earthen bank frequently crashed into the roiling water. Rattlesnakes were common. The heat was punishing and relented only to make way for fierce storms with blinding rain.

As if in some natural tendency toward balance, there was also an incredible abundance of plants and animals, some of which had never been seen by citizens of the United States. The crew's journals are replete with descriptions of seemingly endless flocks of birds and schools of fish. Elk, deer, antelope, and buffalo provided regular fare at meals, as did the berries, plums and cherries growing along the shore.

By August they had passed the Platte River and entered lands inhabited by the various Indian tribes that lived along the northern plains. Jefferson had instructed Lewis and Clark to establish good relations with these tribes, since he hoped to gain control of the fur trade and ensure safe passage to future travelers. Beginning with the Poncas and the Omahas, the expedition began holding councils as it traveled up the river. There was little variation in their methods or message. They typically began with greetings and then, with great solemnity, informed the surprised Indians that they were now in lands claimed by the United States. They impressed upon the tribes the importance and benefits of allying with the United States, handed out gifts, and provided some display meant to reflect America's military might such as firing off the cannon mounted on the keelboat.

By and large these meetings went well, although tensions flared and almost led to bloodshed when they encountered the Teton Lakota. The Lakota were a powerful group of tribes, closely allied with the traders of the British Northwest Company. Jefferson had singled them out as a people on whom "we wish most particularly to make a favorable impression." Eventually, cool heads prevailed and open conflict was avoided. The impression, however, was not favorable for either the Lakota or the expedition.

In late October, with winter coming on fast, the Corps of Discovery finally arrived at the Mandan villages. The Mandan, along with their friends the Hidatsa, were the pivot around which the northern fur trade revolved. They lived in two villages along the river. In summer months it was common to find traders from the British fur companies, French trappers from Canada, an occasional Spanish trader, and Indians from many tribes gathered to exchange goods and supplies for pelts.

Winter months were extremely harsh, more so than any of the men had ever experienced. They quickly built a stockade on the riverbank opposite the village and prepared to face the frigid temperatures they knew would come. For the next four months they hunkered down beside the Mandans and prayed for spring. As he had at Saint Louis, Lewis spent much time attempting to gain knowledge about the river and mountains ahead. Having reached the end of Mckay's map, he was eager to extend it as far as possible. Although the Mandan had never been to the Rocky

317

Mountains, the Hidatsa had and they were happy to share what they knew. What they told Lewis justified his enduring hope regarding the Northwest Passage and must have greatly encouraged him. In his report to Jefferson, Lewis wrote that the "Indians inform us that the country on the Western side of this river consists of open and level plains" and that a river, which he "suposse[d] to be the S[outh] fork of the Columbia" was nearby and navigable to the horizon. Here was proof that a water route to the Pacific existed. All their hard work had paid off. Such thoughts must have warmed him as the arctic winds shrieked across the frozen plains of North Dakota.

By April the party was once again on the river. The keelboat was loaded with specimens of flora and fauna, as well as maps and reports, and sent back to Saint Louis with a detachment of soldiers. The rest of the expedition traveled west in two pirogues and six canoes dug out of cottonwood trees. Joining the group was a young Shoshone woman named Sacagewea and her infant son. As a child she had been captured during a Hidatsa raid on her people. She was familiar with the western mountains and would act as a guide. The commanders also knew they would need horses to make the portage between the Missouri and the Columbia and that Sacagwea's tribe could provide them.

Without the keelboat the Corps made steady progress up the Missouri, though the work continued to be extremely difficult. In May, while scouting ahead, Lewis saw the outline of the distant Rockies. They stood like stony Titans visible from hundreds of miles, much larger than he had imagined. He quickly realized "the difficulties which this snowey barrier would most probably throw in my way..." His misguided belief that the Appalachians were the largest mountain chain on the continent was immediately dispelled. For weeks these snow-covered behemoths waited on the horizon, at once beckoning and foreboding.

By mid-summer the expedition was approaching the foot of the mountains. By then, they had struggled past the great falls of the Missouri in some of the most taxing and frustrating weeks any of them had ever experienced. When the Missouri had forked, they had strained up the rising grade of the Jefferson River as its waters tumbled out of the hills, pushing them back at every stroke of the paddle. They had also become uncomfortably familiar with the stark ferocity of enraged grizzly bears. Now they were sure they only had to cross a single chain of mountains; one last challenge before they reached the much-anticipated Columbia.

It had been over a year since they had left Saint Louis. Many of the men had expected to be on their way back by now. Instead, the mountains stood in front of them like vigilant sentinels of hard packed earth and rock ready to resist their every movement. The impact of the men's ongoing exertions and constant exposure to the elements was exacting a heavy toll. Lewis's medical skills, always in demand for everything from eye infections to malaria, were pressed into service more than ever. Facing the great Rockies and needing every ounce of strength they could muster, the weary expedition resembled what historian Stephen Ambrose called a "walking hospital." They were sick and tired, and the Shoshone, on whose horses they so much depended, were nowhere to be found.

On August 12, 1805, Lewis may have consoled himself with the thought that things would soon be easier. As he and three others scouted ahead, they were about to reach Lemhi Pass, a vantage along a mountain ridge from which they would finally be able to see westward toward the Pacific. Perhaps Lewis would even be able to see the waters of the ocean. It must have been a moment of great expectation as he prepared to blend the geography of his mind with that of his experience. It had been a hard trip—the arduous labor ascending the Missouri, enduring extremes of blistering heat and biting cold, the portages across rocky thickets of prickly cactus, the sickness, the fatigue, the relentless vigilance required in an unknown land far from home. As Lewis approached Lemhi Pass, he hoped the worst was behind them. Soon the rivers would convey them forward, rather than work against them. The Pacific would emerge into view and they would be able to turn around and head home.

When Lewis and his men reached the crest of the pass, however, they did not see a sloping valley with a nearby river leading to the ocean. Instead, as Lewis later wrote in his journal, they saw "immence ranges of high mountains still to the West of us with their tops partially covered with snow." The Bitterroot Mountains—range after range stretched as far as they could see. Patrick Gass of the Corps would remember them as "the most terrible mountains I ever beheld."

There was no Northwest Passage. No river would carry them swiftly to the ocean. Winter would soon be upon them and they had no horses. The journey would be longer and harder than any had imagined.

III

There are times when the road we are on is hard and demanding. As our energies flag we may long for a place of comfort and rest. We may even convince ourselves that if we just cross the next river or scale the next summit our burden will ease and we will be able to cease our exertions. Though the summit may indeed bring relief, sometimes the terrain becomes even more difficult. Wes's journey, like that of Lewis and Clark, would be longer and harder than he expected. There was no Northwest Passage through which he could quickly traverse the landscape of his grief.

"Maybe that's why I never went past Lemhi Pass after Anne died," he said, as though thinking out loud. "Those mountains were so high it hurt just to look at them."

I paused to let his words sink in. "But, by returning to Chicago, you *still* went on."

He looked at me as though his thoughts were impossible to articulate. "You know a lot of people say Lewis had depression most of his life."

I nodded my head.

"I figured if he could keep going even after seeing the Bitterroots, I could go back to Chicago and find my way somehow."

"What about now?" I asked.

He smiled a sad smile. "Guess I'll go back to Florida."

"And find your way somehow?"

"Yeah."

"What do you think will help you do that?"

"Knowing that Shirley is at peace. And that the Pacific is out there somewhere." This time he laughed and his smile was brighter.

His return to Florida did not go well. The old routine of solitary walks and quiet reading that had once helped him build strength and gain perspective no longer worked. He tried socializing but felt awkward. During one of our periodic telephone conversations he wondered if he was simply "running out of gas." In the listlessness of grief, Wes had become lax about taking his medications and was eating only sporadically. He had withdrawn from friends and cut down on his walks. Although he had scrupulously made sure Shirley had never missed a dose of her medication and he had patiently sat beside her every day massaging and exercising her arms and legs, he failed to take care of himself nearly as well as he had taken care of her. He promised to call his doctor and schedule a physical exam, but I suspected he was just humoring me.

About five months later I got a call from his daughter Trudy. She told me Wes was in the hospital after a heart attack. The prognosis was uncertain. "We're just camping out at the hospital," she said, "hoping he'll bounce back, but the doctors say he may not make it."

Lewis and Clark spared no time trying to find their way through the Bitterroots. They found the Shoshones, traded for horses, and struggled forward into the mountains. In the cold autumn shadows, snow covered the ground and game became scarce. The weakened men depleted their food stores and were so desperate they killed and ate some of their precious horses. Morale plummeted along with the temperatures. The ice-covered trees that blocked their way must have seemed like frozen fangs in the jaws of some deadly beast.

By the time they finally stumbled down into the western foothills, they were sick, battered, and near starvation. Bent from the weight of their journey, they probably would have perished if they had not met the Nez Perce Indians. The Nez Perce gave them solace and comfort and protected them in one of their times of greatest need. The Indians watched over them as the weary explorers regained their strength. Without the Nez Perce, Lewis and his men would have died.

Several weeks after I talked with Trudy I got a phone call from Wes. He had moved to Arizona and rented a small apartment about three miles from Trudy and her husband. His granddaughter, grandson-in-law, and three great-grandchildren lived nearby. His voice was surprisingly strong and animated. He laughed about finally being able to wear those Bermuda shorts again now that the doctor had prescribed a "permanent vacation." He missed Shirley and thought about her often, but he was content that her suffering was over. Moreover, he was finding great joy being with his family. After taking care of Shirley for so long, he was in high demand with the great grandchildren as an "expert bath-giver." With winter descending and nearing death, he had found safety with a friendly tribe, his tribe, and gained new comfort and perspective.

After recuperating among the Nez Perce and caching some of their supplies to lighten their load, Lewis and Clark finally headed down the churning Columbia. By early November, Clark recorded in his journal, "Great joy in camp we are in view of the Ocian, this great Pacific Octean which we been so long anxious to See, and the roreing or noise made by waves brakeing on the rockey Shores...may be heard disti[n]tly…" They had finally made it.

Before the first pangs of another winter's fury, the group built a stockade near the Clatsop Indians, not far from the Pacific Coast for what they hoped would be their last cold season away from home. As they ushered in the new year of 1806, they hoped the months until spring would fly by quickly. Many back east assumed the expedition wasn't coming back. Perhaps they were drowned, starved, or frozen to death. Maybe they were killed by Indian warriors or French or Spanish marauders.

As soon as the Columbia was navigable that spring, the men (and Sacagewea and her child) wasted no time jumping into their canoes. They threw themselves into the journey with renewed vigor. Although the return trip was challenging, they knew the way and this time the powerful Missouri River was at their backs. By autumn the Corps of Discovery was paddling in view of Saint Louis. To many, it seemed they had returned from the dead, wiser from their journeys with many wonderful tales to tell.

Wes also had many tales to tell and he found a ready audience in his extended family. His grandchildren were eager to hear about his life as a fireman and his travels. They were also eager to learn about members of his family they would never know, like Shirley, whose stories he cherished and told with love as well as an eye for insightful and humorous detail. He and Trudy even recorded a videotape in which she interviewed him about his experiences, preserving some of these stories for future generations navigating the currents of their own journeys. Like his long time heroes, Wes had continued on from Lemhi Pass. Though the way was hard, his life had continued to hold meaning and his stories continued to inspire others.

The last time I heard from Wes he sent me a card with a painting of a mountain swirling in green, yellow, purple, and gray watercolors. The note inside was like a telegram from the other side of the mountain.

"Made it through the Bitterroots…Pacific Ocean was cold…Home at last."

Conclusion

In late winter of 1816, John Adams sent a letter to Thomas Jefferson in which he asked his friend whether he would choose to live his life all over again. From his plantation in the Virginia mountains, Jefferson responded:

> You ask if I would live my 70, or rather 73, years over again? To which I say Yea. I think with you that it is a good world on the whole, that it has been framed on a principle of benevolence, and more pleasure than pain dealt out to us…I steer my bark with Hope in the head, leaving Fear astern. My hopes indeed sometimes fail; but not oftener than the forebodings of the gloomy. There are, I acknolege, even in the happiest life, some terrible convulsions…I have often wondered for what good end the sensations of Grief could be intended. All our other passions, within proper bounds, have an useful object…I wish the pathologists then would tell us what is the use of grief in the economy, and of what good it is the cause, proximate or remote.

Jefferson, of course, was no stranger to grief. His parents died early in his life, as did his young wife. In the ensuing years, five of the six children to whom his wife had given birth would also die. In the twilight of his life, despite the pleasure he found in his many grandchildren, it is easy to imagine Thomas Jefferson missing loved ones and wishing they were with him.

After his wife died, Jefferson had been gripped by crippling migraine headaches and had withdrawn to his room for weeks, refusing company and conversation, wracked by waves of sobbing. This pattern of intense somatic pain, withdrawal, and private expression of sadness, would attend, in one form or another, many of the losses that lay ahead of him. For all his familiarity with the sometimes callous contours of grief and bereavement, though, Jefferson seemed unable, or unwilling, to acknowledge anything valuable about having traversed such hardship. For him, grief was nothing but a stark shadowland of emotional pain and mental anguish.

It is easy to relate to Jefferson's view. Few people would willingly embrace such pain in exchange for the potential lessons and opportunities that living with an awareness of our own or another's imminent death can bring. Nevertheless, most of us will face such challenges at one time or another. Although there is always the danger that we may get lost in a sea of anger, fear, or guilt, or in the heavy fog of depression or bone-penetrating fatigue, we will do well if we *try* to remain open to the unexpected gifts such times may bring. Gifts which may not be as readily available or as quickly appreciated when the seas are calm, and which will help us ride out the gales that dog us as we navigate through unfamiliar shoals.

Anger will come and go. Anxiety will arrive now and then as surely as sadness and feelings of inadequacy or of being ill-equipped for such a path. Such thoughts and feelings are normal. Although they often feel pervasive and overwhelming, it is important to try to keep them in a larger perspective—that of one's life journey and the relationships one holds dear. If we can do this, as Ray and Lizzie did in Chapter Two, we will see that there are veins of gold beneath the bleakest riverbank.

Of course, it is easy to conceptualize such things from a distance: far easier than acting on them in the midst of gut-wrenching upheaval. Intellectually, one may understand the concept of growth and positive change prompted by suffering, but when one's heart is breaking such prospects can seem remote and counter-intuitive. Finding ways to keep our perspective is hard; it takes practice, and it takes time. In the end, it is enough to do our earnest best while trying to accept that there are many things we cannot control.

As the people whose stories have been remembered in this book learned, it is during the times when we become lost that we may find our way anew; it is when we are losing something or someone we cherish that we may gain a fuller appreciation for life and its wonders. When the days and nights are long—dense with heavy thoughts and weary hearts, there will be moments of transcendent joy, humor, and peace. If we are able to stay attentive, we will welcome their arrival.

Such moments of clarity and wisdom, while they do not take away our suffering, can remind us of the importance of our efforts, however small or ineffective they may seem, to face our challenges well. These moments console us in our limitations, and, at times, move us beyond them, enhancing our knowledge and strengthening our compassion. They remind us that it is enough to act with as much patience and good intention as we can muster on a given day, knowing some days will be harder than others. And they remind us to notice and be grateful for whatever good emerges from the raw landscape of our struggles.

Fundamentally, drawing life-affirming, wisdom-enhancing, lessons from difficult times can change the very stories we tell ourselves about who we are and the possibilities for our lives. As the foregoing chapters have shown, we are immersed in stories every day of our lives, from infancy to old age. As the crisis of death unfolds, people are prone to reflect on their lives and relationships, attempting to make sense of them. They do this largely by telling stories. As Steve Zeitlin and Ilana Harlow put it in their book, *Giving a Voice to Sorrow: Personal Responses to Death and Mourning*: "When death is imminent many people feel an urgency to tell their own life stories, even if only to themselves. They experience an impulse to think back on their lives and to integrate their discrete experiences into a relatively coherent narrative of their time on this earth."

The time surrounding someone's death, as with all transitional times, whether birth, leaving home, marriage, or bereavement, is usually vivid and important for storytelling. Stories generated at such times remain in our minds the longest, often serving, for better or worse, as unconscious or semiconscious maps and blueprints for the way ahead. Maybe this is why people who are in the middle of difficult experiences are often able to integrate helpful themes and metaphors from stories drawn from history, legend, religious tradition, and myth.

Ideally, these stories help a person see his or her life, or understand his or her loss, in a more complete light: As, for example, the story of the Salem witch hunts helped Luke see his life as a journey in which hardships, conflicts, and sacrifices were not signs of failure, but which underscored the value of his quiet determination to live with moral courage and integrity.

When people such as Owen Chase, or the mountain men who plodded through the Rocky Mountains on their way to the yearly Rendezvous, are brought to life and invoked on our modern journeys, we connect with them through our shared humanity. They have gone before us and we can learn from them, just as others who come later may one day learn from our passage.

As valuable as history stories are, those about the people for whom it has been my privilege to serve as hospice social worker are equally important. Though they will not be remembered in future history books, their lives, dreams, and hopes, as well as their wounds and the places they found themselves getting stuck, are as laden with important truths as any found by Cabeza de Vaca during his ordeal in the swamps and deserts of sixteenth century America.

It is here, in the simple stories of everyday lives that the deepest wisdom has always resided. Though these tales are often overshadowed by dramatic narrations about the heroes populating epic, myth, and history, there have always been poets, historians, and tellers of myth who have looked away from the dramatic, to more unassuming lives and humbler heroes for inspiration and illumination. We all have such a story. How we tell it, how we live it, goes a long way toward determining who we are, who we will become, and how we will be remembered.

Philosopher Henry David Thoreau once stated his rather cynical belief that most people lived lives of "quiet desperation." Had he been looking at the lives of people caring for a terminally ill loved one, or of those trying their best to live their last days in a dignified and meaningful way, he may have reconsidered this. Working at hospice and entering the lives and stories of such people reminds one that all lives hold the potential for courage, self-sacrifice, and unassuming heroism. In the end, it is not desperation that defines us, but expressions of quiet strength and love, and moments of loyalty in the face of fear and pain. It is from this reservoir of calm, unpretentious strength that we may draw sustenance and assurance that, however dark the skies may be, the dawn is never far away.

Time and again I have talked with people who have underestimated their ability to weather the long days and gnawing uncertainties of illness, who have misjudged the profound depth of their creativity and resilience. Time and again these people have found that they are capable of doing things they never would have imagined—sitting at the bedside of a dying spouse, retaining the ability to laugh despite the regular arrival of tears, going to a support group to be with others who have had a significant loss: simple acts of courage, hope, and love. It is these things that draw out the truest qualities of our personal narratives and connect us with Osceola as he lay on his deathbed. It is these things that make us part of the larger history of the human family, through which we recognize our shared challenges, and our shared hopes.

I hope that sharing such stories has allowed readers to distill wisdom and perspective from the lives of others, and to see more clearly the still, deep waters within themselves.

The best stories, after all, are the ones that remind us of the best in ourselves. As Paul realized when contemplating the Battle of Horseshoe Bend, inside us all is the indestructible voice of our inner self, our true self. We do not need to experience crisis or suffering to draw out strength and compassion from this bottomless well, we need only bear witness to it when it appears and give thanks. That, perhaps, is the single most important thread running through these stories.

When John Adams replied to Jefferson's letter, he affirmed the Virginian's conclusion that, despite life's inevitable hardships and pains, it was well worth living. Adopting Jefferson's imagery of steering a bark through the waters of life, Adams wrote: "I admire your Navigation and should like to sail with you, either in your Bark or in my own, along side of yours; Hope with her gay Ensigns displayed at the Prow; fear with her Hobgoblins behind the Stern. Hope springs eternal; and Hope is all that endures."

Perhaps Adams would have been happy to learn that it is not just hope that endures. It is also our memories and the stories we carry of those we love.

Bibliography

Allen, John L., "Summer of Decision: Lewis and Clark in Montana, 1805," We Proceeded On, vol. 8, no. 4 (Fall 1976).

Ambrose, Stephen, Undaunted Courage, Meriwether Lewis, Thomas Jefferson, and the Opening of the American West (New York: Simon and Schuster, 1996).

Ashley, Clifford, The Yankee Whaler (New York: Dover Publications, Inc., 1991).

Ayalon, O., "Forward," in Storymaking in Bereavement: Dragons Fight in the Meadow, Alida Gersie (London: Jessica Kingsley Publishers, 1991). Ayalon's use of the terms distancing and involvement is taken from Michael Shiryon's article in Rubin's Bibliotherapy Sourcebook.

Benton, Thomas, "The Last Seminole War" in America: Great Crises In Our History Told by Its Makers, A Library of Original Sources, vol. 6 (Chicago: Americanization Department, Veterans of Foreign Wars of the United States, 1925).

Bonwick, Colin, The American Revolution (Virginia: University of Virginia Press, 1991).

Boyer, Paul and Stephen Nissenbaum, Salem Possessed: The Social Origins of Witchcraft (Cambridge: Harvard University Press, 1974).

Brands, H. W., The Age of Gold: The California Gold Rush and the New American Dream (New York: Doubleday, 2002).

Brown, Dee, Bury My Heart at Wounded Knee: An Indian History of the American West (New York: Holt, Rinehart and Winston, 1972).

Brown, Dee, The American West (New York: Simon and Schuster, 1994).

Byock, Ira, Dying Well: The Prospect for Growth at the End of Life (New York: Riverhead Books, 1997).

Cabeza de Vaca, Alvar Nunez, (Enrique Pupo-Walker, ed) Castaways: The Narrative of Alvar Nunez Cabeza De Vaca (Berkeley: University of California Press, 1993).

Calef, Robert, "Witchcraft in New England," in America: Great Crises In Our History Told by Its Makers, A Library of Original Sources, vol. 2 (Chicago: Americanization Department, Veterans of Foreign Wars of the United States, 1925).

Cappon, Stanley (ed), The Adams-Jefferson Letters: The Complete Correspondence Between Thomas Jefferson and Abigail and John Adams (North Carolina: University of North Carolina Press, 1987).

Chase, Owen, The Wreck of the Whaleship Essex (New York: Harcourt, Brace, and Co., 1999).

Colton, Walter, "The Discovery of Gold in California" in America: Great Crises In Our History Told by Its Makers, A library of Original Sources, vol. 7 (Chicago: Americanization Department, Veterans of Foreign Wars of the United States, 1925).

Davidson, James and Mark Lytle, After the Fact: The Art of Historic Detection, vol. 1 (New York: Alfred Knopf, 1982).

DeVoto, Bernard (ed.), The Journals of Lewis and Clark (Boston: Houghton Mifflin Company, 1953).

DeVoto, Bernard, Across the Wide Missouri (Boston: Houghton Mifflin Company, 1998).

Dolnick, Edward, Down the Great Unknown: John Wesley Powell's 1869 Journey of Discovery and Tragedy

Through the Grand Canyon (New York: HarperCollins, 2001).

Duncan, David, Hernando de Soto: A Savage Quest in the Americas (Norman: University of Oklahoma Press, 1996).

Eckert, Allan A Sorrow in our Hearts: The Life of Tecumseh (New York: Bantam Books, 1993).

Ehle, John, The Trail of Tears: The Rise and Fall of the Cherokee Nation (New York: Doubleday, 1988).

Ellis, Joseph, Founding Brothers: The Revolutionary Generation (New York: Random House, 2002).

Gilbert, Bil, The Old West: The Trailblazers (New York: Times-Life Books, 1973).

Gowans, Fred, Rocky Mountain Rendezvous: A History of the Fur Trade Rendezvous, 1825-1840 (Utah: Peregrine Smith Books, 1985).

Grey Richard, "The Children's Story as Portal for Psychological and Spiritual Healing," Healing Ministry July/August (1998).

Hartley, William and Ellen Hartley, Osceola: The Unconquered Indian (New York: Hawthorn Books, 1973).

Hine, Robert and John Faragher, The American West: A New Interpretive History (Connecticut: Yale University Press, 2000).

Holliday, J. S., The World Rushed in: The California Gold Rush Experience (New York: Simon and Schuster, 1981).

Holm, Don, "Westward With Lewis and Clark: The Great American Adventure," in Water Trails West: The Western Writers of America Donald Duke (ed.) (New York: Avon Books, 1978).

Jackson, Andrew, "Jackson's Defeat of the Creeks: His Official Report," in <u>America: Great Crises In Our History Told by its Makers, A Library of Original Sources</u>," vol. 5 (Chicago: Americanization Department, Veterans of Foreign Wars of the United States, 1925).

Jackson, Andrew, "After The Battle of the Horse Shoe General Jackson Made the Following Address to the Army, March 28, 1814," in America: <u>Great Crises In Our History Told by its Makers, A Library of Original Sources</u>," vol. 5 (Chicago: Americanization Department, Veterans of Foreign Wars of the United States, 1925).

Karlsen, Carol, <u>The Devil in the Shape of a Woman: Witchcraft in Colonial New England</u> (New York: Random House, 1987).

Koch, Adrienne and William Peden (eds), <u>The Life and Selected Writings of Thomas Jefferson</u> (New York: Random House, 1972).

Laycock, George, <u>The Mountain Men: The Dramatic History and Lore of the First Frontiersmen</u> (Connecticut: The Globe Peqout Press, 1996).

Leckie, Robert, <u>George Washington's War: The Saga of the American Revolution</u> (New York: HarperCollins, 1992).

Leckie, Robert, <u>From Sea To Shining Sea: From the War of 1812 to the Mexican War, the Saga of America's Expansion</u> (New York: HarperCollins, 1993).

Levin, David (ed.), <u>What Happened in Salem?</u> (New York: Harcourt, Brace and World, Inc., 1960).

Mahon, John, <u>History of the Second Seminole War: 1835-1842</u> (Florida: University of Florida Press, 1985).

McCullough, David, <u>Mornings on Horseback: The Story of an Extraordinary Family, A Vanished Way of Life,</u>

and the Unique Child Who Became Theodore Roosevelt (New York: Touchstone, 1981).

McCullough, David, The Great Bridge: The Epic Story of the Building of the Brooklyn Bridge (New York: Simon and Schuster, 1982).

McCullough, David, John Adams (New York: Simon and Schuster, 2001).

Melville, Herman, Moby Dick (New York: The New American Library, 1961).

Morgan, Ted, A Shovel of Stars: The Making of the American West—1800 to the Present (New York: Simon and Schuster, 1995).

Neihardt, John (ed.), Black Elk Speaks: Being the Life Story of a Holy Man of the Oglala Sioux (New York: Simon and Schuster, 1972).

Norton, Mary B., In The Devil's Snare: The Salem Witchcraft Crisis of 1692 (New York: Alfred Knopf, 2002).

Philbrick, Nathaniel, In the Heart of the Sea: The Tragedy of the Whaleship Essex (New York: Penguin Books, 2001).

Powell, John W., The Exploration of the Colorado River and its Canyons (New York: Dover Publications, 1961).

Raines, Howell, My Soul is Rested: The Story of the Civil Rights Movement in the Deep South (New York: Penguin Books, 1985).

Slocum, Joshua, Sailing Alone Around the World (New York: Barnes and Noble, Inc., 2000).

Spencer, Ann, Alone at Sea: The Adventures of Joshua Slocum (Buffalo, New York: Firefly Books, Ltd., 1999).

Staloff, Darren, "Lecture 8: New England Society," in The

History of the United States, Part One: Patterns of Settlement and Society (Chantilly, Virginia: The Teaching Company, 1998).

Steltenkamp, Michael, Black Elk: Holy Man of the Oglala (Oklahoma: University of Oklahoma Press, 1993).

B. Tuchman, "The Historian's Opportunity" in Practicing History: Selected Essays, (ed.) Barbara Tuchman (New York: Ballantine Books, 1982).

Utley, Robert, The Lance and The Shield: The Life and Times of Sitting Bull (New York: Random House, 1993).

Ward, Geoffery, The West: An Illustrated History (New York: Little, Brown, and Company, 1996).

Weber, David, The Spanish Frontier in North America (New Haven: Yale University Press, 1992).

Wright, David and David Zoby, Fire on the Beach: Recovering the Lost Story of Richard Etheridge and the Pea Island Lifesavers (New York: Scribner, 2,000).

Wright, Leitch, Creeks and Seminoles (Nebraska: University of Nebraska Press, 1986).

Zeitlin, Steve and Ilana Harlow, Giving a Voice to Sorrow: Personal Responses to Death and Mourning (New York: Perigee, 2001).

Zinn, Howard, A People's History of the United States (New York: HarperCollins).

Additional Resources*

Terminal Illness

Appleton and Henschell, <u>At Home with Terminal Illness: A Family Guide to Hospice in the Home</u>

Albom, Mitch, <u>Tuesdays with Morrie</u>

Byock. Ira, <u>Dying Well</u>

Carson-Reiser, et.al, <u>Dying 101: A Short Course on Living for the Terminally Ill</u>

Hall, Donald, <u>Without</u> (poetry)

Kelly and Callanan, <u>Final Gifts</u>

Kubler-Ross, Elisabeth, <u>On Death and Dying</u>

Kubler-Ross and Warshaw, <u>To Live Until We Say Goodbye</u>

Levine, Stephen, Who Dies: <u>An Investigation of Conscious Living and Conscious Dying</u>

Tolstoy, Leo, <u>The Death of Ivan Ilyich</u>

Zeitlin and Harlow, <u>Giving a Voice to Sorrow</u>

Grief/ For Adults

Colgrove, Melba, <u>How to Survive the Loss of a Love</u>

Ginsburg, Genevieve, <u>Widow to Widow</u>

Golden, Thomas, <u>Swallowed By A Snake</u>

Grollman, Earl, <u>What Helped Me When A Loved One Died</u>

Hichman, Martha, <u>Healing After Loss</u>

Levy, Alexander <u>The Orphaned Adult</u>

McKrachen and Semel, <u>A Broken Heart Still Beats</u> (Death of a Child)

Moffit, Mary Jane, <u>In the Midst of Winter: Selections from the Literature of Mourning</u>

Rando, Therese, <u>How to Go on Living When Someone You Love Dies</u>

Temes, Roberta, <u>Living with an Empty Chair</u>

Grief/ For Teens

Dower, Laura, <u>I Will Remember You</u>

Fitzgerald, Helen, <u>The Grieving Teen</u>

Grollman, Earl, <u>Straight Talk About Death for Teens</u>

Mahon, A.K., <u>Just One Tear</u>

Grief/ For Children

Brown, Laurie and Marc, <u>When Dinosaurs Die</u>

Clifton, Lucille, <u>Everett Anderson's Goodbye</u>

Flynn, Jessie, <u>It's Not Your Fault</u>

Greenlee, Sharon, <u>When Someone Dies</u>

Wright, Betty, <u>The Cat Next Door</u>

For Parents and Adult Helpers

Emswiler, Mary Ann and James, <u>Guiding Your Child Through Grief</u>

Fitzgerald, Helen, <u>The Grieving Child: A Parent's Guide</u>

Mellonie and Ingpen, <u>Lifetimes: The Beautiful Way To Explain Death to Children</u>

Wolfelt, Alan, <u>Healing the Bereaved Child</u>

For Professional Interested in Stories and Counseling

Alida, Gersie, <u>Storymaking in Bereavement: Dragons Fight in the Meadow</u>

Bettelheim, Bruno, <u>The Uses of Enchantment: The Meaning and Importance of Fairy Tales</u>

Burns, George W., <u>101 Healing Stories: Using Metaphors in Therapy</u>

Hesley and Hesley, <u>Rent Two Films and Call Me in the Morning: Using Popular Movies in Psychotherapy</u>

Lankton and Lankton, <u>Tales of Enchantment: Goal-Oriented</u>

Metaphors for Adults and Children in Therapy

Kopp, Richard, <u>Metaphor Therapy: Using Client-Generated Metaphors in Psychotherapy</u>

Remen, Rachel, <u>Kitchen Table Wisdom: Stories that Heal</u>

Rosen, Sidney, <u>My Voice Will Go With You: The Teaching Tales of Milton Erickson</u>

Wallas, Lee, <u>Stories for the Third Ear: Using Hypnotic Fables in Psychotherapy</u>

White and Epston, <u>Narrative Means to Therapeutic Ends</u>

 This, as with any list on these subjects, is incomplete. It is simply a place to start. As for finding and using historical stories, my recommendation is for the reader to find something that interests them and begin learning about it, whether through books, documentaries, courses, etc.** The metaphors and appropriate stories will follow.

*I am indebted to the staff of the Unicorn Bereavement Center, part of Duke University Medical Center, for most of the recommendations pertaining to grief.
**A great place to find college level courses on history in various recorded formats is The Teaching Company in Chantilly, Virginia.

Notes

Introduction

"The light has": McCullough, *Mornings on Horseback*, p. 287. Roosevelt's mother died from typhoid, his wife from Bright's disease: an acute inflammation of the kidneys.

"more than anything": McCullough, *Mornings on Horseback*, p. 330.

"Stories are the": Byock, p. xiv.

"The story and": Tuchman, p. 55.

"our stories, tales": Grey, p. 18.

"The working out": O. Ayalon, p. 16.

"I happened to": Raines, 61.

Chapter One–Cabeza de Vaca: Growth Within Suffering

Cabeza de Vaca's Moroccan companion Estaban's name is also recorded as Estabanico and Esquivel.

"They indicated to": Cabeza de Vaca, p. 14.

"besides great fatigue": Cabeza de Vaca, p. 20.

"Never miss[ed] anything": Cabeza de Vaca, p. 25.

"in such a": Cabeza de Vaca, p. 27.

"caulked with palmetto": Cabeza de Vaca, p. 29.

"scarcely half a": Cabeza de Vaca, p. 39.

"stomach ailment afflicted": Cabeza de Vaca, p. 46.

"owing to the…as I liked": Cabeza de Vaca, p. 52.

"Everywhere I went": Cabeza de Vaca, p. 52.

"shed our skin": Cabeza de Vaca, p. 75.

"to be brought…other will suffice": Cabeza de Vaca, p. 108.

"felt such sorrow": Cabeza de Vaca, p.p. 98-99.

"developed great sores": Cabeza de Vaca, p. 75.

"did not even": Weber, p. 44.

"all the people": Cabeza de Vaca, p.108.

"They went on": Cabeza de Vaca, p. 110.

"we came from": Cabeza de Vaca, p. 114.

"For the rest": Duncan, p. 218.

"one of the": Duncan, pp.215-16.

Chapter Two–California Gold Rush: Golden Moments in a Frigid River

"was caught by": Holliday, p. 33.

"the blacksmith dropped": Colton, p. 115.

"The accounts of": Morgan, p. 168.

"Cholera is the": Holliday, p. 97.

"would make your": Holliday, p. 146.

"If there is": Holliday, p. 146.

"abundant and unmerciful": Holliday, p. 161.

"The stories of": Holliday, pp. 195-96.

"team-killing, back-breaking": Brands, p. 188.

"There was scarcely": Holliday, pp. 253-54.

"you will shed": Holliday, p. 291.

"the various arts": Ward, p. 146.

"rushed to the": Holliday, pp. 313-14.

"traverse the same": Holliday, p. 361.

"You have friends": Holliday, p. 404.

"If it were": Holliday, p. 169.

Chapter Three–Joshua Slocum in the Strait of Magellan: Creating Positive Change in the Face of Resistance

"there were not": Slocum, p. 34.

"had not the": Slocum, p. 39.

"sleep in the": Spencer, pp 92-93.

"drifting into loneliness": Slocum, p. 51.

"tremendous wave...many waves": Slocum, p. 94.

"a mountain of": Slocum, p. 94.

"blowing a gale...scene": Slocum, p. 95, p. 97.

"worth more than": Slocum, p. 99.

"compressed gales of...ends": Slocum, p. 100.

"plunged into the": Slocum, p. 106.

"No other ship": Slocum, p. 106.

"Any landsman seeing": Spencer, p. 128.

"than others that...regrets": Slocum p. 132.

"He would have": Slocum, p. 184.

"tired, tired, tired": Slocum p. 247.

"I secured her": Slocum, p. 250.

Chapter Four–Salem Witch Trials: Affirming Life at the End of One's Journey

"sundry odd postures": Calef, p. 281. Based on comments by Cotton Mather and John Hale, many historians believe that the girls were experimenting with magic and fortune telling prior to the initial episodes of apparent bewitchment. Mather said the girls were "led away with little sorceries," and that they dabbled in "conjuration with sieves and keys, and peas, and mails, and horseshoes." Hale said they were interested in predicting "what trade their sweethearts should be of" and they concocted a device from a jar of water and an egg for divination. Other historians are reluctant to draw firm conclusions from these comments.

"the Devil hath": Norton, p. 20. Many historians identify Tituba as a black slave, usually from the Caribbean. At the time, however, in addition to importing black slaves, it was common for New Englanders to enslave Indians native to the region. Although seventeenth-century New Englanders often described Indians as black, Mary Norton points out that primary sources like Robert Calef and John Hale consistently describe Tituba as an Indian.

"sit still and": Norton, p. 20.

"most grievously": Norton, p. 22.

"Q. Sarah Good what": Levin, p. 4. Punctuation has been modernized.

"to look upon…were all tormented": Levin, p. 4.

"her master did": Calef, p. 282.

"struck with consternation": Norton, p. 64.

"if ye are": Norton, p. 72.

"if they were": Norton, p. 71.

"a very critical": Norton, p. 213.

"long train of": Norton, p. 213.

"persons of good…will be condemned": Norton, pp. 216-17.

"I am no": Boyer and Nissenbaum, pp. 7-8.

"Those who were": Davidson and Lytle, p. 33.

"he would not": Levin, p. 62.

"thought he confessing": Calef, p. 285.

"Accusers and our…our Innocent Bloods": Levin, p. 62.

"it seemed to": Calef, p. 283.

"hotly and madly": Levin, p. xvi.

"wished herself in...propounded": Norton, p. 263.

"I petition your": Boyer and Nissenbaum, p. 8.

"we can say": Staloff.

"The Devill had": Karlsen, p. 41.

Chapter Five–The Voyage of the Essex: On the Persistence of Old Wounds

"presents the curious": Melville, p. 401.

"the Sperm Whale": Ashley, p. 82.

"came down upon": Chase, p. 11.

"tenfold fury and": Chase, p. 12.

"wandered around in": Chase, p. 20.

"as though...it": Philbrick, p. 103.

"violence of raving" Chase, p. 37.

"having no way": Philbrick, p. 125.

"increased to a...destruction": Chase, pp. 42-43.

"Our suffering during": Chase, p. 49.

"Their physical torments": Philbrick, pp. 133-34.

"Never have my": Philbrick, p. 135.

"Our bodies had": Chase, p. 56.

"either feed our bodies": Chase, p. 71.

"were so feeble": Philbrick, p. 177

"Our sufferings were" Chase, pp. 78-79

"prey to the": Philbrick, p. 216.

"Human madness is": Melville, p. 186. The character of Captain Ahab is purely fictional, in no way based on Owen Chase.

Chapter Six–The Battle of Horseshoe Bend: When Defenses Become a Trap

"Let the white...Back!": Eckert, p. 942.

"Two mighty warriors": Eckert, p. 942.

"their vermilion war": Ehle, p. 104.

"Determined to exterminate": Jackson, Jackson's Defeat of the Creeks: His Official Report, p. 238.

"It is difficult": Jackson, Jackson's Defeat of the Creeks: His Official Report, p. 237.

"By their yells": Jackson, After the Battle of the Horse Shoe General Jackson made the Following Address to the Army, March 28, 1814, p. 240.

"Five hundred fifty-seven": Ehle, p. 120. The figures given for those killed in the water may be too high. Leckie (*From Sea to Shining Sea*) estimates that probably about two hundred were killed in the river.

Chapter Seven–Jefferson and Adams: Reconciliation and Forgiveness

The irony of Jefferson being elected Adams's Vice President has to do with the electoral process of the time. Until the passage of the twelfth amendment in 1804, whichever Presidential candidate received the second highest number of votes became Vice President.

"these United Colonies": Bonwick, Colin, p. 93.

"Reason first: you": McCullough, *John Adams*, p. 119.

"fighting fearlessly for": McCullough, *John Adams*, p. 135.

"hang together, or": Leckie, George Washington's War, p. 256.

"gives me great": Cappon, p. 13.

"appeared to me": McCullough, *John Adams*, p. 311.

"I shall part with": McCullough, *John Adams*, p. 329.

"The departure of": Cappon, p, 23.

"the only person": Cappon, p. 14.

"intimate Correspondence with": Cappon, p. 177.

"The Americans in": McCullough, *John Adams*, pp. 383-84.

"in terms of": Ellis, p. 16.

"could not be": Cappon, p. 274.

"addressed a short": McCullough, *John Adams*, p. 600.

"no other objection…prophecy": McCullough, *John Adams*, p. 600.

"not fail to": Ellis, p. 221.

"I have ardently": Cappon, p. 285.

"second [Rush's] efforts": Koch, p. 612.

"No circumstances have": Cappon, p, 292.

"sensible fatigue": Cappon, p. 553.

"separation cannot be": McCullough, *John Adams*, p. 624.

"running for 70": Ellis, p. 226.

"Thomas Jefferson survives": McCullough, *John Adams*, p. 646.

Chapter Eight–The Mountain Man Rendezvous: Finding Community in the Midst of Isolation

"make my living": Gilbert, p. 72.

"Eight pound [of meat]": DeVoto, *Across the Wide Missouri*, p. 42.

"Why do you": DeVoto, *Across the Wide Missouri*, p. 159.

"in the desolate": Gilbert, p. 72.

"ever-ready death": Gowans, p. 51.

"an anthill until": Morgan, p. 139.

"a species of": Gowans, p. 156.

"solitude had given": DeVoto, *Across the Wide Missouri*, p. 44.

"the arrival of": Gowans, p. 27, p. 30. By the middle 1830s, the American Fur Company had established a virtual monopoly on the supply caravan. Prior to that, it was common for more than one company to send trade goods. Thus the Rocky Mountain and Hudson Bay companies might have set up tents near those of the American Company.

"I put in": Laycock, p. 122.

Chapter Nine–The U.S. Life-Saving Service and the Wreck of the Newman: Staying Connected in the Pitch of a Storm

"Mondays and Thursdays": Wright and Zoby, p. 209.

"Robert Tolar discoverd": Wright and Zoby, p. 227. Punctuation modernized.

"From the moment": Wright and Zoby, p. 284.

"Although it seemed": Wright and Zoby, p. 294.

"Keeper Richard Ethridge": Wright and Zoby, p. 297. Punctuation modernized

Chapter Ten–Osceola and the Second Seminole War: When it is Time to Stop Fighting

"The Treaty of": Mahon, pp. 73-74.

"This, you may": Wright, p. 275.

"I had not": Zinn, pp. 143-44.

"leaky, drafty shacks": Mahan, p. 175.

"the greater portion": Hine and Faragher, p. 180.

"swampy, hammocky, low": Mahon, p. 179.

"baffled the exertions": Benton, p. 255.

"If I have": Mahon, pp. 198-99.

"seemed to be": Hartley and Hartley, p. 247.

"shook hands with": Hartley and Hartley, p. 247.

"He made a": Hartley and Hartley, p. 248.

Chapter Eleven–Building the Brooklyn Bridge: Legacy and Asking for Help

"Before the accident...father": McCullough, *The Great Bridge*, p. 100.

"huge diving bell": McCullough, *The Great Bridge*, p. 173.

"was of a": McCullough, *The Great Bridge*, p. 195.

"good enough to": McCullough, *The Great Bridge*, p. 316.

"could never have": McCullough, *The Great Bridge*, p. 329.

"At first I": McCullough, *The Great Bridge*, p. 452.

"I have carried": McCullough, *The Great Bridge*, p. 371.

"unsubstantial fabric of": McCullough, *The Great Bridge*, p. 486.

"has been for": McCullough, *The Great Bridge*, p. 492.

"Mrs. Roebling elevated": McCullough, *The Great Bridge*, p. 518.

"Long ago I": McCullough, *The Great Bridge*, p. 560.

"I don't know": McCullough, *The Great Bridge*, p. 519.

Chapter Twelve–Black Elk at Harney Peak: Trusting One's Inner Voice

"would rove all": Utley, p. 115.

"like some fearful": Neihardt, p. 7.

"every one was": Neihardt, p. 7.

"The Great Spirit": Hine and Faragher, p. 251.

"No white person": Brown, Bury My heart at Wounded Knee, p. 261.

"I was out...home": Neihardt, p. 15.

"A voice is...roaring": Neihardt, p.16.

"the voices would": Neihardt, p. 17.

"swollen badly...puffed up": Neihardt, p. 18.

"white clouds were": Neihardt, p. 19.

"the Powers of": Neihardt, p. 21.

"nation on the": Neihardt, p. 25.

"I saw that": Neihardt, p. 36.

"I was sad": Neihardt, p.39.

"Your boy there": Neihardt, p. 41.

"sacred and incomprehensible": Utley, p. 26.

"felt happy, as": Neihardt, p. 52.

"flowing into the": Neihardt, p. 68.

"[M]y father told": Neihardt, p. 77.

"I thought of": Neihardt, pp. 89-90. Estimates of the number of Indians vary, but generally range between 5,000 and 8,000 with around 3,000 warriors.

"I stayed there": Neihardt, pp. 92-93.

"[I]t made me": Neihardt, p. 116.

"prayed for help": Neihardt, p. 133.

"All our people": pp. 181-82.

"I went up": Brown, The American West, p. 365.

"maybe it was": Neihardt, p. 197.

"I did not": Neihardt, p. 230.

"related (Bible) passages": Steltenkamp, p. 47.

"a pitiful old": Neihardt, p. 230.

"Again, and maybe": Neihardt, p. 233.

"We who listened": Neihardt, p. 233.

"world where there": Neihardt, p. 71.

"I am old": Steltenkamp, p 128.

"was just one": Steltenkamp, p 132.

Chapter Thirteen–John Wesley Powell Exploring the Grand Canyon: Letting Go of Fear, Anger, and Mistrust

"bold enough...to": Dolnick, p. 51.

"staunch and firm": Powell, p. 119.

"We knew nothing": Dolnick, p. 24.

"untried as we": Powell, p. 134.

"the wildest rapid": Dolnick, p. 62

"Our rations are": Dolnick, p. 98.

"There is nothing": Dolnick, p. 98.

"minded to call": Powell, p. 191.

"We start up": Powell p. 168. Inexplicably, in his published account of this episode for *Scribner's* magazine, and in *The Exploration of the Colorado River and its Canyons*, Powell places this event at Steamboat Rock, rather than Desolation Canyon. Dolnick suggests this may have been to highlight the incident's drama.

"To run it": Powell, p. 279

Chapter Fourteen–Lewis and Clark at Lemhi Pass: When a Tough Journey Gets Tougher

"The object of": Ward, p. 37.

"the geography of": Allen, p. 10.

"was hot and": Holm, p. 85

"we wish most" Ambrose, p. 154.

"Indians inform us...Columbia": Ambrose, p 209.

"the difficulties which": DeVoto, *The Journals of Lewis and Clark*, p. 118.

"walking hospital": Ambrose, p. 261.

"immence ranges of": DeVoto, *The Journals of Lewis and Clark*, p 189.

"the most terrible": Ambrose, p. 291.

"Great joy in": DeVoto, *The Journals of Lewis and Clark*, p. 279. It turned out that Clark was mistaken. He was actually seeing the vast sound that leads into the Pacific Ocean, rather than the ocean itself.

Conclusion

"You ask if": Cappon, p. 467.

"When death is": Zeitlin and Harlow, p. 61.

"I admire your": Cappon, p. 471.